THE THEORY OF FUNCTIONS OF A REAL VARIABLE

This textbook leads the reader by easy stages through the essential parts of the theory of sets and theory of measure to the properties of the Lebesgue integral. The first part of the book gives a general introduction to functions of a real variable, measure, and integration, while the second part treats the problem of inverting the derivative of continuous functions, leading to the Denjoy integrals, and studies the derivates and approximate derivates of functions of a real variable on arbitrary linear sets. The author considers the presentation of this second part as the main purpose of his book.

H. L. JEFFERY, who holds degrees from Acadia University and Cornell University, was for many years Professor of Mathematics and Head of the Department of Mathematics at Queen's University, Kingston. He is now Professor of Mathematics at Acadia University, Wolfville, Nova Scotia. He is the author of other important works in mathematics, *Calculus* and *Trigonometric Series: A Survey,* published by the University of Toronto Press.

MATHEMATICAL EXPOSITIONS

Volumes Published

No. 1. *The Foundations of Geometry* by G. DE B. ROBINSON
No. 2. *Non-Euclidean Geometry* by H. S. M. COXETER
No. 3. *The Theory of Potential and Spherical Harmonics* by W. J. STERNBERG and T. L. SMITH
No. 4. *The Variational Principles of Mechanics* by CORNELIUS LANCZOS
No. 5. *Tensor Calculus* by J. L. SYNGE and A. E. SCHILD
No. 6. *The Theory of Functions of a Real Variable* by R. L. JEFFERY
No. 7. *General Topology* by WACLAW SIERPINSKI (translated by C. CECILIA KRIEGER)
No. 8. *Bernstein Polynomials* by G. G. LORENTZ
No. 9. *Partial Differential Equations* by G. F. D. DUFF
No. 10. *Variational Methods for Eigenvalue Problems* by S. H. GOULD
No. 11. *Differential Geometry* by ERWIN KREYSZIG (out of print)
No. 12. *Representation Theory of the Symmetric Group* by G. DE B. ROBINSON
No. 13. *Geometry of Complex Numbers* by HANS SCHWERDTFEGBR
No. 14. *Rings and Radicals*, by NATHAN J. DIVINSKY
No. 15. *Connectivity in Graphs* by WILLIAM T. TUTTE
No. 16. *Introduction to Differential Geometry and Riemannian Geometry* by ERWIN KREYSZIG

MATHEMATICAL EXPOSITIONS, No. 6

THE THEORY OF FUNCTIONS OF A REAL VARIABLE

by

R. L. JEFFERY

SECOND EDITION

UNIVERSITY OF TORONTO PRESS

Reprinted 2017
ISBN 978-1-4875-9204-2 (paper)

First Edition 1951
Second Edition 1953
Reprinted 1962, 1968

TO NELLIE

PREFACE

THE introductory chapter of this book discusses and illustrates the problems involved in the foundations of number systems, but does not go deeply into these problems. The main work of the book, which begins with Chapter I, is based on the assumption of the real number system and the Dedekind partition of the real numbers.

The fundamental purpose of the book is to give a detailed study of the problem of inverting the derivative of a continuous function, and to give an exhaustive and comprehensive consideration of derived numbers and derivatives of arbitrary functions over arbitrary sets. This is the content of Chapters VI and VII. The work of the earlier chapters is an attempt to give, in concise form, such information on functions, point sets, and integration as is necessary to accomplish the main purpose and make the book complete in itself. In Chapters I–V inclusive the author also has in mind the reader who is not especially interested in the abstract theory, but who wants, in short space, to acquire a fundamental knowledge of the basic principles for use in special fields, statistics, Fourier series, harmonic analysis, for example. In particular the work of these chapters is being used for purposes of instruction in classes made up of fourth year honours students and first year graduate students, in the fields of statistics, physics, applied mathematics, and pure mathematics; and it is gratifying to observe that the students in fields other than pure mathematics show a keen interest in the theory for its own sake.

The presentation adheres closely to the early classical form of the point set theory, and to Lebesgue's own formulation of the integral. There have been later formulations of the Lebesgue integral from a point of view other than his, notably those by Carathéodory, Riesz, McShane and Graves. These developments are of great interest and elegance, and it would be a distinct loss were they not in the literature. Nevertheless, the Lebesgue integral, in its original form, grew out of a need for more penetrating tools with which to handle the problems of the day. In this respect it was highly successful, and it is the author's belief, grown out of long experience, that Lebesgue's formulation is the best for handling present day problems. There is a modification of terminology which is briefly described in the introduction to Chapter II.

There are some acknowledgements to make. The idea of the book grew out of research work that the author was doing under a grant from the Carnegie corporation to Acadia University. Then came the war. With the added responsibilities and duties that this brought, together with the great increase in student body at its end, progress on the book was slow. It would have been at a standstill had it not been for the enthusiasm and assistance of one of my students, Colin Blyth, and for the fact that during part of the summer of 1946 the Arts Research Committee of Queen's University granted funds to finance the able assistance of another of my students, Eric Immel. I also wish to thank Professor Israel Halperin, who read the earlier drafts of Chapters II–IV and contributed valuable suggestions. In references to other works no attempt has been made to give original sources.

Finally I wish to express my gratitude to the University of Toronto Press for undertaking the publication of a book of this nature, and to Professors H. S. M. Coxeter and G. de B. Robinson of the University of Toronto who kept encouraging me to keep the project moving. My thanks are due also to Professors W. J. R. Crosby and W. J. Webber who read the manuscript and made valuable suggestions, and to Professor G. G. Lorentz who has kindly assisted in the correction of the proofs, and who has suggested many fundamental improvements.

R. L. JEFFERY

Queen's University
April 14, 1951

CONTENTS

INTRODUCTION

SECTION		PAGE
0.1.	The positive integers	3
0.2.	The fundamental operations on integers	4
0.3.	The rational numbers	7
0.4.	The irrational numbers	9
0.5.	The real number system	12
	Problems	18

I. SETS, SEQUENCES, AND FUNCTIONS

1.1.	Bounds and limits of sets and sequences	20
1.2.	Functions and their properties	30
1.3.	Sequences of functions and uniform convergence	36
	Problems	41

II. METRIC PROPERTIES OF SETS

2.1.	Notation and definitions	45
2.2.	Descriptive properties of sets	46
2.3.	Metric properties of sets	48
2.4.	Measurability and measurable sets	54
2.5.	Further descriptive properties of sets	60
2.6.	Measure-preserving transformations and non-measurable sets	61
2.7.	A non-measurable set	62
	Problems	64

III. THE LEBESGUE INTEGRAL

SECTION PAGE
3.1. Measurable functions 66
3.2. The Lebesgue integral 67
3.3. The Riemann integral 69
3.4. The extension of the definition of the Lebesgue integral to unbounded functions 73
3.5. Further properties of measurable functions 76
Problems 78

IV. PROPERTIES OF THE LEBESGUE INTEGRAL

4.1. Notation and conventions 81
4.2. Properties of the Lebesgue integral 81
4.3. Definitions of summability and their extension to unbounded sets 88
4.4. The integrability of sequences 92
4.5. Integrals containing a parameter 95
4.6. Further theorems on sequences of functions 97
4.7. The ergodic theorem 100
Problems 106

V. METRIC DENSITY AND FUNCTIONS OF BOUNDED VARIATION

5.1. The Vitali covering theorem 110
5.2. Metric density of sets 114
5.3. Approximate continuity 118
5.4. Functions of bounded variation 118
5.5. Upper and lower derivatives 122
5.6. Functions of sets 125
5.7. The summability of the derivative of a function of bounded variation 127
5.8. Functions of sets 131
Problems 137

VI. THE INVERSION OF DERIVATIVES

SECTION		PAGE
6.1.	Functions defined by integrals, $F(x) = L(f,a,x)$	140
6.2.	The inversion of derivatives which are not summable	146
6.3.	The integrals of Denjoy and other generalized integrals	158
6.4.	Descriptive definitions of generalized integrals	159
	Problems	162

VII. DERIVED NUMBERS AND DERIVATIVES

7.1.	Derivatives or derived numbers	165
7.2.	The Weierstrass non-differentiable function	168
7.3.	A function which has no unilateral derivative	172
7.4.	The derived numbers of arbitrary functions defined on arbitrary sets	181
7.5.	Approximate derived numbers over arbitrary sets	187
7.6.	Approximate derived numbers of measurable functions, and relations between arbitrary functions and measurable functions	199

VIII. THE STIELTJES INTEGRAL

8.1.	The Riemann-Stieltjes Integral	204
8.2.	Properties of the Riemann-Stieltjes integral	205
8.3.	Interval functions and measure functions	211
8.4.	Linear functionals	212

BIBLIOGRAPHY 221

INDEX OF SUBJECTS 225

INDEX OF AUTHORS 231

THE THEORY OF FUNCTIONS OF A REAL VARIABLE

INTRODUCTION

Introduction: This introductory chapter is a brief survey of the real number system based on geometrical considerations. For an abstract approach see G. de B. Robinson [55]* which is number 1 of this series. No consideration is given to the deep philosophical questions which underlie the foundations of number systems. For a penetrating study of these the reader is referred to Bertrand Russell [56, 57]. The main work of the book, which begins with Chapter I, is based on the assumptions of the real numbers and the Dedekind section of the real numbers.

0.1. The positive integers. We start with the positive integers, sometimes called natural numbers because they have come to enter into the natural process of counting. The fundamental operations on integers are then defined by means of geometrical constructions, and these in turn lead to the introduction of numbers other than integers. This procedure appears to be based on fundamental concepts, but in reality much is presupposed even in taking the integers for granted; besides, considerable use is made of the concepts of plane geometry,† in particular the problems of constructing a line parallel to a given line, of dividing a line segment into any number of equal parts, and the theorems on similar triangles. Our assumptions, however, are grounded in what we have come to think of as reality, and are, therefore, intellectually acceptable. Furthermore, the procedure supplies a clear-cut illustration of the way in which the necessity for extending any given number system arises. Also, the rules of signs and the reason why division by zero is not defined come out in a natural way.

*Numbers in brackets refer to the bibliography at the end of the book.

†It has been pointed out by Professor H. S. M. Coxeter that the constructions used do not require the full machinery of Euclidean geometry, but only the simpler affine geometry; compasses are not needed, but only an instrument for drawing parallel lines. This, in theory, requires only the axioms 1-7 and 16-18 of Robinson (1), Chapter V. Axioms 10-15 are not involved.

The first step is to take for granted a line segment and use it as a unit of length to associate with each integer a point on a horizontal line l. Choose O any point on l and let the point one unit distance to the right of O be associated with the integer 1, the point two units distance to the right with the

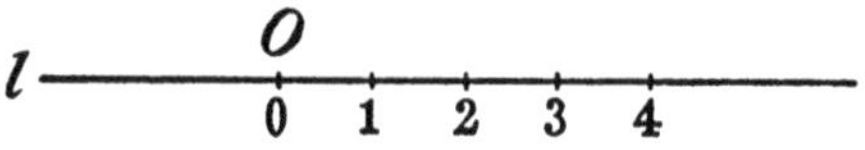

FIG. 1

integer 2, and so on. We shall now speak interchangeably of these points and the symbols to which they correspond. Thus when we speak of the integer 3 we have in mind the third symbol in the set 1, 2, 3, . . . and also the point three units to the right of O. Corresponding remarks apply to any further associations which we shall make between sets of symbols and points on l.

An integer a is greater than, equal to, or less than an integer b (in symbols $a > b$, $a = b$, $a < b$) according as the point a is to the right of, in coincidence with, or to the left of the point b.

0.2. The fundamental operations on integers. The operation of adding an integer b to an integer a is that of locating by means of the unit length a point c which is b units to the right of a.

It is evident that c is an integer, and that c is also the result of adding a to b. The integer c is called the sum of the integers a and b. In symbols, $a + b = b + a = c$.

The operation of subtracting an integer b from an integer a is that of locating a point c which is b units to the left of a. If $b < a$, in the sense defined above, then c is a positive integer. In symbols $a - b = c$. But if $b \geq a$, (b is greater than or equal to a) the point c is to the left of or in coincidence with the point O, and consequently is not a positive integer. Hence if the operation of subtracting one number from another is to always lead to a number, it is necessary to extend the number system of positive integers with which we started. Accordingly, we associate with the point O the symbol 0 (zero), with the point one unit distance to the left of O the symbol -1 (minus one), with the point two units to the left of O the symbol -2, and so on. The set of symbols $-1, -2, -3, \ldots$ and the corresponding points, are the negative integers. A negative number is said to have a negative sign, or minus sign; a positive number a positive sign or plus sign.

The set of numbers $\ldots, -2, -1, 0, 1, 2, \ldots$ we designate by N. Thus, if x is a number in N, x can be a positive or negative integer or zero. The order relations between any two numbers in N are determined in the same way as the order relations between two positive integers; if x and x' are two numbers in N then x is greater than, equal to, less than x' according as x is to the right of, coincident with, or to the left of x'. Likewise the operation of adding a positive integer a to, or subtracting a positive integer a from a number x in N is that already given for the case when x is a positive integer. The operation of adding a negative number $-a = (-a)$ to a number x in N is that of locating a point x' that is a units to the left of x, $x' = x + (-a) = x - a$. The operation of subtracting a negative number $(-a)$ from a number x in N is that of locating a point x' that is a units to the right of x; $x' = x - (-a) = x + a$.

The operations of addition and subtraction have now been defined for numbers in N, and it is evident that these operations lead to numbers in N. It is also true that the operation of adding a negative integer is the same as that of subtracting the corresponding positive integer, and that of subtracting a negative integer is the same as that of adding the corresponding positive integer; indeed these operations could have been defined in this way.

The next considerations are the operations of multiplication and division for numbers in N. Let l' be a line distinct from l and intersecting l in O. Let the positive integers be placed upward on l', the negative integers downward. The point O is the same for both lines. Let x be a number on l, x' a number on l'. Join the point 1 on l' (the unit point on l') to the point x, and draw a line through x' parallel to the joining line to intersect l at x_1. The number x_1 is the result of multi-

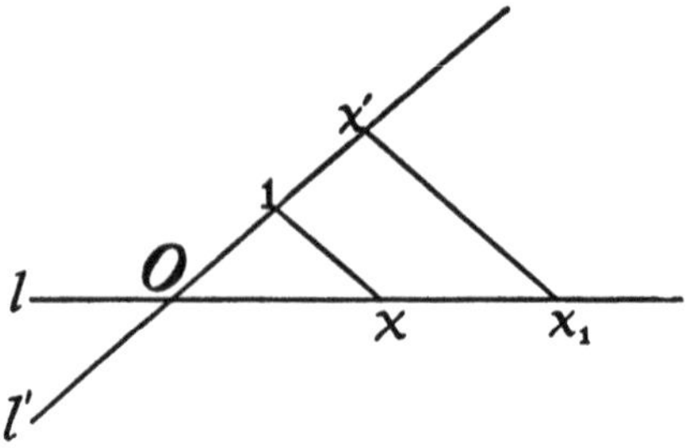

FIG. 2

plying the number x by the number x'. By using theorems in elementary plane geometry it is easily verified that x_1 is also the result of multiplying x' by x. In symbols $x'x = xx' = x_1$. The number x_1 is called the product of x and x'. It is also easily verified that the product of any two numbers in N is a number

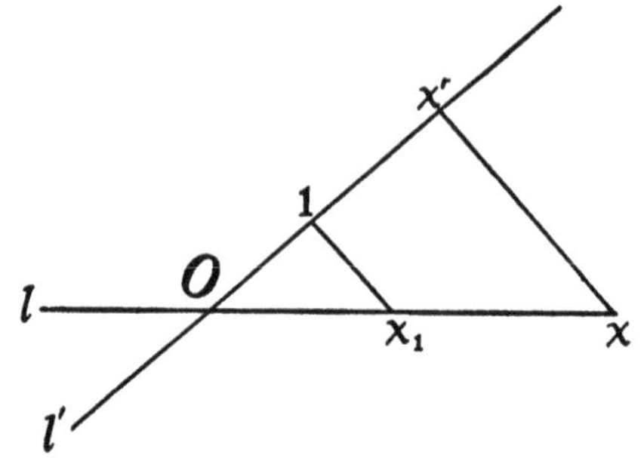

FIG. 3

in N. Furthermore, it follows from the constructions used in defining the operation of multiplication that

(i) $x0 = 0x = 0$

(ii) $x1 = 1x = x$.

(iii) The product of two numbers with like sign is positive and with unlike sign is negative.

Result (iii) is known as the rule of signs.

The operation of division is the inverse of multiplication. The points x and x' are located on l and l' respectively as in multiplication. The point x' is joined to x and through the unit point on l' a line is drawn parallel to the joining line to cut l at x_1. The point x_1 is the result of dividing x by x'. It is sometimes true, but not always, that the result of dividing x by x' is a number in N. The methods of plane geometry can be used to show that if $x = 6$, $x' = 3$, then $x_1 = 2$. But if $x' > x$ it is evident that x_1 is a point on l between zero and the unit point and therefore is not in N. Thus again we have come to the place where circumstances call for an extension of the number system.

0.3. The rational numbers. With the point x_1 which is the result of dividing x by x' we associate the symbol x/x'. The set of symbols thus obtained and the corresponding points we shall designate by N^* and call them the rational numbers. It should be noted, however, that a variety of symbols x/x' is associated with each point of N^*, which now includes the set N. For example, it is easily verified geometrically that $2/3 = 4/6$, and that $5 = 10/2$. The number x/x' is called the quotient of x by x', and when we speak of the point a/b or $-(a/b)$ we shall have in mind the smallest positive integers a and b for which a/b represents the point.

The order relations for numbers in N^* are determined in the same way as the order relations for the numbers in N, and likewise for the operations of addition, subtraction, multiplication, and division (except division by zero). These operations lead to numbers in N^*.

If x is a number in N^* and $x' = 0$, the operation of dividing x by x' is not defined. For if $x \neq 0$ (x is different from 0) the line through the unit point on l' parallel to the line joining x' to x does not cut l. If $x = 0$, $x' = 0$ there is no unique line joining x to x'. Hence division by zero is meaningless.

It can be verified by the methods of plane geometry that for the operation of division

(i) $0/x = 0,\ x \neq 0$

(ii) $x/1 = x$

(iii) If x and x', $x' \neq 0$, are two numbers in N^* with like sign, then x/x' is positive. If x and x' are with unlike sign then x/x' is negative.

Each number in the set N^* is a point on the line l. The question now arises as to whether or not each point on the line l is a number in N^*. This is not easy to settle conclusively, but we shall make it plausible that the answer is in the negative. All the rational numbers between zero and unity are included in the following array:

$$
\begin{array}{llllll}
 & \frac{1}{2} & & & & \\
 & \frac{1}{3}, & \frac{2}{3} & & & \\
 & \frac{1}{4}, & \frac{3}{4} & & & \\
(0.1) & \frac{1}{5}, & \frac{2}{5}, & \frac{3}{5}, & \frac{4}{5} & \\
 & \ldots & & \ldots & & \\
 & \frac{1}{n} \ldots & \frac{k}{n} \ldots & \frac{n-1}{n} & & \\
 & \ldots & \ldots & & &
\end{array}
$$

where n represents the nth positive integer. Let α be a line segment whose length is less than half that of the unit segment. Let $\alpha_1, \alpha_2, \ldots$ be a sequence of line segments each half as long as its predecessor (the predecessor of α_1 being α) centred at $\frac{1}{2}, \frac{1}{3}, \frac{2}{3}, \frac{1}{4}, \ldots$ respectively. Clearly all the points in the array (0.1) are included in the segments $\alpha_1, \alpha_2, \ldots$. Let PQ be the segment α.

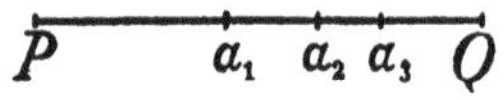

FIG. 4

Bisect PQ at a_1, a_1Q at a_2, a_2Q at a_3, and so on. Then $Pa_1 = \alpha_1$, $a_1a_2 = \alpha_2$, $a_2a_3 = \alpha_3, \ldots$, and it is clear that the total length of the segments $\alpha_1, \alpha_2, \ldots$ is α, which has length less than one half that of the unit segment. Thus the rational points on the unit segment can be included in line segments whose total length is less than one half that of the unit segment. Consequently we are unwilling to believe that the rational points are all the points on the unit segment. The segment a was any segment with length less than one half that of the unit segment, which means that the length of a can be as small as we wish. This leads us to suspect that the rational points constitute a negligible part of the unit segment, and this, as we shall see later, is indeed the truth of the matter. For a geometrical proof of the fact that there are points on l not represented by the rational numbers, see Hardy and Wright [26].

0.4. The irrational numbers. The fundamental operations on rational numbers lead to rational numbers; consequently, from this point of view, there is no necessity for a further extension of our number system. We have become convinced, however, that the representation of the rational numbers does not require all the points on the line; this leads us to wonder if there are reasons for defining operations other than those of addition, subtraction, multiplication and division, which require further extensions of the number system.

Let r and r_1 be two distinct rational points between zero and unity. An examination of the array (0.1) reveals that for n sufficiently great there is at least one number $r_2 = k/n$ of the array which is nearer to the point r than one half the distance between r and r_1. Similarly there is a number r_3 of the array which is nearer to r than one half the distance between r_2 and r. A continuation of this reasoning gives a sequence $r_1, r_2, \ldots$ of rational numbers for which r_n approaches r as n increases; in symbols $r_n \to r$ as $n \to \infty$, or briefly $r_n \to r$.

This rational number r associated with the sequence of rational numbers $r_1, r_2, \ldots$ we shall call the limit of the sequence. It is evident that there is no point other than r on the line l which is such that the distance between it and r_n becomes closer to zero as n increases. Next let μ be a point between zero and unity which is not a rational point, and let r_1 be a rational point between zero and unity. Reasoning as in the case just discussed in which the point in question was a rational point r, it is seen that there is a rational point r_2 nearer to μ than half the distance between r_1 and μ, a rational point r_3 closer to μ than half the distance between μ and r_2, and so on indefinitely. For the sequence $r_1, r_2, \ldots$ obtained in this way, $r_n \rightarrow \mu$, and there is no other point on the line l which r_n approaches as n increases. Hence, since μ is not a rational point, it cannot be said that the sequence $r_1, r_2, \ldots$ has a limit in the set N^* of rational numbers. We are thus led to make the following extension of our number system.

In contrast to the rational numbers, the point μ is called an irrational number, and a symbol for the number μ is the sequence of rational numbers $r_1, r_2, \ldots$. The irrational number μ is the limit of the sequence of rational numbers $r_1, r_2, \ldots$; in symbols $r_n \rightarrow \mu$.

By this extension it results that every point on l represents a number, since every point P on l is either a rational number or there is a sequence of rational numbers $r_1, r_2, \ldots$ such that r_n approaches P. The set of rational and irrational numbers is called the real number system, and we shall denote it by R. The order relations for numbers in R are determined in the same way as the order relations for numbers in N^*. Likewise for the definitions of the fundamental operations, and these operations lead to numbers in R. The results (i), (ii), (iii), under multiplication and division for numbers in N^* hold for numbers in R.

The irrational numbers have now been defined, but it appears that we are rather badly off for symbols with which to represent them. The best we have so far offered is a sequence of rational numbers, and indeed, apart from a few special cases, this is the best that can be done. It is also clear from the way in which we located the sequence $r_1, r_2, \ldots$ of rational numbers defining μ, that there are many such sequences of rational numbers with r_n approaching μ. Hence the representation we have given is not unique. It is true, however, that if $r_1, r_2, \ldots$ and $r'_1, r'_2, \ldots$ are two sequences of rational numbers each defining μ, then $r_n - r'_n \rightarrow 0$. It is also true that for any given sequence defining μ, $r_n - r_m \to 0$ as m and n increase without limit, independently of each other. This raises the question as to whether every sequence $r_1, r_2, \ldots$ of rational numbers for which $r_n - r_m$ tends to zero as m and n increase without limit is such that r_n tends to a limit. An affirmative answer to this is given in Chapter I.

There are symbols other than sequences of rational numbers for some special irrational numbers, $\sqrt{2}, \sqrt[5]{7}$, for example. For these symbols there are some rules of operation. For example, using $\times$ as a symbol for multiplication,

$$\sqrt{2} \times \sqrt[5]{7} = 2^{1/2} \times 7^{1/5} = 2^{5/10} \times 7^{2/10} = \sqrt[10]{2^5 \times 7^2}.$$

There are also symbols such as π and e which represent special irrational numbers. But for these there are no rules of operation. For example if we wish to multiply π by 5 the best we can do is to multiply by 5 each term of the sequence.

$$3\frac{1}{10}, \; 3\frac{14}{100}, \; 3\frac{141}{1000}, \ldots \tag{0.2}$$

which represents π. Another annoying characteristic of a sequence which represents an irrational number is the fact that we cannot at once write in the decimal system any given term of the sequence. There are many who could write the first six terms of the sequence (0.2); but most would fail on the seventh. The writer was acquainted with a person who could give thirty-five terms of this sequence, but failed on the thirty-sixth. On the other hand if a sequence $r_1, r_2, \ldots$ in the decimal system is such that r_n tends to a rational point, any required term can easily be given. For example, the sequence

$$\frac{3}{10}, \; \frac{33}{100}, \; \frac{333}{1000}, \ldots \tag{0.3}$$

is such that r_n tends to $1/3$, and the fifteen-hundredth term could be written in a short time. The terms of the sequences (0.2) have, with much labour, been determined to at least the thousandth, and the fifteen-hundredth term could be determined; but the advantage of knowing it is not worth the work required to determine it.

In these geometrical definitions of the real numbers and operations on them, such puzzling things as the rules of signs and the fact that division by zero is impossible come out as natural consequences. The definitions will appear unusual to all but the trained mathematician. They are by no means a makeshift, however, for they stand up to all the demands of the real variable theory. One reason for introducing them is that they serve to illustrate the way in which operations in any number system give rise to the necessity for extending the system. Another is that they serve to introduce the rules of signs in a natural way.

Now that we have each point on the line representing a number, it is natural to hope that we have a number system adequate for all ordinary purposes. But this is not the case. Indeed we do not get beyond grade school mathematics before we have to consider a number x which is such that its square is -2. According to the definition of multiplication given above, the square of any real number is positive. Hence x cannot be among the real numbers, and if we are to have a solution to the equation $x^2 + 2 = 0$ the number system must again be extended. It is at this point that the complex numbers are introduced. This, too, can be done geometrically but to discuss such an extension here is to go beyond the purpose of this book.

What we have so far said about the set of real numbers is intended to be illustrative rather than fundamental or exhaustive. It is not our purpose to go deeply into the foundations of number systems, but rather to deal in a special way with some phases of the real variable theory. Nevertheless, at this point the reader is urged to study thoroughly the problems involved, philosophical and logical, in a systematic formulation of the real number system. For sources for such a study other than those already mentioned see [14, 19, 20, 28, 31, 40].

0.5. The real number system. In what follows we shall assume the real number system and the knowledge of the arithmetical operations on real numbers that is acquired in elementary mathematics including the calculus. To this we add:

AXIOM 0.1 (THE DEDEKIND SECTION OF THE REAL NUMBERS). *If all real numbers are divided into two classes* R_1, R_2 *in such a way that:* (i) *there are numbers in both classes;* (ii) *every number* r_1 *in* R_1 *is less than any number* r_2 *in* R_2*; then there is a single real number* ν *such that every number less than* ν *is in* R_1 *and every number greater than* ν *is in* R_2.

It is our hope that this axiom appears to the reader to be consistent with common sense. With it as a starting point many of the basic theorems of the real variable theory can be easily obtained, as we shall show in Chapter I. We point out that the number ν, since it is a real number, must be in R_1 or in R_2, and that it can be in either. It is then clear that ν must be either the largest number in R_1 or the smallest in R_2. We point out, too, that there are other starting points that would serve as well as Axiom 0.1. It will be more convenient, however, to call attention to these as the work progresses, rather than to mention them here.

We conclude this chapter with a consideration of some further properties of the real numbers. The totality of real numbers, or any part of this totality, is called a set. Thus we speak of the set of all rational numbers, the set of all numbers between zero and unity, the set consisting of all numbers of the form $1/n, n = 1, 2, \ldots$, etc. We shall use capitals, $A, B, C, \ldots$ to denote sets. If a and b are two real numbers $a < b$, then these numbers define sets called intervals according to the following notation:

$$[a, b] \ : \ a \leq x \leq b.$$
$$(a, b) \ : \ a < x < b.$$
$$[a, b) \ : \ a \leq x < b.$$
$$(a, b] \ : \ a < x \leq b.$$

The first interval is said to be closed, the second open, the last two half open. The letter ω will also be used to denote a single open interval.

DEFINITION 0.1. *If the set* A *is contained in the set* B, A *is dense on* B *if every interval that contains a point of* B *also contains a point of A. If on every interval ω which contains a point of B there is an interval ω′ which contains a point of B but contains no point of A, then A is non-dense on B.*

THEOREM 0.1. *The set of rational numbers is dense on the set of real numbers.*

Let (a, b) be an interval on l. If n is a positive integer for which $1/n < b - a$, then there is at least one value of k, a positive integer or zero, for which either the rational number k/n or $-k/n$ falls in (a, b). Thus every interval contains rational numbers, and it follows from Definition 0.1 that the rational numbers are dense on the set of real numbers.

DEFINITION 0.2. *A set of points is denumerable if it consists of a finite number of points or if the points of the set can be put into one to one correspondence with the positive integers.*

THEOREM 0.2. *A denumerable set of denumerable sets is denumerable.*

Let the denumerable sets be $A_1, A_2, \ldots$. A denumerable set can be symbolized by a sequence $a_1, a_2, \ldots$, where the subscript is the integer which corresponds to the element of the set. Hence it is possible to write

$$\begin{array}{l} A_1 = a_{11}, a_{12}, a_{13}, \ldots \\ A_2 = a_{21}, a_{22}, a_{23}, \ldots \\ A_3 = a_{31}, a_{32}, a_{33}, \ldots \\ \quad \ldots \qquad \ldots \end{array}$$

These sets can now be arranged in the order $a_{11}, a_{21}, a_{12}, a_{31}, a_{22}, a_{13}, a_{41}, \ldots a_{14}, \ldots$ which shows that the points of the sets can be put into one to one correspondence with the positive integers.

THEOREM 0.3. *The rational numbers form a denumerable set.*

It will first be shown that the rational numbers on $[0, 1)$ form a denumerable set. Associate the integer 1 with zero. Then, referring to the array (0.1), associate the integer 2 with 1/2, the integer 3 with 1/3, the integer 4 with 2/3, the integer 5 with 1/4, and so on. It is thus seen that corresponding to every rational number on $[0, 1)$ there is an integer, and corresponding to every integer there is a rational number on $[0, 1)$, and the same can be shown for each of the intervals $(-1, 0]$, $[1, 2)$, $[-2, -1)$, $[2, 3)$, ... By associating the integer 1 with the first of these intervals, the integer 2 with the second, the integer 3 with the third, and so on, we see that this set of intervals is denumerable. It then follows from Theorem 0.2 that the rational numbers form a denumerable set.

NOTE 0.1. The method of Theorem 0.2 can be adapted to show that various combinations of elements of a denumerable set form denumerable sets. For example the set consisting of all pairs, or of all triples, of rational numbers, is a denumable set. Let the rational numbers be r_1, r_2. . . . . Form the array

$$\begin{array}{l} r_1r_1,\ r_1r_2,\ r_1r_3,\ \ldots \\ r_2r_1,\ r_2r_2,\ r_2r_3,\ \ldots \\ \quad\ldots \qquad \ldots \end{array}$$

It is evident that this array contains every pair of rational numbers and can be arranged in a denumerable set A_1, A_2, ... Now consider the array

$$\begin{array}{l} A_1r_1,\ A_1r_2,\ A_1r_3,\ \ldots \\ A_2r_1,\ A_2r_2,\ A_2r_3,\ \ldots \\ \quad\ldots \qquad \ldots \end{array}$$

This is a denumerable array which includes every triple of rational numbers. Since the pairs of rational numbers form a denumerable set it follows that the set of all intervals with rational end-points forms a denumerable set. These intervals are referred to as the rational intervals.

THEOREM 0.4. *The irrational numbers on the interval (0, 1) are non-denumerable.*

Suppose there is a set of rules which will determine all the real numbers on $(0, 1)$ and arrange them in a sequence a_1, a_2, a_3, ... Since certain rational numbers can be represented by means of a decimal in which after some fixed place all the digits are zeros, and also by a decimal in which after some fixed place all the digits are nines, let us suppose the latter mode of representation excluded. The numbers of the set a_1, a_2, a_3, . . . can then be written as follows:

$$\begin{aligned} a_1 &= .a_{11}a_{12}a_{13}\ldots \\ a_2 &= .a_{21}a_{22}a_{23}\ldots \\ a_3 &= .a_{31}a_{32}a_{33}\ldots \\ \ldots & \qquad \ldots \end{aligned}$$

where each a_{ik} stands for one of the integers 0, 1, 2, . . . , 9. Consider the number $\bar{a} = .\bar{a}_{11}\bar{a}_{22}\bar{a}_{33}\ldots$, where $\bar{a}_{11} \neq a_{11}$, $\bar{a}_{22} \neq a_{22}$, $\bar{a}_{33} \neq a_{33}$, . . . , and $\bar{a}$ has not a repetition of nines after some fixed place. Clearly this number does not occur in the original sequence. Thus we have shown that the real numbers are not denumerable. Since the rational numbers are denumerable, it follows from Theorem 0.3 that the irrational numbers are non-denumerable.

We have shown that while the rational numbers are denumerable they are, nevertheless, dense on the real numbers. We now give an example of a non-denumerable set on (0, 1) which is non-dense on this interval. For the reason that this example will be referred to in later work, it will be given in considerable detail.

EXAMPLE 0.1 (THE CANTOR TERNARY SET). Let u^0 be the closed interval [0, 1]. Let α^0 be the interior of the middle third of u^0. Let u^1 be the two closed intervals u_{11}, u_{12} which remain after α^0 is removed. Let α^1 be the two open intervals α_{11}, α_{12} where α_{1i} is the interior of the middle third of u_{1i} $i = 1, 2$. If this process is continued there is obtained:

(i) α^n: $\alpha_{n1}, \alpha_{n2}, \ldots, \alpha_{n2^n}$; u^n: $u_{n1}, u_{n2}, \ldots, u_{n2^n}$

(ii) length of α_{ni} is $\dfrac{1}{3^{n+1}}$; length of u_{ni} is $\dfrac{1}{3^n}$.

Let G be the set which remains when this process has been carried out indefinitely. The set G is not empty; it contains at least the end-points of each interval u_{ni}.

The set G is non-dense on (0, 1). Let ω be an interval containing points of G. Take n so great that $1/3^n$ is less than the length of ω. Then the length of an interval u_{ni} is less than the length of ω, and since u_{ni} is separated from u_{nj} $(i \neq j)$ by at least one interval of the set $\alpha^0, \ldots, \alpha^{n-1}$, there is at least one open interval α_{jk} of this set with a point on the open interval ω.

Hence there is an interval ω' on ω which contains no points of G. It follows from Definition 0.1 that G is non-dense on (0, 1).

The points of G are non-denumerable. Any point of (0, 1) can be represented in the scale of three by $0.a_1a_2\ldots$ where a_i is one of the digits 0, 1, 2. For certain points such as 1/3 there are two representations, one consisting of all zeros after a certain place, the other consisting of all twos after a certain place. We shall agree to use the latter representation, and thus designate 1/3 by .022 . . . rather than .100 . . .

The points of α^0 contain all points with $a_1 = 1$ except $1/3 = .100\ldots = .022\ldots$. The points of α^1 contain all points with $a_2 = 1$ except $1/27 = .00100\ldots = .00020\ldots$ etc. Continuing, all points are removed except those which can be represented by zeros and twos and these are the points of G. Thus the points of G may be represented in the form $.a_1a_2\ldots$, where a_i is one of 0,2. Attempting to enumerate the points of G, we display them as follows:

$$\begin{array}{l} .\,a_{11}a_{12}a_{13}\ldots \\ .\,a_{21}a_{22}a_{23}\ldots \\ .\,a_{31}a_{32}a_{33}\ldots \\ \ldots \qquad \ldots \end{array}$$

Now consider the number $.\bar{a}_{11}\bar{a}_{22}\bar{a}_{33}\ldots$, where $\bar{a}_{nn} \neq a_{nn}$ and a_{nn} is one of 0, 2. Clearly this is a point of G not contained in the array. Hence the set G is non-denumerable.

The real number system, as it has been developed above, consists of rational numbers and irrational numbers. We remark briefly on an alternative classification. Consider the equation

$$a_0x^n + a_1x^{n-1} + \ldots + a_{n-1}x + a_n = 0 \tag{0.4}$$

where n is a positive integer, and the coefficients $a_0, a_1, \ldots, a_n$ are positive or negative integers or zero. Any real number which is a root of an equation of this type is an algebraic number. An integer n is an algebraic number, for it satisfies the equation $x - n = 0$. Any rational number p/q is an algebraic number, for it satisfies the equation $qx - p = 0$. Many irrational numbers are algebraic. The numbers $\sqrt{2}$, $\sqrt{7}$ respectively satisfy the equations $x^2 - 2 = 0$, $x^2 - 7 = 0$. The question then comes up: Does every real number satisfy some equation of the form (0.4)? The answer is negative, and we come by this information in an indirect way. We show that the algebraic numbers are denumerable. Then, since the real numbers are non-denumerable, it follows that there are numbers which do not satisfy (0.4).

To show that the algebraic numbers are denumerable, let $|a_0| + |a_1| + \ldots + |a_n| + n$ be called the rank of (0.4). Obviously there can be only a finite number of equations with rank less than a given positive integer n, and, since every such equation has a finite number of roots, it follows from Theorem 0.2 that the algebraic numbers are denumerable.

It has thus been easy to show that numbers which do not satisfy any equation of type (0.4) exist. Such numbers are called transcendental. To show that any given number is transcendental is sometimes difficult. This has been accomplished for π, and for e which is the limit of $(1 + 1/n)^n$ as n increases without limit. These proofs, and in fact the arithmetical formulation of the irrational numbers, have all come within the memory of men now living. Cantor and Dedekind formulated theories of irrational numbers which were published in 1872. It was not until 1883 that Lindemann succeeded in showing that π is transcendental.

Problems

0.1. Using the definitions of the fundamental operations laid down in this introduction, prove

(i) Addition is associative: $(a + b) + c = a + (b + c)$.

(ii) Multiplication is commutative: $ab = ba$.

(iii) Multiplication is associative: $(ab)c = a(bc)$.

(iv) Multiplication is distributive: $a(b + c) = ab + ac$.

(v) The law of cancellation: $ma/mb = a/b$, $m \neq 0$.

0.2. Show that a repeating decimal represents a rational number.

0.3. Continue the following table to arrive at the square root of 2 correct to two decimal places.

Square less than 2	$\frac{4}{3}$	$\frac{5}{4}$	$\frac{7}{5}$	$\frac{9}{7}$	$\frac{11}{8}$	$\frac{13}{9}$	. . .
Square greater than 2	$\frac{5}{3}$	$\frac{7}{4}$	$\frac{8}{5}$	$\frac{10}{7}$	$\frac{13}{8}$	$\frac{14}{9}$	. . .

0.4. If m and n take on all positive integral values, show that the set consisting of all pairs (m, n) is denumerable.

0.5. Show that the points in the plane with rational coordinates form a denumerable set.

0.6. Let r_1, r_2 be the elements of two classes R_1, R_2 of a Dedekind section representing the real number ν, and let r'_1, r'_2 be the elements of two classes R'_1, R'_2 of a section representing the real number ν'. Show that the sets of numbers $r_1 + r'_1$, $r_2 + r'_2$ are elements of the classes R''_1, R''_2 which represent the real number $\nu + \nu'$. What are the elements of the two classes of the partition which represents the product $\nu\nu'$?

0.7. If the two sequences $a_1, a_2, \ldots$ and $b_1, b_2, \ldots$ represent real numbers a and b, show how to represent the sum $a + b$, the product ab, and the quotient a/b in terms of these sequences.

0.8. Show that the set of open intervals deleted from the interval $[0, 1]$ in the construction of the set G of Example 0.1 is a denumerable set.

0.9. If $\epsilon > 0$ is given, show that there is a finite set of mutually exclusive open intervals $\omega_1, \omega_2, \ldots, \omega_n$, which contain all the points of the set G of Example 0.1 with the sum of their lengths less than ϵ.

0.10. If ω is an open interval which contains a point of the set G defined in Example 0.1, show that ω contains an infinite number of the points of G.

CHAPTER I

SETS, SEQUENCES, AND FUNCTIONS

Introduction: In this chapter we define the concepts of limit and function and obtain fundamental results involving these concepts. The methods used illustrate the usefulness and power of Axiom 0.1, the Dedekind section axiom.

1.1. Bounds and limits of sets and sequences.

DEFINITION 1.1. *Let S be a set of numbers. The numbers s in S are the elements of S. The set S is bounded above if there is a number M such that $s < M$ for all s in S. The set S is bounded below if there is a number m such that $s > m$ for all s in S. If the set S is bounded above and below it is bounded, and there is a number M such that $|s| < M$ for all s in S.*

DEFINITION 1.2. *If M is a number such that $s \leq M$ for every s in S, and if for every number $M' < M$ there is an element s in S with $s > M'$, then M is the least upper bound or supremum of the set S, $M = \sup S$. If there is a number m such that $s \geq m$ for every s in S, and if for every $m' > m$ there is an element s in S for which $s < m'$, then m is the greatest lower bound or infimum of the set S, $m = \inf S$.*

THEOREM 1.1. *The numbers $\sup S$, $\inf S$ exist, finite or infinite, for every set S and $\inf S \leq \sup S$. If the set is bounded above, $\sup S < \infty$, if bounded below $\inf S > -\infty$.*

If the set S is not bounded above then $s \leq \infty$ for every s in S, and if M' is any number with $M' < \infty$ there exists an element s in S with $s > M'$. Consequently $\sup S = \infty$. Similarly if S is not bounded below $\inf S = -\infty$. Let S be bounded above, $s < M < \infty$ for all s in S. Let all real numbers x be divided into two classes R_1 and R_2 in the following way. If x is such that there is an element s of S with $s > x$, then x is in class R_1. Otherwise x is in class R_2. If S is not empty there are numbers in both classes. For if $x > M$ then x is in R_2; if s is an element of S and $x < s$ then x is in R_1.

If r_1 is an element of R_1 and r_2 an element of R_2 then $r_1 < r_2$ for all r_1 and r_2. For suppose there are two numbers r_1 and r_2 with $r_1 \geq r_2$. Since r_2 is in R_2 there is no element s of S with $s > r_2$. Since $r_1 \geq r_2$ there is then no element s of S with $s > r_1$. Hence r_1 is not in R_1, which is a contradiction. We conclude, therefore, that $r_1 < r_2$ for all r_1 in R_1 and all r_2 in R_2.

It can now be stated that the classes R_1 and R_2 constitute a Dedekind section of the real numbers. Consequently by Axiom 0.1 there is a real number ν such that every number less than ν is in R_1 and every number greater than ν is in R_2.

The number ν defined by the section R_1, R_2 is the supremum of the set S under Definition 1.2. First, $s \leq \nu$ for every s in S. For suppose there is s in S with $s > \nu$. There is then a number x with $\nu < x < s$. This means that x is in R_1, which contradicts the fact that every number greater than ν is in R_2. Again, let M' be any number with $M' < \nu$. Then M' is in R_1 and there is an element s in S with $s > M'$. Thus $M = \nu$ qualifies under Definition 1.2 as the supremum of the set S, $\nu = M = \sup S$.

It can be shown in a similar way that if a set S is bounded below it has an infimum. We can conclude, therefore, that the numbers $\sup S$ $\inf S$ exist, finite or infinite, for every non-empty set S. The remaining parts of the theorem follow immediately from Definition 1.2.

DEFINITION 1.3. *If a set of numbers S is such that there is a first number s_1, a second number s_2, and so on, the set S is called a sequence. The sequence is denoted by $s_1, s_2, \ldots$, and the corresponding set of numbers by $S = (s_1, s_2, \ldots)$. A number s_n is a term of the sequence. Let*

$$M(n) = \sup (s_n, s_{n+1}, \ldots), \quad m(n) = \inf (s_n, s_{n+1}, \ldots),$$
$$\bar{s} = \inf [M(1), M(2), \ldots], \quad \underline{s} = \sup [m(1), m(2), \ldots].$$

Then the numbers $\bar{s}$, $\underline{s}$ are respectively the limit superior and the limit inferior of the sequence $s_1, s_2, \ldots$,

$$\bar{s} = \limsup_{n \to \infty} s_n, \quad \underline{s} = \liminf_{n \to \infty} s_n.$$

If for any sequence $\bar{s} = \underline{s}$ *the common value* s *is the limit of the sequence,*

$$s = \lim_{n \to \infty} s_n.$$

THEOREM 1.2. *The numbers* $\bar{s}$, $\underline{s}$ *exist, finite or infinite, for every sequence* $s_1, s_2, \ldots$ *and* $\underline{s} \leq \bar{s}$. *If the sequence is bounded above* $\bar{s} < \infty$, *if bounded below* $\underline{s} > -\infty$.

That $\bar{s}$, $\underline{s}$ exist for every sequence follows from Theorem 1.1. To prove that $\underline{s} \leq \bar{s}$ we note that $M(n)$ does not increase, $m(n)$ does not decrease as n increases, and that for every n $m(n) \leq M(n)$ by Theorem 1.1. The supposition that $\underline{s} > \bar{s}$ easily leads to a contradiction of this relation. Hence $\underline{s} \leq \bar{s}$. The remainder of the theorem follows from Theorem 1.1.

The foregoing definition of the limits $\bar{s}$, $\underline{s}$ and s relative to a sequence $s_1, s_2, \ldots$ is concise and comprehensive, in fact too comprehensive to be useful in all instances as a working tool. We now state a group of definitions, which are more practical, and the limits given by them are easily seen to be identical with those of Definition 1.3.

DEFINITION 1.3.1. *If the sequence* $s_1, s_2, \ldots$ *is such that for every number* M *there is an integer* n *with* $s_n > M$ *then the limit superior of the sequence is*

$$\bar{s} = \limsup_{n \to \infty} s_n = \infty.$$

If there is a number $\bar{s}$ *with* $-\infty < \bar{s} < \infty$ *which is such that for any* $\epsilon > 0$ *there are not more than a finite number of terms of the sequence with* $s_n > \bar{s} + \epsilon$ *and an infinite number of terms of the sequence with* $s_n > \bar{s} - \epsilon$, *then* $\bar{s}$ *is the limit superior of the sequence,*

$$\bar{s} = \limsup_{n \to \infty} s_n.$$

DEFINITION 1.3.2. *If the sequence* $s_1, s_2, \ldots$ *is such that for every number* M *there is an integer* n *with* $s_n < M$ *then the limit inferior of the sequence is*

$$\underline{s} = \liminf_{n \to \infty} s_n = -\infty.$$

If there is a number s *with* $-\infty < \underline{s} < \infty$ *which is such that for* $\epsilon > 0$ *there are not more than a finite number of terms of the sequence with* $s_n < \underline{s} - \epsilon$ *and an infinite number of terms of the sequence with* $s_n < \underline{s} + \epsilon$, *then* $\underline{s}$ *is the limit inferior of the sequence,*

$$\underline{s} = \liminf_{n \to \infty} s_n.$$

DEFINITION 1.3.3. *If the sequence* $s_1, s_2, \ldots$ *is such that for every number* M *there exists an integer* n_M *for which* $s_n > M$ *when* $n > n_M$, *then the sequence has the limit*

$$s = \lim_{n \to \infty} s_n = \infty.$$

DEFINITION 1.3.4. *If the sequence* $s_1, s_2, \ldots$ *is such that for every number* M *there exists an integer* n_M *for which* $s_n < M$ *when* $n > n_M$, *then the sequence has the limit* $s = -\infty$,

$$s = \lim_{n \to \infty} s_n = -\infty.$$

DEFINITION 1.3.5. *If the sequence* $s_1, s_2, \ldots$ *is such that there is a number* s *with* $-\infty < s < \infty$ *such that for* $\epsilon > 0$ *there exists an integer* n_ϵ *for which*

$$|s - s_n| < \epsilon$$

when $n > n_\epsilon$, *then this number* s *is the limit of the sequence,*

$$s = \lim_{n \to \infty} s_n.$$

The limits $\bar{s}$, $\underline{s}$ and s of Definitions 1.3.1—1.3.5 are easily seen to be identical with the corresponding limits of Definition 1.3. Hence for these definitions the limits $\bar{s}$, $\underline{s}$ exist for every sequence and $\underline{s} \leq \bar{s}$. If the sequence is bounded $-\infty < \underline{s} \leq \bar{s} < \infty$.

DEFINITION 1.4. *If the sequence* $s_1, s_2, \ldots$ *is such that as* n *increases* s_n *does not increase, or does not decrease, then the sequence is monotone.*

THEOREM 1.3. *If the sequence* $s_1, s_2, \ldots$ *is monotone then it has a limit* s.

Let the sequence be non-decreasing. By Theorem 1.2, $\underline{s}$ and $\bar{s}$ exist and $\underline{s} \leq \bar{s}$. If $\underline{s} < \bar{s}$ there is a number a with $\underline{s} < a < \bar{s}$. It follows from Definition 1.3.1 that there is an integer n_1 with $s_{n_1} > a$. It then follows from Definition 1.3.2 that there is an integer $n_2 > n_1$ with $s_{n_2} < a$. Hence $s_{n_2} < s_{n_1}$, $n_2 > n_1$, and this contradicts the hypothesis that the sequence is non-decreasing. We conclude, therefore, that $\underline{s} = \bar{s}$. Their common value s is then the limit of the sequence under Definition 1.3. The proof is similar when the sequence is non-increasing.

DEFINITION 1.5. *If the sequence $s_1, s_2, \ldots$ is such that for $\epsilon > 0$ there exists n_ϵ with*

$$|s_m - s_n| < \epsilon, \quad m, n > n_\epsilon$$

the sequence is a Cauchy sequence.

THEOREM 1.4. *If the sequence $s_1, s_2, \ldots$ is a Cauchy sequence then it has a finite limit s, and conversely.*

Let $\epsilon > 0$ be given. There is then n_ϵ for which

$$-\epsilon < s_m - s_n < \epsilon, \quad n, m > n_\epsilon.$$

If an integer n_1 is fixed with $n_1 > n_\epsilon$ then for $n > n_1$

$$s_{n_1} - \epsilon < s_n < s_{n_1} + \epsilon, \quad n > n_1.$$

Since the number of terms of the sequence with $n \leq n_1$ is finite it follows that the sequence is bounded. It then follows from Theorem 1.2 that $-\infty < \underline{s} \leq \bar{s} < \infty$. If $\underline{s} < \bar{s}$ let $\bar{s} - \underline{s} = \eta > 0$. Fix n_η so that

$$| s_m - s_n | < \frac{\eta}{2}, \quad m, n > n_\eta.$$

By Definition 1.3.1 there exists $n_2 > n_\eta$ with $s_{n_2} > \bar{s} - \eta/4$, and by Definition 1.3.2 there exists $n_3 > n_2 > n_\eta$ with $s_{n_3} < \underline{s} + \eta/4$. Hence

$$| s_{n_2} - s_{n_3} | > \eta/2, \quad n_2, n_3 > n_\eta,$$

which is a contradiction. We conclude, therefore, that $\bar{s} = \underline{s} = s$, and the sequence has a limit under Definition 1.3.5. /If $s_n \rightarrow s$ then for $\epsilon > 0$ there is n_ϵ such that $| s_n - s | < \epsilon$, $| s_m - s | < \epsilon$, $m, n > n_\epsilon$. These inequalities combine to give $| s_m - s_n | < 2\epsilon$, if $n, m > n_\epsilon$. Hence s_n is a Cauchy sequence.

NOTE 1.1. The proof of Theorem 1.3 involves the use of Axiom 0.1, but Theorem 1.3 could be taken as an axiom and the existence of the number ν which is postulated in Axiom 0.1 could then be established in the following way:

Let every real number be in one or other of two classes R_1 and R_2 which are such that (i) there are numbers in both classes and (ii) any number in R_1 is less than every number in R_2. Let a be a number in R_1, b a number in R_2. Divide the interval $[a, b]$ in halves. Then, on account of (ii), not more than one of the closed halves of $[a, b]$ can contain points of both R_1 and R_2. If this half is $[a_1, b_1]$ it also follows from (ii) that every number less than a_1 is in R_1 and every number greater than b_1 is in R_2. Likewise not more than one of the closed halves $[a_2, b_2]$ of $[a_1, b_1]$ contains points of both R_1 and R_2, with every number less than a_2 in R_1 and every number greater than b_2 in R_2. Continuing there is obtained a sequence of closed intervals $[a_n, b_n]$ each of which contains all of the succeeding intervals, and for each value of n every number less than a_n is in R_1 and every number greater than b_n is in R_2, and $b_n - a_n \to 0$ as $n \to \infty$. Also $a_n \leq a_{n+1} < b$, $a < b_{n+1} \leq b_n$. Hence by Theorem 1.3 a_n tends to a limit λ and b_n tends to a limit λ'. Furthermore, since $a_n < b_n$ and $b_n - a_n \to 0$ it follows that $\lambda = \lambda' = \nu$. If x is a number less than ν, then for n sufficiently great $a_n > x$, and it follows that x is in R_1. Similarly if $x > \nu$ then x is in R_2. Hence ν is the number postulated by Axiom 0.1.

Thus Theorem 1.3, as well as Axiom 0.1, can be, and sometimes is, taken as a starting point for the real variable theory. Such a procedure is, perhaps, desirable for the reason that Theorem 1.3 is more readily taken as evident. There is a third possible starting point which we shall state as

AXIOM 1.1. *If* $[a_n, b_n]$ *is a sequence of closed intervals such that each interval contains all the succeeding intervals and such that* $b_n - a_n \to 0$, *then there is a single point* ν *which is on every interval of the sequence.*

This axiom would lead to the existence of the number ν postulated by Axiom 0.1 as in the foregoing proof, and Theorem 1.3 would then follow. For further comments on this procedure see [19, pp. 68-69].

As we have already remarked, the terms of the sequence $s_1, s_2, \ldots$ may be considered as a set of points A on the line l. We now study the problem of limits from this angle.

DEFINITION 1.6. *The point P is a limit point of the set A if every interval which contains P as an interior point also contains points of A other than P. The point P may or may not belong to A.*

It is an immediate consequence of the definition that every interval which has P on its interior contains an infinite number of points of A.

DEFINITION 1.7. *If all the limit points of a set A belong to A or if A has no limit point, then the set A is closed.*

A set consisting of a finite number of points has no limit point in the sense of Definition 1.6 and is, therefore, closed. Likewise a denumerable set $a_1, a_2, \ldots$ for which $a_n \to \infty$ has no limit points and is therefore closed.

DEFINITION 1.8. *If A is any set, then the set consisting of A and its limit points is the closure of A and is denoted by $\bar{A}$.*

DEFINITION 1.9. *If every point of a closed set A is a limit point of A, then A is perfect.*

DEFINITION 1.10. *If the set A is such that each of its points is interior to an interval all of whose points belong to A, then A is an open set.*

NOTE 1.2. The concepts open and closed are neither inclusive nor mutually exclusive. A set may be neither open nor closed, for example, the rational numbers. A set may be both open and closed. This is the case for the set of all points on the line l. As another example of such a set, consider the points A on the circumference of a circle, and in Definition 1.6, 1.7, and 1.10 replace "interval" by "arc of a circle". Then the set A is both open and closed.

DEFINITION 1.11. *If a point P of a set A is such that there exists an interval containing P on its interior and containing no other points of A, then P is an isolated point of the set A.*

DEFINITION 1.12. *The set A is bounded if there is an interval (a, b) which contains A.*

THEOREM 1.5. (THE BOLZANO-WEIERSTRASS THEOREM). *Every bounded set which has more than a finite number of points has at least one limit point.*

Let A be an infinite set of points on the interval (a, b).

Divide all real numbers x into two classes R_1 and R_2 in the following way: If there is an infinite number of points of A to the right of x then x goes in class R_1. If there are no points of A or only a finite number of points of A to the right of x then x goes in R_2. There are points in both classes, for points to the left of a are in R_1 and points to the right of b are in R_2. The rules for determining into which class x goes put every point x on the line l into one or other of the two classes. Finally, any point in R_1 is to the left of every point in R_2. For suppose there is a point r_1 in R_1 to the right of or coinciding with a point r_2 of R_2. Since r_1 is in R_1 there is an infinite number of points of A to the right of r_1, and consequently an infinite number of points of A to the right of r_2. But this puts r_2 in R_1, which is a contradiction. We can now conclude that the classes R_1 and R_2 constitute a Dedekind section. If ν is the real number defined by this section, every number to the left of ν is in R_1 and every number to the right of ν is in R_2. It then follows that for every ϵ there is an infinite number of points of A on the interval $\nu - \epsilon < x < \nu$. Hence every interval which contains ν as an interior point contains points of A other than ν. Consequently the number ν qualifies as a limit point P of the set A under Definition 1.6. Thus we have shown that A has at least one limit point. It is clear that the set A can have more than one limit point.

NOTE 1.3. An examination of the proof of the Bolzano-Weierstrass theorem reveals that the limit point established in that proof is the right-hand limit point of the set A. An obvious modification of the manner of assigning points x to the classes R_1 and R_2 leads to the left-hand limit point of A. It is clear that these are not necessarily the only limit points of A. For example, if A is the set of rational numbers on $(0, 1)$ every point of $[0, 1]$ is a limit point of A.

It is also clear that the right-hand limit point of A is not necessarily the least upper bound of A. It is if there are no points of A to the right of this limit point; otherwise A has a right-hand point which is the least upper bound of A.

Finally, the Bolzano-Weierstrass theorem can be used to

prove Theorem 1.3 when the sequence $s_1, s_2, \ldots$ is bounded. The elements of the sequence then constitute a bounded set A on the line l. This bounded set A has at least one limit point P, and since the sequence is monotone it readily follows that P is the only limit point and is also the limit of the sequence according to Definition 1.3.5.

THEOREM 1.6 (HEINE-BOREL THEOREM). *If each point of the closed and bounded set A is interior to an interval of the infinite family F of open intervals, there can be selected from F a finite number of intervals having the same property.*

Since A is closed, it has a first point a. Let (a_1, b_1) be an interval of F which has a as an interior point. Since A is closed, there is a first point b'_1 (which may be b_1) of A to the right of (a_1, b_1). Let (a_2, b_2) be an interval of F which has b'_1 as an interior point. We shall show that it is possible to choose in this way a finite set of intervals of F: $(a_1, b_1), \ldots, (a_n, b_n)$, containing all the points of A.

Let ξ be the least bound of points of A which cannot be reached by a finite set of such intervals. Since A is closed, ξ belongs to A. Let (a', b') be an interval of F which has ξ as an interior point. From the definition of ξ, we can find a finite set of intervals $(a_1, b_1), \ldots, (a_n, b_n)$ of F which contain as interior points all points x of A with $x \leq (a' + \xi)/2$. Let (a', b') be the interval (a_{n+1}, b_{n+1}). Then $b_{n+1} > \xi$, and ξ is not the lower bound of points of A which are not included in a finite set of intervals of the family F. This contradicts the definition of ξ and the theorem follows.

That the conditions (i) A be closed and bounded, and (ii) F be a family of open intervals, are necessary is shown by the following examples.

EXAMPLE 1.1. Let $A = (0, 1)$ and let F consist of all open intervals of the form (a_i, b_i) where $0 < a_i < b_i < 1$. Then F covers A but no finite subset of F does. The condition that A be a closed set is not satisfied.

EXAMPLE 1.2. Let A be the closed set $-\infty < x < \infty$ and let F consist of all finite intervals (a, b) covering A. No finite subset of F covers A. The condition that A be a bounded set is not satisfied.

EXAMPLE 1.3. Let A be the closed set consisting of the points $0, 1/r, r = 1, 2, \ldots$. If F is taken equal to A then F covers A but no finite subset of F does. The condition that F be a set of open intervals is not satisfied.

DEFINITION 1.13. *The point x is a condensation point of a set A if every interval containing x contains a non-denumerable subset of A.*

THEOREM 1.7. *A non-denumerable set A contains at least one condensation point and the condensation points of A form a closed set.*

Suppose the set A contains no condensation points of A. If x is a point of A there is then an interval with rational endpoints which contains x on its interior and which contains not more than a denumerable set of the points of A. By Note 0.1 the rational intervals form a denumerable set. It then follows from Theorem 0.2 that the set A is denumerable, and the first part of the theorem is established.

If E is the set of condensation points of A and ξ a limit point of E, then on every interval ω with ξ as an interior point there is a point of E and consequently a non-denumerable subset of A. This makes ξ a condensation point of A. Consequently ξ belongs to E and E is closed.

THEOREM 1.8. *If A is closed and non-denumerable then A consists of a perfect set and a denumerable set.*

Let E be the set of condensation points of A. By Theorem 1.7 E is closed. The set E is perfect. For suppose ξ is an isolated point of E. Then there is an open interval ω containing ξ and containing no other points of E. Let F be the family of intervals with rational endpoints which are on ω and do not contain ξ. There is at most a denumerable set belonging to A on each interval, for otherwise such an interval would contain a point of E by Theorem 1.7. The family F is denumerable by Note 0.1, and contains all of ω except ξ. Hence the points of A on ω are denumerable by Theorem 0.2, giving a contradiction.

The theorem is proved if it can now be shown that $A - E$ is denumerable where $A - E$ denotes the points which belong to A but not to E. Let F be the family of intervals with rational end-points which contain no points of E. Then F contains all of $A - E$. For, since E is closed, if x is a point of $A - E$ then x is on an open interval ω which contains no points of E, and consequently on an interval of F. Since the family F is denumerable it follows from Theorem 0.2 that $A - E$ is denumerable.

1.2. Functions and their properties. In a relation such as $y = 3x^2 + x - 9$, or such as $y = \sin 2x + e^x$, the value of y depends on that of x. This is expressed by the statement "y is a function of x", in symbols $y = f(x)$. In these cases, to each value of x there corresponds a single value of y, and y is called a single valued function of x. The relation $x^2 + y^2 = 9$ is satisfied by two values of y for each value of x for which $-3 < x < 3$ and y is called a double valued function of x. For $y = \arcsin x$ there are infinitely many values of y. More generally, if to each value of x there is more than one value of y, y is called a multiple valued function of x. Furthermore, the relation $y = \arcsin x$ has meaning only when $-1 \leq x \leq 1$.

Functional relations are many and varied. In the examples just given, the relation between y and x is determined by a single expression, but this is not always the case. If $y = 1$ for x rational and $y = -1$ for x irrational, y is a function of x. If t is time and T is the temperature of the atmosphere, then T depends on t, $T = f(t)$. But in neither of these cases is there a formula from which the function can be computed when x, or t, is given. In the early days of the development of mathematical analysis and the theory of functions there was considerable controversy as to what constituted a function. Out of this there emerged a brief and comprehensive definition which has proved adequate for the demands made upon it. This we now state, and it can be easily verified that it covers the illustrations given above.

DEFINITION 1.14. *Let the real variable x range over the set A. The variable y is a function of x, $y = f(x)$, if for each value of x of the set A there is a set of rules for determining the value or values of y.*

In this study we shall be concerned with single valued functions of the real variable x defined for values of x on a set A. Some of the definitions and theorems are variants of those of Section 1.1. For the sake of variety and emphasis we give them independently of those of Section 1.1.

DEFINITION 1.15. *A function $f(x)$ defined on a set A is bounded above if there is a number M such that $f(x) \leq M$ for all x on A, it is bounded below if there is a number m such that $f(x) \geq m$ for all x on A. If $f(x)$ is bounded both above and below it is bounded on the set A and there exists a positive number M such that $|f(x)| < M$.*

If a number M bounds a function above so does any number greater than M, and if a number m bounds a function below so does any number less than m. For functions, as for sets of numbers, there are special bounds called the supremum or least upper bound and infimum or greatest lower bound. A description of these bounds can be inferred from Definition 1.2, for the set of values taken on by a function is a set of numbers. We shall, for emphasis, describe them in terms of the function $f(x)$ in the following definition:

DEFINITION 1.16. *The number M is the supremum of $f(x)$, $M = \sup f(x)$, if $f(x) \leq M$ for every x on A, and for every $M' < M$ there is a value of x on A for which $f(x) > M'$. The number m is the infimum of $f(x)$, $m = \inf f(x)$, if $f(x) \geq m$ for every x on A, and if for every $m' > m$ there is a value of x on A for which $f(x) < m'$.*

THEOREM 1.9. *If the function $f(x)$ is defined on the set A then $f(x)$ has a supremum and an infimum. Also $\inf f(x) \leq \sup f(x)$, and $\sup f(x) < \infty$ if $f(x)$ is bounded above, $\inf f(x) > -\infty$ if $f(x)$ is bounded below.*

If the function $f(x)$ is not bounded above it follows from Definitions 1.15 and 1.16 that $\sup f(x) = \infty$, and if not bounded below that $\inf f(x) = -\infty$. If the function $f(x)$ is bounded above divide all real numbers y into two classes, R_1 and R_2, in the following way: If y is a number such that there are values of x on the set A for which $f(x) \geq y$, then y goes in class R_1. Otherwise y goes in class R_2.

Since $f(x)$ has a value y for each value of x, and since $f(x)$ is bounded above, there are numbers in both classes; also every real number y is in one or other of the two classes, and it can be shown as in Theorem 1.1 that every value r_1 of y in R_1 is less than any value r_2 of y in R_2. Consequently the classes R_1 and R_2 constitute a Dedekind section which defines a real number ν, and this number ν is such that every number less than ν is in R_1 and every number greater than ν is in R_2.

If ϵ is given and $\nu - \epsilon < y < \nu$, then y is in R_1 and consequently there is some x in A for which $f(x) \geq y > \nu - \epsilon$. If $y > \nu$, y is in R_2 and there is no x in A for which $f(x) \geq y$. Hence $f(x) \leq \nu$ for all x in A. This establishes ν as the supremum of $f(x)$ according to Definition 1.16. The existence of inf $f(x)$ may be established in a similar way. The remaining parts of the theorem follow at once from Definitions 1.15 and 1.16.

In the following three definitions the function $f(x)$ is defined on a set A and a is a limit point of A.

DEFINITION 1.17. *If there is a finite number b which is such that for every $\epsilon > 0$ there exists $\delta > 0$ for which $|f(x) - b| < \epsilon$ when $0 < |x - a| < \delta$, then b is the limit of $f(x)$ as x tends to a. The notation for this is*

$$\lim_{x \to a} f(x) = b.$$

DEFINITION 1.18. *If for every $M > 0$ there exists $\delta > 0$ such that $f(x) > M$ when $0 < |x - a| < \delta$, then $f(x)$ becomes positively infinite as x tends to a. There is a corresponding definition for $f(x)$ becoming negatively infinite. In symbols*

$$\lim_{x \to a} f(x) = \infty, \quad \lim_{x \to a} f(x) = -\infty.$$

DEFINITION 1.19. *If there is a number $\bar{b}$ such that for $\epsilon > 0$ every interval with a as an interior point contains a point $x \neq a$ for which $f(x) > \bar{b} - \epsilon$ and if there exists $\delta > 0$ which is such that $f(x) < \bar{b} + \epsilon$ when $0 < |x - a| < \delta$ then $\bar{b}$ is the limit superior or upper limit of $f(x)$ as x tends to a. If for every M and every $\delta > 0$ there exists x_δ with $0 < |x_\delta - a| < \delta$ and with $f(x_\delta) > M$ then as $x \to a$ the limit superior or upper limit of $f(x)$*

is $\bar{b} = \infty$. *There are corresponding definitions for the limit inferior or lower limit* $\underline{b}$. *In symbols*

$$\limsup_{x \to a} f(x) = \bar{b}, \qquad \liminf_{x \to a} f(x) = \underline{b}.$$

If both these limits are finite and if $\bar{b} = \underline{b}$ the common value is the limit of $f(x)$ under Definition 1.17.

Definitions 1.17, 1.18 and 1.19 can be combined in a single definition in a manner similar to that of Definition 1.3.

DEFINITION 1.20. *Let* $f(x)$ *be defined on the set* A *and let* a *be a limit point of* A *which belongs to* A. *If for a given* $\epsilon > 0$ *there exists* $\delta > 0$ *such that* $|f(x) - f(a)| < \epsilon$ *when* $|x - a| < \delta$, x *being a point of* A, *then* $f(x)$ *is continuous on* A *at* $x = a$.

DEFINITION 1.21. *The function* $f(x)$ *is continuous on* A *at a point* a *of* A *if for every sequence of values* $x_1, x_2, \ldots$ *of* x *with* $x_n \to a$, x_n *a point of* A, $f(x_n) \to f(a)$.

NOTE 1.4. Are Definitions 1.20 and 1.21 equivalent? Obviously the first implies the second. Suppose the second holds. If the first does not hold let $\delta_1 > \delta_2 > \ldots$ be a sequence of positive numbers with $\delta_n \to 0$, and let A_n be the set of points x of A for which $\delta_n < |x - a| \leq \delta_{n-1}$. If Definition 1.20 does not hold there is, for $\epsilon > 0$, an infinite set A_{n_k} of the sets A_n each of which contains one or more values of x with $|f(x) - f(a)| \geq \epsilon$. Choose one value x_k from each such set A_{n_k}. Then, since $\delta_k \to 0$, $x_k \to a$, and since $|f(x_k) - f(a)| \geq \epsilon$ it follows that $f(x_k)$ does not tend to $f(a)$. Consequently Definition 1.21 is denied, and we conclude, therefore, that Definition 1.20 holds.

While this method of proof appears satisfactory to most readers, it has, nevertheless, been questioned by eminent mathematicians. The difficulty is this: the point is reached where there is at least one value of x on each of the mutually exclusive sets A_k which satisfies $|f(x) - f(a)| \geq \epsilon$. The next step is to choose one of these values from each set. But which one? There is no rule by which a particular value of x satisfying the relation can be selected. If, for example, the set x

satisfying the relation in question were closed, the least point of the set could be selected. It has been maintained that this method of proof is not acceptable because it is not possible to specify the value of x that is selected from each A_k. This objection was raised long ago and led to the formulation of what has been called the *principle of selection*, first stated by Zermelo [69] in 1904. This principle is also called the Zermelo axiom.

For every aggregate M consisting of sets E, non-empty and mutually exclusive, there exists an aggregate N containing one, and only one, element from each set E.

The principle of choice has proved to be of considerable importance and has never led to a contradiction. The reader would do well to distinguish the instances where it is used.

DEFINITION 1.22. *The function $f(x)$ defined on the set A is continuous on A if it is continuous under Definition 1.21 at each point of A which is a limit point of a.*

DEFINITION 1.23. *Let the function $f(x)$ be defined on a set A and let a be a limit point of A. For $\eta > 0$ let ω be an interval with length less than η which contains the point a. Let $s(a, \eta) = \sup |f(x') - f(x)|$ for every pair x, x' on A* and on ω, *and for all such intervals ω. Then $s(a, \eta) \geq 0$ and does not increase as η decreases. Hence as $\eta \to 0$ $s(a, \eta)$ tends to a limit $s(a) \geq 0$. This limit $s(a)$ is the saltus of $f(x)$ at the point a.*

NOTE 1.5. Definitions 1.20—1.22 do not explicitly define continuity of $f(x)$ at isolated points of A. However, Definition 1.23 implies that if $f(x)$ is defined on A and a is an isolated point of A then $f(x)$ is continuous at $x = a$. While the function $f(x)$ is defined only on the set A, the saltus of $f(x)$ is determined by Definition 1.23 at every point of the set $\bar{A}$, the closure of A. If a is a point of A then $s(a)$ can be taken as a measure of the discontinuity of $f(x)$ at $x = a$. In particular, if $s(a) = 0$ then $f(x)$ is continuous at $x = a$.

THEOREM 1.10. *If $f(x)$ is defined on the bounded set A and at every point where the saltus of $f(x)$ is defined it is less than λ then there exists $\delta > 0$ such that $|f(x) - f(x')| < \lambda$ when x, x' are any two points of A with $|x - x'| < \delta$.*

Suppose the contrary to be true. Let $\delta_1 > \delta_2 > \ldots$ be a sequence of positive numbers with $\delta_n \rightarrow 0$. There then exist for each positive integer n two points x_n, x'_n of A with $|x_n - x'_n| < \delta_n$ and $|f(x_n) - f(x'_n)| \geq \lambda$. By Theorem 1.2 the set $x_1, x_2, \ldots$ has a limit point x_0. Let ω be any interval with x_0 on its interior. Then since x_0 is a limit point of $x_1, x_2, \ldots$ and since $|x_n - x'_n| \rightarrow 0$ as n increases, it follows that there are two points x_n, x'_n of A which are interior to ω and for which $|f(x_n) - f(x'_n)| \geq \lambda$. Since there is no restriction on the length of ω it follows that at x_0 the saltus of $f(x)$ is not less than λ. This is a contradiction, and the theorem follows.

DEFINITION 1.24. *Let $f(x)$ be defined on the set A. If for a given $\epsilon > 0$ there exists $\delta > 0$ such that*

$$|f(x) - f(x')| < \epsilon$$

when x, x' are any two points of A with $|x - x'| < \delta$ then $f(x)$ is uniformly continuous on A.

THEOREM 1.11. *If $f(x)$ is continuous at each point of the bounded and closed set A it is uniformly continuous on A.*

This theorem is a consequence of Theorem 1.10. For if A is closed $s(x)$ is defined only at the points of A, and since $f(x)$ is continuous on A, $s(x) = 0$ at each point x of A. Hence any number $\epsilon > 0$ can replace λ in Theorem 1.10 to give Theorem 1.11.

THEOREM 1.12. *If $f(x)$ is continuous on the closed and bounded set A it is bounded on A. Furthermore $f(x)$ assumes its supremum for at least one value of x on A, and $f(x)$ assumes its infimum for at least one value of x on A.*

Let A be on the interval (a, b). Let $\epsilon > 0$ be given, and choose δ so that $|f(x) - f(x')| < \epsilon$ when $|x - x'| < \delta$. Divide (a, b) into n subintervals each of length less than δ and let $[x_k, x'_k]$ be the intervals of this set which contain points of A. Let ξ_k be a point of A on $[x_k, x'_k]$. Then the finite set of values $f(\xi_k)$ has a maximum M, and since for x on $[x_k, x'_k]$, $|f(x) - f(\xi_k)| < \epsilon$ it follows that $|f(x)| < M + \epsilon$ for x on A. This establishes the first part of the theorem.

To prove the second part of the theorem let $M = \sup f(x)$

for x on A, and let $M_1 < M_2 < \ldots < M$ be an increasing sequence of numbers with $M_n \rightarrow M$. From the definition of $\sup f(x)$ it follows that there is a point x_n on A with $f(x_n) > M_n$. It then follows from the Bolzano-Weierstrass theorem that the set $x_1, x_2, \ldots$ has at least one limit point x_0. Since A is closed x_0 belongs to A. There is then a subsequence x_{n_i} of x_n with $x_{n_i} \rightarrow x_0$, and since $f(x)$ is continuous on A it follows that $f(x_{n_i}) \rightarrow f(x_0)$ as $i \rightarrow \infty$. But

$$M_{n_i} < f(x_{n_i}) \leq M$$

where $M_{n_i} \rightarrow M$. From these relations it follows that $f(x_0) = M$. It can be shown in a similar way that there is a point x_1 on A for which $f(x_1) = \inf f(x)$. This completes the proof of the theorem.

1.3. Sequences of functions and uniform convergence. Let $s_1(x)$, $s_2(x), \ldots$ be a sequence of functions defined on the set A. If for each x on A, $s_n(x)$ tends to a limit $s(x)$ under Definition 1.3.5 then $s(x)$ is a function of x defined on the set A. In this connection a situation arises which often proves troublesome. If x is fixed, $x = x_0$, the sequence $s_1(x_0)$, $s_2(x_0), \ldots$ is a sequence of constants to which Definition 1.3.5 applies. Consequently for a given $\epsilon > 0$ there exists n_ϵ such that

$$|s_n(x_0) - s(x_0)| < \epsilon, \quad n > n_\epsilon.$$

There is no guarantee, however, that this inequality will hold if x_0 is replaced by another value of x on the set A. For this new value of x Definition 1.3.5 may require a larger value of n_ϵ. Indeed cases arise in which for a sequence of values x_0, x_1, $x_2, \ldots$ of x the corresponding values $n_\epsilon^0, n_\epsilon^1, n_\epsilon^2, \ldots$ of n_ϵ satisfying Definition 1.3.5 are such that n_ϵ^i increases without limit as i increases.

EXAMPLE 1.4. Consider

$$s_n(x) = 1 - nx, \quad 0 \leq x < 1/n, \quad s_n(x) = 0, \quad 1/n \leq x \leq 1.$$

Thus $s(x) = 0$, $x \neq 0$, $s(0) = 1$. Let $\epsilon = 1/4$. Then if $x = 1/3$ we can take $n_\epsilon = 3$. But if $x = 1/7$, n_ϵ must be at best as great as 6. Now $S_6(1/7) = 1 - 6/7 = 1/7$ and $s_5(1/7) = 1 - 5/7 = 2/7 > 1/4$. It is easily verified that for $\epsilon = 1/4$, as x takes on the values of the sequence $1/2, 1/3, 1/4, \ldots$ the n_ϵ required by Definition 1.3.5 continues to increase.

There are sequences for which the situation is not so complicated, as the next example illustrates.

EXAMPLE 1.5. For $0 \leq x \leq 1$ let $s_n(x) = (n - 1)/n + x^2$. It is easily verified that $s_n(x)$ tends to $1 + x^2$ as $n \to \infty$. Then if $\epsilon = 1/4$ and $n_\epsilon = 5$,

$$|s_n(x) - s(x)| < \epsilon, \quad n > n_\epsilon \tag{1.1}$$

for all x on $0 \leq x \leq 1$. In general, for a given ϵ if n_ϵ is fixed so that $n_\epsilon > 1/\epsilon$ then (1.1) holds for all x on $0 \leq x \leq 1$.

The sequences that behave like that of Example 1.5 are sufficiently numerous and important to be classified by

DEFINITION 1.25. *The sequence $s_1(x), s_2(x), \ldots$ defined on the set A converges uniformly to the function $s(x)$ if for a given $\epsilon > 0$ there exists n_ϵ such that for all $x \in A$*

$$|s_n(x) - s(x)| < \epsilon, \quad n > n_\epsilon.$$

This definition says that it is possible to make a single choice of n_ϵ such that the inequality of the definition holds for all x of the set A.

In the following theorem the idea of uniform convergence is fundamental. The theorem itself is of considerable importance.

THEOREM 1.13. *Let the sequence of functions $s_1(x), s_2(x), \ldots$ defined on the set A converge uniformly to $s(x)$ and be such that for each n, $s_n(x)$ is continuous on A. Then the limit function $s(x)$ is continuous on A.*

Let $\epsilon > 0$ be given. Fix n_ϵ so that

$$|s_n(x) - s(x)| < \epsilon/3 \tag{1.2}$$

when $n > n_\epsilon$. Let x_0 be a point of A. Fix $n > n_\epsilon$ and then fix δ such that

$$|s_n(x_0) - s_n(x)| < \epsilon/3 \tag{1.3}$$

when $|x - x_0| < \delta$, x on A. This is possible because $s_n(x)$ is continuous over A. Now $|s(x_0) - s(x)| \leq |s(x_0) - s_n(x_0)| +$

$|s_n(x_0) - s_n(x)| + |s_n(x) - s(x)|$. By (1.2) the first and third term on the right are each less than $\epsilon/3$; by (1.3) the second is less than $\epsilon/3$, provided $|x - x_0| < \delta$, x on A. Hence for x on A and $|x - x_0| < \delta$, $|s(x_0) - s(x)| < \epsilon$, and $s(x)$ is continuous over A at x_0 by Definition 1.20.

While uniform convergence of the sequence $s_n(x)$ is sufficient for continuity of the limit function it is not necessary, as the following example shows.

EXAMPLE 1.6. Consider

$$s_n(x) = nxe^{-nx}, \quad 0 \leq x \leq 1.$$

It is easily verified that for each n, $s_n(x)$ is continuous in x. The curve $y = s_n(x)$ has a maximum point at $x = 1/n$, at which point $y = 1/e$. Hence if $\epsilon < 1/e$, no matter how great n_ϵ is taken, there is for $n > n_\epsilon$ a corresponding $x = x_n$ for which $|s(x) - s_n(x)| = 1/e > \epsilon$. Hence the convergence is not uniform on [0,1]. Nevertheless $s(x) = \lim s_n(x) = 0$ and consequently $s(x)$ is continuous.

The question now arises as to whether it is possible to determine conditions which are both necessary and sufficient for the limit function of a sequence of continuous functions to be continuous.

Let $s_n(x)$ be a sequence of continuous functions, defined on an interval $[a, b]$, which converges to $s(x)$. Suppose that for each x_0 and each $\epsilon > 0$ there exist $m = m_{\epsilon x_0}$ and an interval $\omega_1 = (x_0 - \delta_1, x_0 + \delta_1)$ such that $|s(x) - s_m(x)| < \epsilon$, x on ω_1. Since $s_m(x)$is continuous, an interval $\omega_2 = (x_0 - \delta_2, x_0 + \delta_2)$ contained in ω_1, can be found, such that

$$|s_m(x_0) - s_m(x)| < \epsilon, \quad x \text{ on } \omega_2.$$

Then

$$|s(x) - s(x_0)| \leq |s(x) - s_m(x)| + |s_m(x) - s_m(x_0)| + |s_m(x_0) - s(x_0)| < 3\epsilon, \quad x \text{ on } \omega_2.$$

Since ϵ is arbitrary, it follows that $s(x)$ is continuous at x_0.

Now suppose that $s(x)$ is continuous, and let $\epsilon > 0$ be given. For x_0, fix $m = m_{\epsilon x_0}$ such that

$$|s(x_0) - s_m(x_0)| < \frac{\epsilon}{3}.$$

Fix $\omega_1 = (x_0 - \delta_1, x_0 + \delta_1)$ so that for x on ω_1

$$|s(x) - s(x_0)| < \frac{\epsilon}{3}, \ |s_m(x_0) - s_m(x)| < \frac{\epsilon}{3}.$$

We now have, for x on ω_1

$$|s(x) - s_m(x)| \leq |s(x) - s(x_0)| + |s(x_0) - s_m(x_0)| + |s_m(x_0) - s_m(x)| < \epsilon.$$

We have thus proved

THEOREM 1.14. *A necessary and sufficient condition for the continuity of the limit function of a convergent sequence of continuous functions defined on* $[a, b]$ *is that for each* x_0 *and any* $\epsilon > 0$ *there exist* $m = m_{\epsilon x_0}$ *and an interval* $\omega = (x_0 - \delta, x_0 + \delta)$ *such that* $|s(x) - s_m(x)| < \epsilon$, x *on* ω.

We have shown that if $\epsilon > 0$ is given then for each x there exists an interval $\omega_{\epsilon x}$ containing x, and an integer $m = m_{\epsilon x}$ such that for x on $\omega_{\epsilon x}$ $|s(x) - s_m(x)| < \epsilon$. Thus each point x of $[a, b]$ is interior to an interval $\omega_{\epsilon x}$. From the infinite set of intervals thus defined on $[a, b]$ there is, by the Heine-Borel theorem, a finite set $\omega_1, \omega_2, \ldots, \omega_n$ of these intervals such that each point of $[a, b]$ is interior to at least one interval of the finite set. Corresponding to ω_i there is an integer m_i such that for x on ω_i

$$|s(x) - s_{m_i}(x)| < \epsilon.$$

Hence we can state

THEOREM 1.15. *If* $s_1(x), s_2(x), \ldots$ *is a sequence of continuous functions which converges to* $s(x)$ *on the interval* $[a, b]$, *then a necessary and sufficient condition for the continuity of* $s(x)$ *is that for* $\epsilon > 0$ *there exists a finite set of intervals* $\omega_1, \ldots, \omega_n$ *covering* $[a, b]$ *and a corresponding set of integers* $m_1, m_2, \ldots, m_n$ *such that for* x *on* ω_i, $|s(x) - s_{m_i}(x)| < \epsilon$, $i = 1, 2, \ldots n$.

For a more extended study of the convergence of sequences and series see [29, pp. 99-171].

If in a sequence of functions $s_n(x)$ the subscript n which takes on only integer values is replaced by a continuous variable t, which could be time for example, there arises a function $s_t(x) = s(t, x)$ of the two real variables t and x. *This function is continuous in the two variables* t, x *at* (t_0, x_0) *if as* $t \to t_0$, $x \to x_0$, *the function* $s(t, x) \to s(t_0, x_0)$ *where* $t \to t_0$ *and* $x \to x_0$ *in any manner whatever.* It is with some surprise that we learn that a function $s(t, x)$ can be such that $s(t_0, x)$ is continuous in x for each fixed t_0, and $s(t, x_0)$ is continuous in t for each fixed x_0, but at some points $s(t, x)$ fails to be continuous in the two variables under this definition.

EXAMPLE 1.7. Consider the function defined on $0 \leq t \leq 1$, $0 \leq x \leq 1$,

$$s(t, x) = \frac{2tx}{t^2 + x^2}, \quad t, x \text{ not both zero;}$$

$$s(0, 0) = 0.$$

It is easily verified that this function is continuous in one of the variables when the other is fixed. But if the point (t, x) tends to the origin along the line $t = x$ the function $s(t, x)$ tends to unity, which is different from the value of $s(t, x)$ at the origin. A sketch of the surface defined by this function shows that if $0 < \epsilon < 1$ there is no positive number δ such that for all t on $0 \leq t \leq 1$,

$$|s(t, 0) - s(t, x)| < \epsilon$$

for $0 < x < \delta$. In other words, $s(t, x)$ is not continuous in x at $x = 0$ uniformly with respect to t; or to say it in another way, $s(t, x)$ does not converge to $s(t, 0)$ uniformly with respect to t. It is of importance to know under what conditions this convergence is uniform. The example given above shows that continuity in each variable separately is not sufficient. It is, however, possible to prove the following:

THEOREM 1.16. *If on a rectangle* $a \leq t \leq b$, $c \leq x \leq d$ *the function* $s(t, x)$ *is continuous in the two variables then* $s(t, x)$ *tends to* $s(t, x_0)$ *uniformly with respect to* t *for each* x_0 *on* $c \leq x \leq d$.

Suppose for some x_0 the theorem is false. Let $\delta_1 > \delta_2 > \ldots$ be a sequence of positive numbers with $\delta_n \to 0$. Since the theorem is false there is some $\epsilon > 0$ such that there corresponds to δ_n at least one value t_n of t and at least one value x_n of x such that

$$|s(t_n, x_0) - s(t_n, x_n)| \geq \epsilon \tag{1.4}$$

with $|x_0 - x_n| < \delta_n$. The set $t_1, t_2, \ldots$ is bounded and, by the Bolzano-Weierstrass theorem, has at least one limit point t_0. Hence there is a subsequence $t'_1, t'_2, \ldots$ of the sequence $t_1, t_2, \ldots$ with $t'_n \to t_0$ as $n \to \infty$. Also the values x'_n of the sequence $x_1, x_2, \ldots$ which correspond to t'_n are such that $|x_0 - x'_n| < \delta_n$. Hence the point (t_n, x_n) tends to (t_0, x_0) as $n \to \infty$. Then, since $s(t, x)$ is continuous at (t_0, x_0) it follows that for n sufficiently great

$$|s(t'_n, x_0) - s(t_0, x_0)| < \frac{\epsilon}{2},$$

$$|s(t_0, x_0) - s(t'_n, x'_n)| < \frac{\epsilon}{2}.$$

Combining these gives $|s(t'_n, x_0) - s(t'_n, x'_n)| < \epsilon$, which contradicts (1.4). Hence the theorem is established.

Problems

1.1. Use the Dedekind section to show that if $n_1, n_2, \ldots$ is an increasing sequence of positive integers there is a number ξ such that $\Sigma 1/n_i^p$ diverges for $p < \xi$ and converges for $p > \xi$.

1.2. Let the function $f(x)$ be defined on the set A, and let a be any positive real number. Show that the points x at which the saltus of $f(x)$ is greater than or equal to a form a closed set. Construct an example to show that the points x at which the saltus of $f(x)$ is greater than zero do not necessarily form a closed set.

1.3. Let A be a bounded set such that about each point x of an interval $[a, b]$ containing A there is an interval ω which contains at most a denumerable number of the points of A. Show that the set A is denumerable.

1.4. Show that every point of the Cantor set G of Example 0.1 is a limit point of the set.

1.5. Let $f(x) = x$ at the points x of the set G of Example 0.1. On each interval (a_i, b_i) deleted from $[0, 1]$ in the construction of G let $f(x)$ be constant and equal to a_i. Show that $f(x)$ is non-decreasing on $[0, 1]$ and that $f(x)$ has a denumerable set of discontinuities.

1.6. Show that the function $f(x)$ of the preceding problem is continuous at points of G which are not right-hand end-points of the intervals deleted in the construction of G.

1.7. Discuss the continuity of the limit function and the uniformity of convergence for the following sequences:

$$\text{(a)}\quad S_n(x) = \frac{1}{1+nx}, \qquad 0 \leq x \leq 1.$$

$$\text{(b)}\quad S_n(x) = n^2 x e^{-nx}, \qquad 0 \leq x < \infty.$$

$$\text{(c)}\quad S_n(x) = nx(1-x)^n, \qquad 0 \leq x \leq 1.$$

$$\text{(d)}\quad S_n(x) = x\frac{1-e^{-nx}}{1-e^{-n}}, \qquad 0 \leq x < \infty.$$

$$\text{(e)}\quad S_n(x) = \frac{n^2 x}{1+n^3x^2}, \qquad 0 \leq x \leq 1.$$

1.8. (The Weierstrass test for uniform convergence). The series $u_0(x)+u_1(x)+\ldots$ converges uniformly if the sequence $s_n(x)=u_0(x)+\ldots+u_{n-1}(x)$ converges uniformly. If there exists a convergent series of positive constants $a_0+a_1+\ldots$ such that $|u_n(x)| \leq a_n$, show that the series $u_0(x)+u_1(x)+\ldots$ converges uniformly.

1.9. Given the series

$$\text{(a)}\ \sum_{n=1}^{\infty} \frac{\sin nx}{n^2}, \quad \text{(b)}\ \sum_{n=1}^{\infty} \frac{1}{n^p}(1-x^2)^n$$

show that (a) converges uniformly on $-\infty < x < \infty$, and that if $p > 1$, (b) converges uniformly on $-1 \leq x \leq 1$.

1.10. (Abel's lemma). Let the real numbers $a_0, \ldots, a_n$ be such that $a_0 \geq a_1 \geq \ldots \geq a_n > 0$. Let $u_0, \ldots, u_n$ be any n real numbers, $s_1 = u_0+u_1$, $s_2 = u_0+u_1+u_2, \ldots, s_n = u_0+u_1+\ldots+u_n$. If U is the maximum, u the minimum of the numbers $s_1, \ldots, s_n$ then $ua_0 \leq a_0u_0+a_1u_1+\ldots+a_nu_n \leq Ua_0$. ([22], p. 153.)

1.11. (Abel's test). Let $u_0+u_1+\ldots$ be a series such that $s_n = u_0+\ldots u_{n-1}$ is bounded. Let $a_0, a_1, \ldots$ be a sequence of positive numbers for which $a_{n-1} \geq a_n$ and for which $a_n \to 0$. Then the series $a_0u_0+a_1u_1+\ldots$ converges. ([22], p. 148).

1.12.(Dirichlet's test). If the series $u_0 + u_1 + \ldots$ converges and $a_0, a_1, \ldots$ is a monotone sequence of positive numbers such that a_n tends to a finite limit then the series $a_0u_0 + a_1u_1 + \ldots$ converges. ([22], p. 350.)

1.13. (Cauchy's test). If $a_0 + a_1 + \ldots$ is a series of positive terms for which there is a number λ with $0 < \lambda < 1$ and a positive integer n_1 for which $\sqrt[n]{a_n} < \lambda$, $n > n_1$, show that the series converges. ([22], p. 333.)

1.14. If $a_0 + a_1 + \ldots$ is a series of positive terms for which a_{n+1}/a_n tends to a limit then $\sqrt[n]{a_n}$ tends to the same limit.

1.15. If the power series $a_0 + a_1x + a_2x^2 + \ldots$ converges on the interval (a, b) then it converges uniformly on any interval (a', b') for which $a < a' < b' < b$.

1.16. (Abel's theorem). Show that if the series

$$\sum_{n=0}^{\infty} a_n$$

converges and has the value a then the series

$$\sum_{n=0}^{\infty} a_nx^n$$

is uniformly convergent on $0 \leq x \leq 1$, and

$$\lim_{x \to 1} \sum_{0}^{\infty} a_nx^n = a,$$

([62], p. 9.)

1.17. Show that if the numbers a_n are positive and $a_{n-1} \geq a_n$, then the necessary and sufficient condition that the series

$$\sum a_n \sin nx$$

should be uniformly convergent throughout any interval is that $na_n \to 0$. ([53], p. 6.)

1.18. Let $s_1(x), s_2(x), \ldots$ be a sequence of functions which converges to the function $s(x)$. Let ω be an interval containing the point x, let $\sigma_n(\omega) = \sup |s(x') - s_n(x')|$ for x' on ω,

$$\sigma(\omega) = \limsup_{n \to \infty} \sigma_n(\omega),$$

and let $\sigma(x) = \lim\sup \sigma(\omega)$ as the length of the interval ω containing x tends to zero. The function $\sigma(x)$ is the measure of non-uniform convergence of the sequence $s_1(x)$, $s_2(x)$, . . . at the point x. Prove the following:

(a) The points x at which $\sigma(x) \geq k > 0$ form a closed set.

(b) The set at which $\sigma(x) > 0$ is not necessarily closed. Construct an example to show this.

(c) If the functions $s_n(x)$ are continuous, and x_0 is a point for which $\sigma(x_0) = 0$, then $s(x)$ is continuous at x_0.

(d) Let the functions $s_n(x)$ be continuous and converge to a continuous function $s(x)$ on the interval $[a, b]$. Then the set of points x for which $\sigma(x) \geq k > 0$ is non-dense on $[a, b]$.

1.19. If the function $f(x, y)$ is continuous on the rectangle $a \leq x \leq b$, $c \leq y \leq d$, then for $\epsilon > 0$ this rectangle can be divided into a finite set of rectangles with lines parallel to the coordinate axes such that for the points (x, y), (ξ, η), both in the same subrectangle, $|f(x, y) - f(\xi, \eta)| < \epsilon$.

1.20. Let $f(x)$ be defined on $[a, b]$ and let $s(x)$ be the saltus of $f(x)$ at the point x. If $s(x)$ is bounded, show that there is at least one point x on $[a, b]$ at which $s(x)$ takes on the value of its supremum.

CHAPTER II

METRIC PROPERTIES OF SETS

Introduction: In this chapter metric properties of sets and the definitions of measure and measurability are considered. These definitions are based on outer Lebesgue measure. Outer measure and inner measure are contrasting terms which were introduced during the early stages of the work on measure theory. In the definitions of this chapter inner measure does not enter. It seems appropriate, therefore, to use some other designation for what has been called outer measure, and for this the term "metric of a set" is adopted. Two sets A and B are metrically separated if there is an open set containing A and an open set containing B with the metric or outer measure of the common part of the two open sets arbitrarily small. A set A is measurable if A and the set of all points which do not belong to A are metrically separated.

This approach to the problem of measure is made precise in Definitions 2.3, 2.5 and 2.6, and it there becomes clear that it is equivalent to the definitions usually adopted. It was not introduced here for the sake of novelty, but because it is concise, and because it had already been found useful [33, 34, 35, 53].

2.1. Notation and definitions. Sets of points on a line are called linear sets, and it is to these that we shall direct our attention, referring them to the line l of the introduction or to the x-axis of the Cartesian coordinate system. Nearly all the results of Chapters II–IV are valid in two or more dimensions; but the formulation is for linear sets because it is simpler, and because extensions to dimensions of higher order are for the most part obvious. Exceptions to this will be noted as they occur.

DEFINITION 2.1. *If A and B are two sets on l then $A + B$ represents the set of points which belong to either of the sets, and is called the sum or union of the sets A and B. The symbol AB indicates the points that are in both A and B and is called the product or intersection of A and B. If A and B are any sets on* *the line l then the set of points belonging to A but not to B is denoted by $A - B$; $A \subset B$, $B \supset A$ imply that A is a part of B, $A = B$ that A and B are identical, and $AB = 0$ indicates that A and B have no points in common. The latter is also described by saying that A and B are mutually exclusive, or disjoint. Finally, $A \in B$, $B \ni A$ are used to denote that A is an element of B.*

DEFINITION 2.2. *If A is a set on l the set of all points not belonging to A is called the complement of A and is denoted by $\tilde{A}$. If E is used to denote subsets of some fundamental set A then $A - E$ is denoted by $\tilde{E}$ provided the meaning is clear from the context.*

2.2. Descriptive properties of sets. Sets which are closed, or open, have been defined, Definitions 1.7 and 1.10, and it was pointed out in Note 1.1 that the concepts "closed" and "open" are not mutually exclusive. That there is, however, a relation between the two concepts follows from

THEOREM 2.1. *If the set A is open then $\tilde{A}$ is closed, and if A is closed then $\tilde{A}$ is open.*

If A is open and P is a point of A there is an open interval ω with $P \in \omega \subset A$. Hence P cannot be a limit point of $\tilde{A}$. Consequently $\tilde{A}$ contains all its limit points or has no limit point and is, therefore, closed by Definition 1.7. Let A be closed. If $P \in \tilde{A}$ it follows from the definitions of a closed set that P is not a limit point of A. Hence there is $\omega \ni P$ with $\omega \subset \tilde{A}$, and consequently $\tilde{A}$ is open by Definition 1.10.

THEOREM 2.2. *The product of a finite number of open sets and the sum of a finite or infinite set of open sets are again open sets. The product of a finite or infinite set of closed sets and the sum of a finite number of closed sets are again closed sets.*

This theorem follows immediately from the definitions of open and closed sets. It is easy to construct examples which show that the product of an infinite set of open sets is not necessarily open, and examples which show that the sum of an infinite set of closed sets is not necessarily closed.

THEOREM 2.3. *An open set is a denumerable set of non-overlapping open intervals.*

If A is open and P is a point of A there is an interval containing P all of whose points belong to A. Then, since the rational points are dense on l, there are rational points on this interval and consequently A contains rational points. Let the rational points on l be arranged in the sequence $r_1, r_2, \ldots$ and let r_{i_1} be the first member of this sequence which is in A. Since $\tilde{A}$ is closed there is a first point $a_1 \in \tilde{A}$ to the left of r_{i_1} and a first point $b_1 \in \tilde{A}$ to the right of r_{i_1}. Furthermore all points in the open interval (a_1, b_1) belong to A.

Let r_{i_2} be the first point of the sequence of rational numbers which is in A but not in (a_1, b_1). There is a first point $a_2 \in \tilde{A}$ to the left of r_{i_2} and a first point $b_2 \in \tilde{A}$ to the right of r_{i_2}, all points of the open interval (a_2, b_2) belong to A, and the open intervals (a_1, b_1), (a_2, b_2) have no points in common.

This process can be continued to obtain the finite or denumerably infinite set of non-overlapping intervals (a_1, b_1), $(a_2, b_2), \ldots$. In the exceptional case when A is the line l then A is the single interval $(-\infty < x < \infty)$. Whatever is the open set A, these intervals $(a_1, b_1), (a_2, b_2), \ldots$ contain all the points of A. For suppose P is a point of A which is not in any of these intervals. There is then an interval (a', b') with P on its interior, and with all its points belonging to A, and it follows that there is a rational point $r \in A$ and interior to (a', b'). But r precedes some r_{i_n} and therefore is in some interval (a_i, b_i) of the set $(a_1, b_1), (a_2, b_2), \ldots$. Hence (a', b') and consequently P is in (a_i, b_i) which is a contradiction. We conclude, therefore, that the finite or denumerably infinite set of non-overlapping open intervals $(a_1, b_1), (a_2, b_2), \ldots$ is the set A and the theorem is established.

THEOREM 2.4. *A set of non-overlapping intervals is denumerable.*

If the intervals are open they form an open set by Theorem 2.2 and the theorem follows at once from Theorem 2.3. If some or all of the intervals are not open, delete the end-points from these intervals. The resulting set of open intervals is denumerable and consequently the same is true of the original set.

In case the set A of intervals of Theorem 2.4 is a bounded set, there is an alternative proof which is of some interest.

Let A_n be the intervals of A whose length is greater than $1/n$, n a positive integer. Since the intervals of the set are non-overlapping and all are contained in an interval (a, b), for a given n there can be only a finite number of intervals in the set A_n. Hence $A = A_1 + A_2 + \ldots$, which is a denumerable set of intervals by Theorem 0.2.

2.3. Metric properties of sets. For the purpose of arriving at a definition of a metric of a set some notation will first be introduced. Let $\mathfrak{J}$ be the class of sets $I, J, K, \ldots$. which possess a representation of the form

$$I = I_1 + I_2 + \ldots,$$

where each I_i is an open, closed, or half open interval or a single point, and $I_iI_j = 0$, $i \neq j$. The set I can be finite or denumerably infinite. The letters, $\alpha, \beta, \gamma, \ldots$ will be used to denote open sets. By Theorem 2.3

$$\alpha = \alpha_1 + \alpha_2 + \ldots$$

where each α_i is an open interval, $\alpha_i\alpha_j = 0$, $i \neq j$, and consequently $\alpha \in \mathfrak{J}$. Whenever it is desirable to use a single symbol to denote different sets of open intervals this will be done by means of primes or superscripts, α' or

$$\alpha^i = \alpha_{i1} + \alpha_{i2} + \ldots, \quad \alpha_{ij}\alpha_{ik} = 0, \quad j \neq k.$$

The letters u, v, w will be used in a similar way to denote sets of closed intervals. As previously mentioned, the letter ω will be used to denote a single open interval. If a, b are the end-points of an interval, $a < b$, then the length of the interval is $b - a$. Thus the length of an interval is the same whether it is open, closed, or half open.

DEFINITION 2.3. *If A is an interval then the metric of A is the length of the interval, denoted by $|A|°$. If A is a single point or the empty set, the metric of A is zero, $|A|° = 0$. If A is an* *element of class* $\mathfrak{I}$, $A = I = I_1 + I_2 + \ldots$, *then the metric of* A *is given by* $|A|^\circ = \Sigma|I_i|^\circ$.

Evidently if $A = I \in \mathfrak{I}$ then A can be represented in more than one way as the union of sets of mutually exclusive intervals and points. The question then arises: Does the foregoing definition of metric assign the same value to $|A|^\circ$ regardless of the representation of the set A? The definition is not satisfactory unless this is the case. Suppose that

$$I = I_1 + I_2 + \ldots, \quad I = I'_1 + I'_2 + \ldots$$

are two representations of the set $A = I$. Then

$$I_i = \sum_j I_i I'_j, \quad I'_j = \sum_i I_i I'_j,$$

where $I_i I'_j$ is an interval or a point, or is empty. Since each $|I_i I'_j|^\circ$ is positive or zero, the two series

$$\sum_i \sum_j |I_i I'_j|^\circ, \quad \sum_j \sum_i |I_i I'_j|^\circ$$

converge to the same value, finite or plus infinity. If it can be shown that when $J = J_1 + J_2 + \ldots$ is an interval then $\sum|J_i|^\circ$ is the length of the interval, then the first of these is $\sum|I_i|^\circ$ and the second is $\sum|I'_j|^\circ$. If J is an interval the addition of one or two points to either side of

$$J = J_1 + J_2 + \ldots$$

will change neither the length of J nor the value of $\sum|J_i|^\circ$. Consequently there is no loss of generality in taking J as a closed interval.

Let $\epsilon > 0$ be given, and let $\epsilon_i > 0$ be such that $\Sigma\epsilon_i < \epsilon$. Put J_i in an open interval α_i with $|\alpha_i|^\circ - |J_i|^\circ < \epsilon_i$. Every point of J is then interior to an interval of the family of open intervals α_i. Hence by the Heine-Borel Theorem there exists a finite set $\alpha_1, \alpha_2, \ldots, \alpha_n$ of these intervals covering J. Obviously

$$|J|^\circ \leq \sum_{i=1}^{n} |\alpha_i|^\circ \leq \sum_{i=1}^{\infty} |\alpha_i|^\circ < \sum_{i=1}^{\infty} |J_i|^\circ + \epsilon.$$

Since ϵ is arbitrary it then follows that $\sum|J_i|^\circ \geq |J|^\circ$. But for every positive integer n it is obvious that

$$\sum_{i=1}^{n} |J_i|^\circ \leq |J|^\circ.$$

From these two relations it follows that $|J|^\circ$, the length of the interval J, is $\sum |J_i|^\circ$. Hence if A is in class $\mathfrak{J}$ Definition 2.3 assigns the same value to $|A|^\circ$ regardless of the representation of A.

We have now defined $|A|^\circ$, the metric of A, for every set $A \in \mathfrak{J}$. For such sets it is evident that $0 \leq |A|^\circ \leq \infty$. If $A = I = I_1 + I_2 + \ldots$, where $\sum |I_i|^\circ$ converges than $|A|^\circ < \infty$. If $A \in \mathfrak{J}$ is bounded, then $|A|^\circ < \infty$. If A is an open set it follows from Theorem 2.3 that $A \in \mathfrak{J}$. Hence Definition 2.3 assigns a metric to open sets α.

Our next step is the formulation of a definition of metric for any set A. We note first that if A is any set then there are open sets $\alpha \supset A$. For example $(-\infty, \infty)$ is an open set which contains every set A. It is clear that every bounded set A is contained in a bounded set α.

DEFINITION 2.4. *If A is any set then the metric of A is the infimum of $|\alpha|^\circ$ for all sets $\alpha \supset A$.*

From this definition it follows at once that if A is bounded then $|A|^\circ < \infty$, and if $A \subset B$ then $|A|^\circ \leq |B|^\circ$.

We now obtain a result for sets in class $\mathfrak{J}$ which will be useful in establishing the metric properties of all sets.

THEOREM 2.5. *If I and J are two sets in class $\mathfrak{J}$ then $I + J$, IJ are in class $\mathfrak{J}$ and*

$$|I + J|^\circ = |I|^\circ + |J|^\circ - |IJ|^\circ.$$

If I and J are elements of class $\mathfrak{J}$ each consisting of a finite number of points and intervals, it is evident that for such sets the theorem is true. Furthermore, it is evident that for such finite sets $I + J$, $I - J$ are in class $\mathfrak{J}$, and it should be noted that the last relation holds necessarily only when the sets are finite; if, for example, I is the interval (0, 1) and $J = J_1 + J_2 + \ldots$ is the set of rational numbers on (0, 1), then I and J are in class $\mathfrak{J}$ but $I - J$ is not in $\mathfrak{J}$. Continuing with the case in which at least one of the sets I, J is denumerably infinite, let

$$I_1 + J_1 = K^1, \quad I_1 + J_1 + I_2 + J_2 = K^1 + K^2,$$

where $K^2 = (I_2 + J_2) - K^1$. Then $K^1K^2 = 0$, and since there are only finite sets of class $\mathfrak{J}$ entering into the definitions of K^1

and K^2, it follows that K^1 and K^2 are in class $\mathfrak{J}$. If this process is continued there is obtained,

$$I(n) = I_1 + \ldots + I_n,\ J(n) = J_1 + \ldots + J_n,$$
$$I(n) + J(n) = K^1 + \ldots + K^n,$$

where $K^iK^j = 0$, $i \neq j$, and K^i is in class $\mathfrak{J}$, $i = 1, 2, \ldots, n$. Since each K^i consists of at most a finite number of points and intervals and since $K^iK^j = 0$, $i \neq j$, it follows that

$$|I(n) + J(n)|^\circ = \sum_{i=1}^{n} |K^i|^\circ. \tag{2.1}$$

Also, for the reason that $I(n)$ and $J(n)$ are each finite sets in class $\mathfrak{J}$,

$$|I(n) + J(n)|^\circ = |I(n)|^\circ + |J(n)|^\circ - |I(n)J(n)|^\circ. \tag{2.2}$$

Furthermore, the set $I + J = \sum K^i$ and $\sum K^i$ is a denumerable set of mutually exclusive intervals and points. Consequently $I + J$ is in class $\mathfrak{J}$. Also, since $K^iK^j = 0$, $i \neq j$, and since each set K^i consists of a finite number of intervals and points it follows that

$$|I + J|^\circ = \sum |K^i|^\circ. \tag{2.3}$$

It then follows from (2.1) and (2.3) that

$$|I(n) + J(n)|^\circ \to |I + J|^\circ. \tag{2.4}$$

Again,

$$I(n)J(n) = \sum_{l=1,\, m=1}^{n} I_lJ_m, \tag{2.5}$$

where I_lJ_m is a single interval or point, and the sets I_lJ_m and I_jJ_k are mutually exclusive if $l, m \neq j, k$. Furthermore

$$IJ = \sum_{l,\, m} I_lJ_m.$$

Hence $IJ \in \mathfrak{J}$ and by the definition of metric of a set in $\mathfrak{J}$,

$$|IJ|^\circ = \sum_{l,\, m} |I_lJ_m|^\circ.$$

It follows from (2.5) that

$$|I(n)J(n)|^\circ \to |IJ|^\circ. \tag{2.6}$$

Again from the definition of metric,

$$|I(n)|^\circ \to |I|^\circ,\ |J(n)|^\circ \to |J|^\circ. \tag{2.7}$$

Relations (2.2), (2.4), (2.6) and (2.7) now give

$$|I + J|^\circ = |I|^\circ + |J|^\circ - |IJ|^\circ,$$

which is the theorem.

THEOREM 2.6. *If A is a denumerable set of points then* $|A|^\circ = 0$.

This follows from the definition of metric, and the fact that the metric of a point is defined to be zero.

NOTE 2.1. Sets with zero metric are called null sets. Null sets are of frequent occurrence, for the most part as exceptional sets. If a property holds for all points of a set A except for a null set, it is said to hold *for almost all of A*, or to hold *almost everywhere on A*. Finally if a set A is a null set we emphasize the fact that by the definition of zero metric there exists $\alpha \supset A$ with $|\alpha|^\circ$ arbitrarily small.

Theorem 2.6 establishes the fact that a denumerable set is a null set. But sets which are non-denumerable can also be null sets. This is the case with the set G of Example 0.1. This set is on $u_{n1} + u_{n2} + \ldots + u_{n2^n}$ for every n, and $\sum_i |u_{ni}|^\circ = (2/3)^n$, which tends to zero as n increases. It readily follows that for $\epsilon > 0$ and arbitrary there exist $\alpha \supset G$ with $|\alpha|^\circ < \epsilon$, which shows that G is a null set.

DEFINITION 2.5. *Two sets A and B are metrically separated if for $\epsilon > 0$ there exists $\alpha \supset A$ and $\beta \supset B$ with $|\alpha\beta|^\circ < \epsilon$.*

THEOREM 2.7. *If A and B are any two sets then*

$$|A + B|^\circ \leq |A|^\circ + |B|^\circ.$$

If A and B are metrically separated the equality holds. If $A = A_1 + A_2 + \ldots$ then $|A|^\circ \leq \sum |A_i|^\circ$. If A_i and A_j are metrically separated, $i \neq j$, then the equality holds.

If at least one of the numbers $|A|^\circ$, $|B|^\circ$ is infinite the equality sign holds regardless of whether or not the sets are metrically separated. Hence we need to consider only the case in which both $|A|^\circ$ and $|B|^\circ$ are finite. Let $\alpha \supset A$, $\beta \supset B$ with

$$|\alpha|^\circ < |A|^\circ + \epsilon, \; |\beta|^\circ < |B|^\circ + \epsilon.$$

Then $\alpha + \beta \supset A + B$. Furthermore the sets α and β belong to class $\mathfrak{I}$ and consequently satisfy Theorem 2.5. Hence

$$|A + B|^\circ \leq |\alpha + \beta|^\circ = |\alpha|^\circ + |\beta|^\circ - |\alpha\beta|^\circ$$
$$\leq |\alpha|^\circ + |\beta|^\circ < |A|^\circ + |B|^\circ + 2\epsilon.$$

Since ϵ is arbitrary the first part of the theorem follows.

To obtain the second part of the theorem suppose A and B are metrically separated and let $\gamma \supset A + B$ where $|\gamma|^\circ < |A + B|^\circ + \epsilon$. Let $\alpha \supset A, \beta \supset B$ with $|\alpha\beta|^\circ < \epsilon$. Then $\alpha\gamma \supset A$, $\beta\gamma \supset B$ and $|(\alpha\gamma)(\beta\gamma)|^\circ < \epsilon$. Furthermore, since $\alpha\gamma$ and $\beta\gamma$ are open sets and, therefore, are in class $\mathfrak{J}$, we can use Theorem 2.5 to get

$$|A|^\circ + |B|^\circ \leq |\alpha\gamma|^\circ + |\beta\gamma|^\circ$$
$$= |\alpha\gamma + \beta\gamma|^\circ + |(\alpha\gamma)(\beta\gamma)|^\circ$$
$$< |A + B|^\circ + 2\epsilon.$$

Since ϵ is arbitrary, this combines with the first part of the theorem to give, when A and B are metrically separated,

$$|A + B|^\circ = |A|^\circ + |B|^\circ.$$

In proving the third part of the theorem we note first that if $|A_n|^\circ$ is infinite for any n then so is $|A|^\circ$ and the equality holds. Suppose that $|A_n|^\circ$ is finite for every n. Let $\epsilon > 0$ be given, and let $\epsilon'_1, \epsilon'_2, \ldots$ be a sequence of positive numbers with $\sum \epsilon'_n < \epsilon$. Let $\alpha^n \supset A_n$ with $|\alpha^n|^\circ < |A_n|^\circ + \epsilon'_n$. Let $\alpha = \sum \alpha^n$. Then $\alpha \supset A$ and it will be shown that $|\alpha|^\circ \leq \sum_n |\alpha^n|^\circ$. To accomplish this, let (a_j, b_j) be an interval of the open set α. By Theorem 2.3

$$\alpha^n = \alpha_{n1} + \alpha_{n2} + \ldots, \; \alpha_{ni}\alpha_{nj} = 0, \; i \neq j.$$

Let $\alpha_{nij} = \alpha_{ni}(a_j, b_j)$. Let ϵ_j be a positive number with $\sum \epsilon_j < \epsilon$ and $\epsilon_j < (b_j - a_j)/2$. Every point of the interval $[a_j + \epsilon_j, b_j - \epsilon_j]$ is interior to an interval of the set α_{nij}. It then follows from the Heine-Borel theorem that there is a finite set $\alpha_1, \alpha_2, \ldots, \alpha_k$ of these intervals α_{nij} covering $[a_j + \epsilon_j, b - \epsilon_j]$. Consequently, since the intervals $\alpha_1, \ldots, \alpha_k$ are included among the intervals α_{nij},

$$\sum_n \sum_i |\alpha_{nij}|^\circ \geq \sum_{i=1}^{k} |\alpha_i|^\circ > b_j - a_j - 2\epsilon_j,$$

which gives

$$\sum_j \sum_n \sum_i |\alpha_{nij}|^\circ > \sum_j (b_j - a_j) - 2\sum \epsilon_j.$$

The left member of this inequality is a three-way series of positive terms and can, therefore, be summed in any order. Using this and the definition of metric we get

$$\sum_n \sum_i \sum_j |a_{nij}|^\circ = \sum_n \sum_i |a_{ni}|^\circ = \sum_n |a^n|^\circ.$$

From the definition of metric $\sum_j (b_j - a_j) = |a|^\circ$. Then since $\sum \epsilon_j < \epsilon$ where ϵ is arbitrary, it follows that

$$|A|^\circ \leq |a|^\circ \leq \sum |a^n|^\circ < \sum |A_n|^\circ + \sum \epsilon'_n,$$

and since $\sum \epsilon'_n < \epsilon$ where ϵ is arbitrary, it follows that

$$|A|^\circ \leq \sum |A_n|^\circ.$$

Now suppose A_i and A_j metrically separated, $i \neq j$. From the first part of the theorem it follows that

$$\sum_{i=1}^{n} |A_n|^\circ = |\sum_{i=1}^{n} A_n|^\circ \leq |A|^\circ.$$

It then follows that $\sum |A_n|^\circ \leq |A|^\circ$, and this combined with the relation $|A|^\circ \leq \sum |A_n|^\circ$ already obtained, gives $|A|^\circ = \sum |A_n|^\circ$, and the proof of the theorem is complete.

NOTE 2.2. If A and B are such that for $\epsilon > 0$ there is $\alpha \supset A$ except for a null set, and $\beta \supset B$ except for a null set with $|\alpha\beta|^\circ < \epsilon$, then A and B are metrically separated. For by Note 2.1 the exceptional null parts of A and B can be put respectively in open sets α' and β' with $|\alpha'|^\circ < \epsilon$, $|\beta'|^\circ < \epsilon$. Then $\alpha + \alpha' \supset A$, $\beta + \beta' \supset B$, $|(\alpha + \alpha')(\beta + \beta')|^\circ = |\alpha\beta + \alpha\beta' + \alpha'\beta + \alpha'\beta'| < 4\epsilon$, the last relation following from Theorem 2.7. Since ϵ is arbitrary it follows that A and B are metrically separated.

2.4. Measurability and measurable sets.

DEFINITION 2.6. *If the set A is such that A and $\tilde{A}$, the complement of A, are metrically separated then the set A is measurable. The measure of A is denoted by $|A|$ and is equal to $|A|^\circ$, the metric of A.*

THEOREM 2.8. *If the set A is measurable then the set $\tilde{A}$ is measurable, and conversely.*

This follows at once from the definition of measurability.

THEOREM 2.9. *If the set A is open it is measurable. If the* *set A is such that $A(a, b)$ is measurable for every interval (a, b) then A is measurable.*

First let $\epsilon > 0$ be given. Assuming that A is open consider a finite interval (a, b) and let $A(a, b) = \alpha = \alpha_1 + \alpha_2 + \ldots$. Set $\alpha' = \alpha_1 + \ldots + \alpha_n$ where

$$\sum_{n+1}^{\infty} |\alpha_i|^\circ < \epsilon.$$

Since α' is a finite set of open intervals it is possible to put $\tilde{A}(a, b)$ in β with $|\alpha'\beta|^\circ < \epsilon$. Then

$$\alpha \supset A(a, b),\ \beta \supset \tilde{A}(a, b),\ |\alpha\beta|^\circ < 2\epsilon, \tag{2.8}$$

which shows that $A(a, b)$ and $\tilde{A}(a, b)$ are metrically separated, and $A(a, b)$ is measurable. Now let a_i be a sequence of real numbers with $\ldots < a_{-n} < a_{-n+1} < \ldots < a_0 < a_1 < \ldots$, where $a_{-n} \to -\infty$, $a_n \to \infty$, and let $\epsilon_1 > \epsilon_2 > \ldots$ be a sequence of positive numbers such that $\Sigma\epsilon_i < \epsilon$. By (2.8) there exists $\alpha^i \supset A(a_i, a_{i+1})$ and $\beta^i \supset \tilde{A}(a_i, a_{i+1})$, with $|\alpha^i\beta^i|^\circ < \epsilon_i$. Then $\sum \alpha^i = \alpha \supset A$ except possibly for points of the denumerable set a_i, $\sum \beta^i = \beta \supset \tilde{A}$ except possibly for points of the same denumerable set, and

$$|\alpha\beta|^\circ < \sum \epsilon_i < \epsilon.$$

Hence by Definition 2.5 and Note 2.2, A and $\tilde{A}$ are metrically separated. The measurability of A then follows from Definition 2.6. The sequence of intervals (a_i, a_{i+1}) may be used in a similar way to prove the second part of the theorem.

From this point on, when the set A is known to be measurable we shall replace $|A|^\circ$ by the equal number $|A|$. Thus if α and β are open sets it follows from Theorem 2.2. that the sets $\alpha + \beta$ and $\alpha\beta$ are open. Then by Theorem 2.9 these sets are measurable, and their measures, which are also their metrics, can be denoted by $|\alpha + \beta|$, $|\alpha\beta|$ respectively.

THEOREM 2.10. *If the set A is closed then A is measurable.*

If A is closed, then by Theorem 2.1 $\tilde{A}$ is open, and the theorem follows from Theorems 2.8 and 2.9.

THEOREM 2.11. *If A is a null set then A is measurable.*

Let $\epsilon > 0$ be given, and let $\alpha \supset A$ with $|\alpha| < \epsilon$. Let $\beta \supset \tilde{A}$. Then $|\alpha\beta| < \epsilon$, the sets A and $\tilde{A}$ are metrically separated by Definition 2.5, and consequently by Definition 2.6 the set A is measurable.

THEOREM 2.12. *If the sets A and B are measurable, then the sets $A + B$, AB, and $A - B$ are measurable. If A and B are metrically separated then $|A + B| = |A| + |B|$. If $|A|$ is finite and $A \supset B$ then $|A - B| = |A| - |B|$.*

Let $\epsilon > 0$ be given. Since A and B are measurable we have

$$\alpha \supset A,\ \gamma \supset \tilde{A},\ |\alpha\gamma| < \epsilon,$$
$$\beta \supset B,\ \delta \supset \tilde{B},\ |\beta\delta| < \epsilon.$$

Then

$$\alpha + \beta \supset A + B,\ \gamma\delta \supset \tilde{A}\tilde{B} = \widetilde{A + B},$$
$$|\gamma\delta(\alpha + \beta)| \leq |\alpha\gamma\delta| + |\beta\gamma\delta| < 2\epsilon,$$

from which it follows that $A + B$ and $\widetilde{A + B}$ are metrically separated, and consequently $A + B$ is measurable. Then, since $\tilde{A}$ and $\tilde{B}$ are both measurable it follows that $\widetilde{AB} = \tilde{A} + \tilde{B}$ is measurable. Likewise $\widetilde{A - B} = \tilde{A} + AB$ is measurable, and consequently AB and $A - B$ are measurable by Theorem 2.8. That $|A + B| = |A| + |B|$ follows from Theorem 2.7 and the fact that A and B are metrically separated.

If $A \supset B$, we have $A = (A - B) + AB = (A - B) + B$, and since $A - B$ and $AB = B$ are metrically separated it follows from the first part of the theorem that

$$|A| = |A - B| + |B|,\ |A - B| = |A| - |B|.$$

The proof of the theorem is now complete.

THEOREM 2.13. *If $A = A_1 + A_2 + \ldots$ where A_n is measurable and $A_n \supset A_{n-1}$ then A is measurable and*

$$\lim_{n \to \infty} |A_n| = |A|.$$

Since A_n contains A_{n-1} it follows that $|A_n| \geq |A_{n-1}|$. Since $A \supset A_n$ it follows that $|A|^\circ \geq |A_n|$. Consequently if $|A_n|$ is not bounded $|A_n| \to \infty$, $|A|^\circ = \infty$, and $|A_n| \to |A|^\circ$. We next show that this relation holds when $|A_n|$ is bounded, $|A_n| < M$.

Let $E_1 = A_1$, $E_n = A_n - A_{n-1}$, $n = 2, 3, \ldots$. Then E_n is measurable by Theorem 2.12, $E_iE_j = 0$, $i \neq j$, and $E_1 + \ldots + E_n = A_n$. Let $\epsilon > 0$ be given, and let $\epsilon_1, \epsilon_2, \ldots$ be a sequence of positive numbers with $\sum \epsilon_n < \epsilon$. Let $\alpha^n \supset E_n$ with $|\alpha^n - E_n| < \epsilon_n$. Then $\sum \alpha^n \supset A$. Also, since $A = \sum A\alpha^n$, it follows from Theorem 2.7 that

$$|A|^\circ \leq \sum |\alpha^n|^\circ < \sum |E_n| + \epsilon.$$

By Theorem 2.12

$$|E_1| + \ldots + |E_n| = |A_n| < M.$$

From these relations and the fact that ϵ is arbitrary it follows that $|A|^\circ \leq M$, and that for n sufficiently great

$$|A_n| = |E_1| + \ldots + |E_n| > |A|^\circ - \epsilon.$$

We can, therefore, conclude that $|A_n| \to |A|^\circ$, and the theorem is complete when it is shown that A is measurable.

Let (a, b) be any interval and take $A_n = A_n(a, b)$, $A = A(a, b)$. Since A_n is measurable, $A_n \subset A$, and $|A_n| \to |A|^\circ \leq (b - a)$, it is possible to have $\alpha \supset A$, $A_n \subset \alpha^n \subset \alpha$, $|\alpha| < |A|^\circ + \epsilon$, $|\alpha^n| \geq |A_n| > |A|^\circ - \epsilon$, and $\beta \supset \tilde{A}_n$ with $|\alpha^n\beta| < \epsilon$, where ϵ is arbitrary. These relations combine to give, using Theorem 2.12,

$$|\alpha - \alpha^n| = |\alpha| - |\alpha^n| < 2\epsilon.$$

Then, since $\tilde{A}_n \supset \tilde{A}$, we have $\alpha \supset A$, $\beta \supset \tilde{A}$ with

$$|\alpha\beta| = |\alpha^n\beta + (\alpha - \alpha^n)\beta| \leq |\alpha^n\beta| + |\alpha - \alpha^n| < 3\epsilon.$$

Since ϵ is arbitrary it follows that A and $\tilde{A}$ are metrically separated, and consequently $A = A(a, b)$ is measurable. The measurability of A follows from the second part of Theorem 2.9.

THEOREM 2.14. *If $A_1, A_2, \ldots$ is a sequence of measurable sets, the set $A = A_1 + A_2 + \ldots$ is measurable. If $A_iA_j = 0$, $i \neq j$, then $|A| = \sum |A_n|$.*

The set $E_n = A_1 + A_2 + \ldots + A_n$ is measurable by Theorem 2.12, and it is evident that $E_n \supset E_{n-1}$. It follows from Theorem 2.13 and the fact that $A = E_1 + E_2 \ldots$, that the set A is measurable, and $|E_n| \to |A|$. Then by Theorem

2.12, $|A_1|+\ldots+|A_n| \to |A|$. That $|A| = \Sigma|A_n|$ if $A_iA_j = 0$, $i \neq j$, follows from Theorem 2.7.

THEOREM 2.15. *If $A_1, A_2, \ldots$ is a sequence of measurable sets with $A_{n-1} \supset A_n$, then $A = A_1A_2\ldots$ is measurable and $|A_n| \to |A|$ as $n \to \infty$.*

We have $\tilde{A} = \tilde{A}_1+\tilde{A}_2+\ldots$, which is measurable by Theorem 2.14. That A is measurable then follows from Theorem 2.8. If $|A| = \infty$, since $A_n \supset A$ the relation $|A_n| \to |A|$ holds. Suppose that $|A_n|$ is finite for some n. Then, since $A_n \supset A$, $|A|$ is finite, if $E = (A_1-A_2)+(A_2-A_3)+\ldots$ then E is the sum of a denumerable sequence of mutually exclusive measurable sets and it follows from Theorems 2.12 and 2.14 that

$$|E| = \sum|A_n - A_{n+1}| = \sum[|A_n| - |A_{n+1}|] = |A_1| - \lim_{n\to\infty}|A_{n+1}|.$$

Also, $E = A_1 - A$ which gives $|E| = |A_1| - |A|$. Hence $|A_n| \to |A|$.

THEOREM 2.16. *If $A_1, A_2, \ldots$ is a sequence of measurable sets then $A = A_1A_2\ldots$ is measurable.*

Set $E_1 = A_1$, $E_2 = A_1A_2, \ldots$. Then E_n is measurable by Theorem 2.12 and, since $E_{n-1} \supset E_n$, $E = E_1E_2\ldots$ is measurable by Theorem 2.15. But $E_1E_2\ldots = A_1A_2\ldots$. Hence A is measurable.

THEOREM 2.17. *If A is a set with $|A|^\circ$ finite, then there is a measurable set E such that $E \supset A$ and $|E| = |A|^\circ$.*

Let $\alpha^1, \alpha^2, \ldots$ be a sequence of sets of open intervals such that $\alpha^n \supset A$, $\alpha^{n-1} \supset \alpha^n$ and $|\alpha^n| \to |A|^\circ$. Then by Theorem 2.15 the set $E = \alpha^1\alpha^2\ldots$ is measurable and $|\alpha^n| \to |E|$. It then follows that $E \supset A$ and $|E| = |A|^\circ$.

THEOREM 2.18. *If $A = A_1+A_2+\ldots$, where $A_n \supset A_{n-1}$ then $|A_n|^\circ \to |A|^\circ$ as $n \to \infty$.*

Since $A_n \subset A$ it follows that

$$\lim_{n\to\infty} |A_n|^\circ \leq |A|^\circ. \tag{2.9}$$

By Theorem 2.17 there exist measurable sets E_n such that $E_n \supset A_n$ and $|E_n| = |A_n|^\circ$. Set

$$G_n = E_nE_{n+1}\ldots$$

Then G_n is measurable by Theorem 2.16, and, since $A_n \subset E_n$, $A_n \subset A_{n+p}$, $p = 1, 2, \ldots$,

$$G_n \supset G_{n-1},\ E_n \supset G_n \supset A_n. \tag{2.10}$$

It follows from the first relation of (2.10) in conjunction with Theorem 2.13 that

$$E = G_1 + G_2 + \ldots$$

is measurable and that $|G_n| \to |E|$. The second relation of (2.10) in conjunction with the relation $|E_n| = |A_n|^\circ$ gives $|G_n| = |A_n|^\circ$. Hence, since $E \supset A$, $|A_n|^\circ \to |E| \geq |A|^\circ$. This with (2.9) gives the theorem.

THEOREM 2.19. *If the sets A and B are metrically separated there exist measurable sets E and F with $E \supset A$, $F \supset B$ and $|EF| = 0$.*

Let $\epsilon_1 > \epsilon_2 > \ldots$ be a sequence of positive numbers with $\epsilon_n \to 0$. Let $\alpha^n \supset A$, $\beta^n \supset B$ with $|\alpha^n \beta^n| < \epsilon_n$. Let $E = \alpha^1 \alpha^2 \ldots$, $F = \beta^1 \beta^2 \ldots$ Then by Theorem 2.16 E and F are measurable. Since for every n, $EF \subset \alpha^n \beta^n$, we have $|EF| \leq |\alpha^n \beta^n| < \epsilon_n$ for every n. Then, since $\epsilon_n \to 0$, it follows that $|EF| = 0$.

THEOREM 2.20. *Let A be a measurable set and let $A = A_1 + A_2$ where A_1 and A_2 are metrically separated. Then A_1 and A_2 are measurable and $|A| = |A_1| + |A_2|$. Let A and B be two sets with $|A|^\circ$ and $|B|^\circ$ finite which are not metrically separated. If A_1 and B_1 are two sets with $A_1 \subset A$, $B_1 \subset B$ and with $|A_1|^\circ$, $|B_1|^\circ$ sufficiently close to $|A|^\circ$, $|B|^\circ$ respectively, then A_1 and B_1 are not metrically separated.*

Since A_1 and A_2 are metrically separated, it follows from Theorem 2.19 that measurable sets E and F exist such that $E \supset A_1$, $F \supset A_2$ and $|EF| = 0$. The set AE is measurable by Theorem 2.12. Also if $G = AE - A_1$ then $A_1 \subset AE = A_1 + G$. Then $G \subset A_2$ and it follows that $EF \supset G$. This in turn gives $0 \leq |G|^\circ \leq |EF| = 0$. Hence G is measurable and $|G| = 0$. Then by Theorem 2.12 $A_1 = AE - G$ is measurable. This, in turn, gives $A_2 = A - A_1$ measurable, and it then follows from Theorem 2.12 that $|A| = |A_1| + |A_2|$.

Coming to the second part of the theorem, if A and B are not metrically separated there exists $\lambda > 0$ such that if $\alpha \supset A$,

$\beta \supset B$ then $|\alpha\beta| > \lambda$. Now suppose $|A_1|^\circ > |A|^\circ - \lambda/8$, $|B_1|^\circ > |B|^\circ - \lambda/8$. If $\alpha \supset A$, $\beta \supset B$ with $|\alpha| < |A|^\circ + \lambda/8$, $|\beta| < |B|^\circ + \lambda/8$, and $\alpha \supset \alpha' \supset A_1$, $\beta \supset \beta' \supset B_1$, then it is easily verified that $|\alpha'\beta'| > \lambda/2$. Hence A_1 and A_2 are not metrically separated.

THEOREM 2.21. *If A is measurable with $|A|$ finite then corresponding to $\epsilon > 0$ there is a closed set C with $C \subset A$ and $|A - C| < \epsilon$.*

There is an open set $\alpha \supset \tilde{A}$ with $|\alpha - \tilde{A}| < \epsilon$. Putting $C = \tilde{\alpha}$, we have $A - C = \alpha - \tilde{A}$, which gives the result.

2.5. Further descriptive properties of sets.

THEOREM 2.22. *Let $C_1, C_2, \ldots$ be a sequence of bounded closed, non-empty sets which are such that $C_{n-1} \supset C_n$. Then the set $C = C_1C_2\ldots$ is not empty and is closed.*

Suppose that C_1 is contained in an interval (a, b). From each set let the right-hand point be selected. There is obtained a bounded infinite set of points which, by the Bolzano-Weierstrass theorem, has at least one limit point P. It is clear that P is in C_1. Suppose that P is not in C_k. There is then an interval ω about P containing no point of C_k. Thence since $C_k \supset C_{k+l}$, $l = 1, 2, \ldots$, there is no point of C_{k+l} in ω, $l \geq 1$. This contradicts the definition of P. Hence $P \in C_1C_2\ldots = C$. If P is any limit point of C it is a limit point of each of the closed sets $C_1, C_2, \ldots$ and consequently belongs to each of these sets. Hence $P \in C = C_1C_2\ldots$ and it follows that C is closed.

THEOREM 2.23 (BAIRE'S THEOREM). *If C is a non-empty closed set and $C = C_1 + C_2 + \ldots$ where C_n is closed ($n = 1, 2, \ldots$), then there is a closed interval v with centre in C, and a positive integer n such that $vC = vC_n$.*

Suppose that the theorem is false. Consider the aggregate of closed intervals with rational end-points such that there is at least one point of C on the interior of each interval. Since the pairs of rational numbers have been shown in Note 0.1 to be denumerable, this aggregate of intervals is denumerable and may be arranged in the sequence $u_1, u_2, \ldots$.

Since the theorem is supposed to be false, the interior of u_1 contains at least one point ξ of $(C - C_1) \subset \tilde{C}_1$. Since $\tilde{C}_1$ is open by Theorem 2.1, a closed interval $v_1 \subset u_1$ may be formed with ξ as centre and containing only points of $\tilde{C}_1$. Now v_1 contains intervals of the set $u_1, u_2, \ldots$ of which we select the first which contains a point of C. Let the interval selected be denoted by w_1. Then $w_1 \subset \tilde{C}_1$, and using w_1 and C_2 we may repeat the above reasoning to get

$$w_2 \subset \widetilde{C_1 + C_2}; \quad w_1 \supset w_2 \supset, \ldots; \quad w_n C_n = 0; \quad w_n C \neq 0;$$
$$w_n \text{ closed}, \; n = 1, 2, \ldots.$$

It is also true that $w_n C$ is closed, by Theorem 2.2, and $w_{n-1}C \supset w_n C$. If, now, we define $A = w_1 C w_2 C \ldots$ it follows from Theorem 2.22 that A is not empty. If $x \in A$ then $x \in C$ and consequently $x \in C_n$ for some value of n. But if $x \in A$ it is in $w_n C$ for every n. Hence $w_n C_n$ is not empty, which is a contradiction. The truth of the theorem now follows.

THEOREM 2.24. *If C is a denumerable closed set then C is not perfect.*

Let $c_1, c_2, \ldots$ be the members of C. By Baire's Theorem there exists a closed interval v with centre in C and a positive integer n such that $vC_n = vC$. Hence C_n is isolated, and cannot, therefore, be a limit point of C. This proves the theorem.

NOTE 2.3. Returning to Example 0.1, the Cantor set G is closed by Theorem 2.1, since $\tilde{G}$ is the set $\alpha^0 + \alpha^1 + \ldots$ which is open by Theorem 2.2. Every point of G is a limit point of G. For if a point $\xi \in G$ is isolated, it is the end-point of two abutting open intervals of the set $\tilde{G}$. But there is no stage in the construction of the intervals of $\tilde{G}$ at which an interval is taken which abuts another interval of $\tilde{G}$. Hence G is perfect by Definition 1.8. Therefore, by Theorem 2.24, G cannot be denumerable.

2.6. Measure-preserving transformations and non-measurable sets. In the present chapter, and in the two following chapters, considerable use is made of the concepts of measurable sets and measurable functions. This naturally raises the question as to whether or not all sets are measurable. If the answer is in the affirmative there is no point to much of the foregoing discussion. As a matter of fact, the answer is not in the affirmative. While we are not able to give an explicit example of a non-measurable set we are able at least to make it plausible that such sets exist. We first need some results on transformations.

DEFINITION 2.7. *A measure preserving transformation is a transformation T which is one to one, which preserves measure, and which has an inverse T^{-1}; if $x' = Tx_0$ then $x_0 = T^{-1}x'$, and if A is a measurable set then TA, the transform of A, is measurable and $|TA| = |A|$.*

THEOREM 2.25. *If h is a real number, the translation T: $x' = x + h$ is measure preserving.*

If the inverse of T is $T^{-1}: x = x' - h$, then the requirements of T having an inverse and of being one to one are satisfied. For any set A let $TA = A_h$. Then if A is an interval (a, b), A_h is the interval $(a + h, b + h)$, and $|A_h| = |A|$. Hence if α is a non-overlapping set of open intervals, the same is true of α_h and $|\alpha_h| = |\alpha|$.

Now let A be a measurable set. For $\epsilon > 0$ let $\alpha \supset A, \beta \supset \tilde{A}$, with $|\alpha\beta| < \epsilon$. Then $\alpha_h \supset A_h$, $\beta_h \supset \tilde{A}_h$ and $|\alpha_h\beta_h| = |(\alpha\beta)_h| = |\alpha\beta| < \epsilon$. Since ϵ is arbitrary, A_h and $\tilde{A}_h$ are metrically separated, and consequently A_h is measurable. Since $|\alpha_h| = |\alpha|$ it follows that $|A_h| \leq |A|$. Also $A = T^{-1}A_h$, from which it follows that $|A| \leq |A_h|$. Consequently $|A_h| = |A|$, which concludes the theorem.

2.7. A non-measurable set. A set will now be constructed which is not measurable according to Definition 2.6.

Let ω denote the interval $0 < x < 1$ and for $x \in \omega$, let $B(x)$ denote the set of numbers ξ for which $\xi - x$ is rational, $0 < \xi < 1$.

(i) If $x - y$ is irrational then $B(x)B(y) = 0$.

For suppose there is ξ such that $\xi \in B(x)B(y)$. It follows that $\xi - x = r_1$, $\xi - y = r_2$, and $x - y = r_2 - r_1$ is rational. This contradicts the hypothesis that $x - y$ is irrational and (i) is established.

(ii) If $x - y$ is rational then $B(x) = B(y)$.

For suppose $\xi \in B(x)$ with $\xi - x = r_1$. Since $x - y = r_2$ it follows that $\xi - y = r_1 + r_2$ is rational and hence $\xi \in B(y)$. Similarly if $\xi \in B(y)$ it may be deduced that $\xi \in B(x)$, and (ii) is established.

(iii) If $B(x)$, $B(y)$ have one point in common they are identical.

This follows at once from (i) and (ii).

These considerations allow us to conclude that as x moves over ω generating the sets $B(x)$, the members of the aggregate of sets $B(x)$ are distinct. That is to say, to each x on ω there corresponds a single set $B(x)$. The correspondence is not one to one however, for by (ii) every rational number generates the same set.

Let A be a set formed by taking one point from each of the mutually exclusive sets $B(x)$. Thus

(iv) For $x \in \omega$, $AB(x)$ consists of a single point.

Let $r_1, r_2, \ldots$ be the rational numbers on $(-1, 1)$, and let $E_n(x) = x + r_n$ be a transformation defined for $n = 1, 2, \ldots$, so that $E_n(A)$ is the set of all points $x + r_n$, where $x \in A$.

(v) If $m \neq n$, $E_m(A)E_n(A) = 0$.

Suppose $x \in E_m(A)E_n(A)$. Then

$$x = \xi + r_m, \ \xi \in A; \ x = \eta + r_n, \ \eta \in A,$$

which gives $\xi - \eta = r_n - r_m$, a rational number. Consequently by (ii), ξ and η correspond to the same set $B(x)$. But $AB(x)$ is a single point and hence $\xi = \eta$. But this makes $m = n$ which is a contradiction. We conclude that $E_m(A)E_n(A) = 0$ if $m \neq n$.

(vi) If $x \in \omega$ then $x \in E_n(A)$ for some value of n.

Let ξ be the point of $B(x)$ which is in A. Then $x = \xi + r$, where r is some rational number r_n on $(-1, 1)$. Hence $x = \xi + r_n \in E_n(A)$.

If A is measurable, then by Theorem 2.25 $E_n(A)$ is measurable and $|E_n(A)| = |A|$. But $E_m(A)E_n(A) = 0$, $m \neq n$, and $E_n(A) \subset (-1, 2)$. Therefore by Theorem 2.14,

$$|\sum E_n(A)| = \sum |E_n(A)| \leq 3,$$

from which it follows that $|E_n(A)| = 0$, and consequently $\sum |E_n(A)| = 0$. But $\sum E_n(A) \supset \omega$ which makes $\sum |E_n(A)| \geq 1$.

This contradiction leads us to conclude that the set A is non-measurable.

For further insight into the problem of non-measurable sets the reader is referred to [24, 37, 63].

NOTE 2.3. In Section 2.6 it is stated that no explicit rule for defining a non-measurable set has ever been given. In defining the set A of Section 2.7 one point was taken from each of the mutually exclusive sets $B(x)$. The question then comes up: Which point? There is no way of determining this, and again we must have recourse to the axiom of choice which affirms the existence of a set A which contains one and only one point from each of the mutually exclusive sets $B(x)$. To anyone who does not accept this axiom we have not demonstrated the existence of non-measurable sets.

Problems

2.1. The Cantor set G of Example 0.1 is such that $|G| = 0$. If $0 < \lambda < 1$ modify the method of that example to construct a non-dense closed set G with $|G| = \lambda$.

2.2. Let the set E be closed and bounded and let $\epsilon > 0$ be given. Show that there is a finite set of mutually exclusive intervals, $\alpha = \alpha_1, \ldots, \alpha_n$, such that $\alpha \supset E$ and $|\alpha - E| < \epsilon$.

2.3. Let A be any set contained in a finite interval (a, b). The number $b - a - |\tilde{A}(a, b)|^\circ$ is called the inner measure of the set A. If this inner measure is equal to $|A|^\circ$ the set A is said to be measurable. This is the usual definition of Lebesgue measurability. Show that it is equivalent to Definition 2.6.

2.4. Show that $|A|^\circ$ is not less than the inner measure of A, and that the excess of $|A|^\circ$ over the inner measure is the infimum of $|\alpha\beta|$ for all sets $\alpha \supset A$ and $\beta \supset \tilde{A}(a, b)$.

2.5. According to Carathéodory, a set A is measurable if for every set W with $|W|^\circ$ finite the relation

$$|W|^\circ = |AW|^\circ + |W - AW|^\circ$$

holds. Show that this definition is equivalent to Definition 2.6

2.6. Let A be any set. The set of points x which are such that $|A\omega|^\circ > 0$ for every interval ω containing x is a closed set.

2.7. Let A be any set, λ and δ positive numbers with $0 < \lambda < 1$. The set of points x which are such that

$$|A(x, x + h)|^\circ \geq \lambda h, \quad 0 < h \leq \delta,$$

is a closed set.

2.8. Let the function $f(x)$ be continuous on $[a, b]$ and not constant. Let $\epsilon > 0$ be given. If there exist x and x' with $|f(x) - fx')| > 2\epsilon$, show that there is a first point $x_1 > a$ such that $f(x_1) = f(a) + \epsilon$, or $f(x_1) = f(a) - \epsilon$, a first point $x_2 > x_1$ for which $f(x_2) = f(x_1) + \epsilon$ or $f(x_2) = f(x_1) - \epsilon$, and so on. Show that this can be continued to give a finite set $a < x_1 < x_2 < \ldots < x_n$ where $|f(x_n) - f(x)| \leq \epsilon$, $x_n \leq x \leq b$. Hence deduce that $f(x)$ is bounded and uniformly continuous on $[a, b]$.

2.9. Let $f(x)$ be continuous on $[a, b]$ and let $M = \sup f(x)$, x on $[a, b]$. Let E_n be the set for which

$$f(x) \geq M - \frac{1}{n}, \quad n = 1, 2, \ldots .$$

Show that E_n is closed, and that $E_{n-1} \supset E_n$. Then use Theorem 2.22 to establish the existence of a closed set C (which may be a single point) for which $f(x) = M$, $x \in C$.

2.10. Let $\mu(x)$ be a non-decreasing, continuous, bounded function on $(-\infty, \infty)$. Let $\mu(a, b)$ be a function of the interval (a, b) defined by $\mu(b) - \mu(a)$. If in the definitions of metric and measure $\mu(a, b)$ replaces the lengths of intervals (a, b), there results a metric $\mu^\circ(A)$ and a measure $\mu(A)$ corresponding respectively to $|A|^\circ$, $|A|$. Show that $\mu^\circ(A) < \infty$ for all sets A.

CHAPTER III

THE LEBESGUE INTEGRAL

Introduction: In this chapter we first define measurable functions and the integral of Lebesgue. Then, for purposes of comparison and contrast, we define the integral of Riemann. While this reverses the chronological order it does not mean that the Riemann integral has been superseded in usefulness by that of Lebesgue. It is still the tool of elementary calculus and many phases of applied mathematics; but the integral of Riemann is included in that of Lebesgue, and for the purposes of this book there is no point in giving it a separate detailed study.

3.1. Measurable functions.

DEFINITION 3.1. *If $f(x)$ is defined on a measurable set A in such a way that for every real number a the set $E \subset A$ for which $f(x)$ is less than a, $E(f < a)$, is measurable then $f(x)$ is measurable on A.*

THEOREM 3.1. *If $f(x)$ is measurable on the set A, then the sets $E(f \geq a)$, $E(f > a)$, $E(f = a)$ are measurable. If a_1 and a_2 are any two real numbers with $a_1 < a_2$ then the sets $E(a_1 < f < a_2)$, $E(a_1 < f \leq a_2)$, $E(a_1 \leq f \leq a_2)$, $E(a_1 \leq f < a_2)$ are measurable. If e is any measurable subset of A then $f(x)$ is measurable on e.*

The measurability of $E(f \geq a)$ follows from $E(f \geq a) = A - E(f < a)$ and Theorem 2.12. Let $a_1 > a_2 > \ldots > a_n > \ldots > a$ be a sequence of real numbers with $a_n \to a$. Let $E_n = E(f \geq a_n)$. Then by what has just been proved E_n is measurable, and obviously $E_n \supset E_{n-1}$. The measurability of $E(f > a)$ then follows from $E(f > a) = E_1 + E_2 + \ldots$ and Theorem 2.14. Again, $E(f = a) = E(f \geq a) - E(f > a)$, and $E(f \leq a) = A - E(f > a)$, which are measurable sets by Theorem 2.12.

For the set $E(a_1 < f < a_2)$ we have

$$E(a_1 < f < a_2) = E(f < a_2) - E(f \leq a_1)$$

which is measurable by Theorem 2.12. The measurability of

the remaining three sets of this group follows in a similar way.

If e is any measurable subset of A and a is any real number, the part of e for which $f < a$ is the set $e[E(f < a)]$, which is measurable by Theorem 2.12. Hence by Definition 3.1, f is measurable on e.

THEOREM 3.2. *If the function $f(x)$ is measurable on the measurable set A and $c \neq 0$ is any real number, then the functions cf and $c + f$ are measurable on A. If $\varphi(x)$ is a function measurable on A then the set $E(f < \varphi)$ is measurable; also the functions $f + \varphi$ and $f\varphi$ are measurable.*

If c is any real number different from zero, then the set $E(cf < a)$ is the set $E(f < a/c)$ or $E(f > a/c)$ according as c is positive or negative; and the set $E(c + f < a)$ is the set $E(f < a - c)$. These sets are measurable by definition and by Theorem 3.1.

If $f < \varphi$ for a point x, there is a rational number r such that $f < r < \varphi$. Let the rational numbers be arranged in the sequence $r_1, r_2, \ldots$ and let $E_n = E(f < r_n < \varphi)$. The measurability of E_n follows the relation

$$E_n = E(f < r_n)E(\varphi > r_n),$$

and Theorems 2.12 and 3.1. The set $E(f < \varphi) = E_1 + E_2 + \ldots,$ which is measurable by Theorem 2.14. The set $E(f + \varphi < a)$ is the set $E(f < a - \varphi)$, the measurability of which follows from the result just obtained. Hence $f + \varphi$ is measurable on A. To prove that $f\varphi$ is measurable we first note that f^2 is measurable. For the set $E(f^2 < a)$, $a > 0$, is the set $E(-\sqrt{a} < f < \sqrt{a})$ which is measurable by Theorem 3.1. Writing

$$f\varphi = 1/2\,[(f + \varphi)^2 - (f^2 + \varphi^2)],$$

it then follows from the results already obtained that the function on the right is measurable on A. Hence $f\varphi$ is measurable on A. This completes the proof of the theorem.

3.2. The Lebesgue integral.

DEFINITION 3.2. *Let $f(x)$ be bounded and measurable on the bounded and measurable set A. Let m and M be two real numbers such that $m < f < M$ for $x \in A$, and let $a_0 = m < a_1 <$*

$a_2 < \ldots < a_n = M$ *be a subdivision*, Δ, *of* (m, M). *Let* $e_i = E(a_{i-1} \leq f < a_i)$. *The set* e_i *is measurable by Theorem* 3.1. *If* $a_i - a_{i-1} \to 0$ *as* $n \to \infty$ *then*

$$\lim_{n\to\infty} \sum_{i=i}^{n} a_i|e_i| = L(f, A) = \int_A f(x)dx$$

is the Lebesgue integral of $f(x)$ *over* A.

In what follows the two symbols which represent the limit of the sum $\sum a_i|e_i|$ will be used interchangeably. The second symbol will usually, but not always, be used in display.

The statement of the definition implies that to every function bounded and measurable on the bounded and measurable set A there corresponds a number $L(f, A)$ such that

$$\left|\sum a_1|e_i| - L(f, A)\right|$$

is arbitrarily small if the maximum of $a_i - a_{i-1}$ is sufficiently small. We shall show that this is the case.

Let Δ be a subdivision of (m, M) of the type called for by Definition 3.2 and consider the upper and lower sums

$$S = \sum_{i=1}^{n} a_i|e_i|\ , \quad s = \sum_{i=1}^{n} a_{i-1}|e_i|\ .$$

Then

$$m|A| \leq s \leq S \leq M|A|\ ,$$

and

$$S - s = \sum (a_i - a_{i-1})|e_i| < \eta|A|\ ,$$

where η is the maximum of $a_i - a_{i-1}$, $i = 1, 2, \ldots n$. Hence $S - s \to 0$ as $\max (a_i - a_{i-1}) \to 0$. Let $L = \inf S$ for all possible subdivisions of (m, M) and let Δ, Δ' be any two of these subdivisions. Also let $e_{ij} = e_i e'_j$. Then if ξ_{ij} is any point of e_{ij} it follows that

$$a'_{j-i},\ a_{i-1} \leq f(\xi_{ij}) \leq a'_j,\ a_i.$$

Consequently

$$s = \sum_{i=1}^{n} a_{i-1}|e_i| \leq \sum_{i=1}^{n}\sum_{j=1}^{m} f(\xi_{ij})|e_{ij}| \leq \sum_{i=1}^{n} a_i|e_i| = S,$$

$$s' = \sum_{j=1}^{m} a'_{j-1}|e'_j| \leq \sum_{j=1}^{m}\sum_{i=1}^{n} f(\xi_{ij})|e_{ij}| \leq \sum_{j=1}^{m} a'_j|e'_j| = S'.$$

Since the double sums are equal, it follows that any s is less than or equal to every S'. It then follows that every s satisfies $s \leq L$. Hence $s \leq L \leq S$, and since $S - s \to 0$ as $a_i - a_{i-1} \to 0$, it follows that both s and S tend to L as $a_i - a_{i-1} \to 0$.

NOTE 3.1. A second proof of the fact that the sums s and S tend to a limit will now be indicated which is, perhaps, somewhat more direct. Let $L_\eta = \inf S$ for all possible subdivisions Δ with $a_i - a_{i-1} < \eta$. If $\eta_1 < \eta_2$ then $L_{\eta_1} \geq L_{\eta_2}$ and always $L_\eta \leq M|A|$ where $|f(x)| < M$. Let

$$L = \lim_{\eta \to 0} L_\eta.$$

There is then a sequence of subdivisions $\{\Delta\}$ for which the corresponding sequence of sums $\{S\}$ is such that $S \to L$. Then since $S - s \to 0$ it follows that $s \to L$ and consequently the double sum in the first of the relations given above tends to L. Let $\epsilon > 0$ be given and take a subdivision Δ of this special sequence $\{\Delta\}$ for which the corresponding sums s and S satisfy $S - s < \epsilon$. Then the corresponding double sum differs from L by not more than ϵ. Now let Δ' be any subdivision whatever with $a'_j - a'_{j-1}$ sufficiently small to ensure that $S' - s' < \epsilon$. The double sum for this subdivision is equal to that for the particular subdivision Δ, and consequently differs from L by not more than ϵ. It then follows that s' and S' differ from L by not more than ϵ.

3.3. The Riemann integral. For purposes of comparison and contrast we now give the definition of the Riemann integral of a bounded function.

DEFINITION 3.3. *Let the function $f(x)$ be defined and bounded on the closed interval $[a, b]$. Let $a = x_0 < x_1 < \ldots < x_n = b$ be a subdivision, Δ, of $[a, b]$, and let ξ_i be any point such that $x_{i-1} \leq \xi_i \leq x_i$. If as $n \to \infty$ and $x_i - x_{i-1} \to 0$ the sum*

$$\sum_{i=1}^{n} f(\xi_i)(x_i - x_{i-1})$$

tends to a limit, this limit is the Riemann integral of $f(x)$ over $[a, b]$, and is designated by $R(f, a, b)$.

The clause "if the limit exists" implies that it does not

exist for every bounded function, and this is indeed the case, as we shall now show by an example.

EXAMPLE 3.1. For $0 \leq x \leq 1$ let

$$f(x) = 0 \text{ when } x \text{ is rational,}$$
$$f(x) = 1 \text{ when } x \text{ is irrational.}$$

If $x_0 = 0 < x_1 < \ldots < x_n = 1$ is any subdivision of [0, 1], then since both the rational and irrational numbers are dense on [0, 1] each ξ_i can be rational, which makes the sum in Definition 3.3 equal to zero. On the other hand each ξ_i can be irrational which makes this sum unity. Hence this sum does not tend to a limit irrespective of the choice of ξ_i, and it follows that $R(f, 0, 1)$ does not exist.

The Lebesgue integral of the function of Example 3.1 does exist. Since the function is bounded, it is only necessary to show that it is measurable. For any real number a the set $E(f < a)$ is empty, or the rational numbers on [0, 1], or the unit interval. The complement of the empty set is the line l, and consequently the empty set is measurable by Theorem 2.8. By Theorem 2.6 the set of rational numbers is measurable with measure zero. The unit interval is a closed set which is measurable by Theorem 2.10. Hence the function $f(x)$ of Example 3.1 is measurable, and $L(f, 0, 1)$ exists. Since the rational numbers on [0, 1] have measure zero it follows from the definition of measurability and Theorem 2.12 that the irrational numbers on [0, 1] have measure unity. It then follows from the definition of the Lebesgue integral that $L(f, 0, 1) = 1$.

We now obtain some results which throw light on the type of functions for which $R(f, a, b)$ exists. For any subdivision of (a, b), let $M_i = \sup f(x)$, $m_i = \inf f(x)$, $x_{i-1} \leq x \leq x_i$, and let

$$s = \sum_{i=1}^{n} m_i(x_i - x_{i-1}), \quad S = \sum_{i=1}^{n} M_i(x_i - x_{i-1}).$$

THEOREM 3.3. *A necessary and sufficient condition that $R(f, a, b)$ exist is that $S - s \to 0$ as $x_i - x_{i-1} \to 0$.*

The condition is necessary. For if there is a number $d > 0$ such that for some arbitrarily small subdivision the corresponding sums s, S satisfy $S - s > d$ it is then possible to find a sum $\sum f(\xi_i)(x_i - x_{i-1})$ arbitrarily near to s, and to find another such sum arbitrarily near to S. Consequently $\sum f(\xi_i)(x_i - x_{i-1})$ cannot tend to a limit as $x_i - x_{i-1} \to 0$.

The condition is also sufficient. Let R be the infimum of the set of sums S for all possible subdivisions Δ of $[a, b]$. Let Δ, Δ' be two subdivisions of $[a, b]$ and let e_{ij} be the common part of the intervals $[x_{i-1}, x_i]$ and $[x'_{j-i}, x'_j]$. If m_{ij}, M_{ij} are respectively the infimum and supremum of $f(x)$ for x on e_{ij} then

$$m'_j,\ m_i \leq m_{ij} \leq M_{ij} \leq M'_j,\ M_i.$$

Consequently

$$s \leq \sum_i \sum_j m_{ij} |e_{ij}| \leq \sum_i \sum_j M_{ij} |e_{ij}| \leq S,$$
$$s' \leq \sum_j \sum_i m_{ij} |e_{ij}| \leq \sum_j \sum_i M_{ij} |e_{ij}| \leq S'.$$

The corresponding double sums in the first and second relations have the same value. Hence any s is less than or equal to every S' and consequently $s \leq R$. Thus for every subdivision Δ, $s \leq R \leq S$, and since by hypothesis $S - s \to 0$ as the maximum of $x_i - x_{i-1}$ tends to zero, it follows that s and S both tend to R as the maximum of $x_i - x_{i-1}$ tends to zero. Then since

$$s \leq \sum f(\xi_i)(x_i - x_{i-1}) \leq S,$$

it follows that $\Sigma f(\xi_i)(x_i - x_{i-1}) \to R$ as the maximum of $x_i - x_{i-1}$ tends to zero. The method of proof outlined in Note 3.1 can also be followed in this case.

THEOREM 3.4. *If the function $f(x)$ is continuous on the interval $[a, b]$ then $R(f, a, b)$ exists.*

Let $\epsilon > 0$ be given. Making use of Theorem 1.11, there exists $\delta > 0$ such that if Δ is any subdivision of $[a, b]$ with $x_i - x_{i-1} < \delta$ then $|f(x) - f(x')| < \epsilon$ for x, x' any two points on the interval $[x_{i-1}, x_i]$. From this it follows that $M_i - m_i \leq \epsilon$ and that

$$S - s = \sum_{i=1}^{n} (M_i - m_i)(x_i - x_{i-1}) \leq \epsilon(b - a).$$

Consequently, since ϵ is arbitrary, $S - s \to 0$ as $x_i - x_{i-1} \to 0$, and $R(f, a, b)$ exists by Theorem 3.3.

THEOREM 3.5. *If the function $f(x)$ is bounded on (a, b), a* *necessary and sufficient condition that $R(f, a, b)$ exist is that the set of discontinuities of $f(x)$ have zero measure.*

Let $\epsilon > 0$ be given, and let D_ϵ be the set at which the saltus of $f(x)$ is not less than ϵ. It is easily verified that D_ϵ is closed, and since this set is contained in the set of discontinuities of f it follows that $|D_\epsilon| = 0$. If $\alpha_1, \alpha_2, \ldots$ is the set of open intervals complementary to D_ϵ on $[a, b]$, then for n sufficiently great the finite set of closed intervals and points complementary to $\alpha' = \alpha_1 + \alpha_2 + \ldots + \alpha_n$ has measure less than ϵ. It is evident that this finite set of intervals and points can be put interior to a finite set α of non-abutting intervals with $|\alpha| < \epsilon$. It will then be the case that at each point of the finite set u of closed intervals complementary to α the saltus of $f(x)$ is less than ϵ. Hence by Theorem 1.10 there exists $\delta > 0$ such that, if x, x' are two points of an interval of the set u with $|x - x'| < \delta$, then $|f(x) - f(x')| < \epsilon$. Now let (x_{i-1}, x_i) be any subdivision of (a, b) with $x_i - x_{i-1} < \delta$, and (x_j, x'_j) the intervals of this set with points in common with the set α. Then on the remaining intervals (x_k, x'_k) of the subdivision (x_{i-1}, x_i), the saltus of $f(x)$ is less than ϵ and consequently $\sum(M_k - m_k)(x'_k - x_k) < \epsilon(b - a)$. Hence

$$S - s < \epsilon(b - a) + (M - m)(\epsilon + 2p\delta),$$

where m and M are the infimum and supremum, respectively, of $f(x)$ on $[a, b]$, and p is the number of intervals in the set α'. Since ϵ is arbitrary and since δ can be made arbitrarily small independently of p it follows that $S - s$ is close to zero if $x_i - x_{i-1}$ is sufficiently small. Hence by Theorem 3.3, $R(f, a, b)$ exists.

Suppose the set D of discontinuities of $f(x)$ is such that $|D|^o > 0$. Let D_m be the part of D at which the saltus of $f(x)$ is greater than $1/m$. Then $D_m \supset D_{m-1}$. Consequently it follows from Theorem 2.18 that there exists $\lambda > 0$ and a positive integer m such that

$$|D_m|^o > \lambda.$$

Let Δ be any subdivision of $[a, b]$ and $[x_k, x'_k)$ the intervals of Δ which have points of D_m as interior points. Then $M_k - m_k > 1/m$, $\Sigma(x'_k - x_k) > \lambda$, and

$$S - s > \sum(M_k - m_k)(x'_k - x_k) > \lambda/m.$$

It then follows that $S - s$ cannot tend to zero as $x_i - x_{i-1} \rightarrow 0$, and consequently by Theorem 3.3 $R(f, a, b)$ fails to exist. We conclude, therefore, that the conditions of the theorem are necessary.

We note that the non-existence of $R(f, a, b)$ for the function $f(x)$ of Example 3.1 now follows from Theorem 3.5. For the set of discontinuities of $f(x)$ is all the points of $[0, 1]$.

THEOREM 3.6. *If the function $f(x)$ is bounded on $[a, b]$ and has at most a denumerable set of discontinuities, then $R(f, a, b)$ exists.*

This follows from Theorems 2.6, 2.11, and 3.5.

3.4. The extension of the definition of the Lebesgue integral to unbounded functions.

DEFINITION 3.4. *Let $f(x)$ be a measurable function defined on the bounded and measurable set A. Let the measurable set $B \subset A$ be a set over which $f(x)$ is bounded. Then if $L(f, B)$ tends to a limit as $|B|$ tends to $|A|$, this limit is the Lebesgue integral of $f(x)$ over A, $L(f, A)$.*

There are sets B on which $f(x)$ is bounded with $|B|$ arbitrarily near $|A|$. For, let $B_n = E(-n < f < n)$. Then f is bounded on B_n and by Theorem 2.13 $|B_n| \rightarrow |A|$. As a matter of fact, the usual extension of the Lebesgue integral to an unbounded function is based on the set B_n in the following way: let $f_n = f$ on B_n, $f_n = n$ on $A - B_n$. If $L(f_n, A)$ tends to a limit, this limit is the Lebesgue integral of f over A.

We now state an alternative definition of the Lebesgue integral of an unbounded function which is equivalent to that just given, and for many purposes is more serviceable.

DEFINITION 3.5. *Let the function $f(x)$ be measurable on the measurable and bounded set A. Let Δ be a subdivision of the range $(-\infty, \infty)$, and let $e_i = E(a_{i-1} \leq f < a_i)$. If*

$$\sum_{-\infty}^{\infty} a_i |e_i|$$

converges for all sufficiently small $a_i - a_{i-1}$ and tends to a limit *as* $a_i - a_{i-1} \to 0$, *this limit is the Lebesgue integral of* $f(x)$ *over the set* A.

In Chapter IV, Section 4.3, it is shown that the two definitions are equivalent.

DEFINITION 3.6. *If a function* $f(x)$ *is integrable in the Lebesgue sense over a set* A *it is said to be summable over* A, *or summable on* A.

We have now accomplished the definitions of the Riemann and Lebesgue integrals for bounded functions. The essential difference is that the Riemann integral is based on a subdivision of the range over which the function is defined, while the Lebesgue integral is based on a subdivision of the range of the function. This change in point of view proved fortunate. It influenced subsequent developments in real variable theory, and gave to them an elegance and simplicity which they might not otherwise have attained. This particular approach to an integral more general than that of Riemann could easily have been overlooked. At the time of its introduction the stage was set for some new definition of an integral. Many mathematicians were thinking of it from the point of view of basing a definition on some kind of subdivision other than intervals of the range over which the function is defined. Pierpont [50] and W. H. Young [67, 68] succeeded in formulating integrals from this point of view which are at least as general as that of Lebesgue, and these integrals could well have served the needs of the day. However, the work of Lebesgue continued to predominate while the new theory was taking shape and settling down to a permanent form.

Definitions based on a subdivision of the range over which the function is defined are not without interest. That of Pierpont extended by Hildebrandt [27] and the present writer [33] gives a process of integration which is applicable to a wide range of non-measurable functions, and is, therefore, more general than that of Lebesgue. It is equal to the integral of Lebesgue when the function is measurable. Building on these extensions of Pierpont's definition, an integral has been devised by Fan [21] which exists for all bounded functions.

We conclude this section with a definition of the Lebesgue integral which depends upon a subdivision of the range over which the function is defined [36, 42].

DEFINITION 3.7. *Let $f(x)$ be bounded and measurable on the bounded and measurable set A. Let $E_n = e_1 + \ldots + e_n$ be a finite sequence of subsets of A with e_i measurable, $e_i e_j = 0$, $i \neq j$ and such that*

$$\lim_{n \to \infty} |E_n| = |A|, \lim_{n \to \infty} |e_i| = 0, \quad i = 1, 2, \ldots n.$$

Let ξ_i be any point on e_i. If there exists a sequence E_n satisfying these conditions and such that

$$\sum_{i=1}^{n} f(\xi_i) |e_i|$$

tends to a limit T then T is the Lebesgue integral of $f(x)$ over A.

The limit T is unique. To show this let E'_n be another sequence such as E_n, for which the corresponding limit is T'. Let m_i be the infimum, M_i the supremum of $f(x)$ on e_i. It then follows, that

$$s = \sum_{i=1}^{n} m_i |e_i|, \; S = \sum_{i=1}^{n} M_i |e_i|$$

both tend to T, and the corresponding sums S', s' both tend to T'. Now let $e_{ij} = e_i e'_j$. Then

$$m_i, m'_j \leq m_{ij} \leq M_{ij} \leq M_i, M'_j,$$

and

$$\textstyle\sum_i m_i |e_i| \leq \sum_i \sum_j m_{ij} |e_{ij}| \leq \sum_i \sum_j M_{ij} |e_{ij}| \leq \sum_i M_i |e_i|,$$

$$\textstyle\sum_j m'_j |e'_j| \leq \sum_j \sum_i m_{ij} |e_{ij}| \leq \sum_j \sum_i M_{ij} |e_{ij}| \leq \sum_j M'_j |e'_j|.$$

In the first inequality both the left-hand term and the right-hand term tend to T, while in the second both the left-hand term and the right-hand term tend to T′. It then follows that in the first inequality the two middle terms tend to T, and in the second the two middle terms tend to T′. But for each integer n the two middle terms in the first inequality are each equal to the corresponding term of the two middle terms in the second inequality. It follows from this that $T = T'$.

To show that $T = L(f, A)$, let a be the infimum, b the

supremum of the set A, and divide (a, b) into sub-intervals $\delta_1, \ldots, \delta_n$ of equal length. Let (a_{i-1}, a_i) be a subdivision of a range including f. Let $e_i = E(a_{i-1} \leq f < a_i)$, and let $e_{ij} = e_i\delta_j$. Then

$$E_n = e_{11} + e_{12} + \ldots + e_{1n} + e_{21} + e_{22} + \ldots + e_{nn}$$

is a sequence satisfying the condition of Definition 3.7, and if T exists, it is the limit of $\sum_i \sum_j f(\xi_{ij}) |e_{ij}|$. But

$$\sum_i a_{i-1} |e_i| \leq \sum_{ij} f(\xi_{ij}) |e_{ij}| \leq \sum_i a_i |e_i| .$$

This shows that T does exist, and that it is equal to $L(f, A)$.

3.5. Further properties of measurable functions.

THEOREM 3.7. *If $f_n(x)$ is a sequence of measurable functions defined on the measurable set A, then lim sup $f_n(x)$ and lim inf $f_n(x)$ are measurable. In particular, if the sequence approaches a limit, this limit is measurable.*

Let $f(x) =$ lim sup $f_n(x)$ and let a be any real number. Let

$$E_n = E(f_n > a) + E(f_{n+1} > a) + \ldots$$

Since f_n is measurable, it follows from Theorem 2.14 that E_n is measurable. If $E = E_1E_2 \ldots$ then E is measurable by Theorem 2.16, and $E = E(\limsup f_n \geq a)$. The measurability of $E(\limsup f_n < a)$ now follows as in Theorem 3.1 and we conclude that lim sup f_n is measurable. That lim inf f_n is measurable may be proved in a similar way. In case f_n tends to a limit this limit is both lim sup f_n and lim inf f_n, and consequently it, too, is a measurable function.

THEOREM 3.8. *If the function $f(x)$ is defined on the measurable set A and if the set D of discontinuities of $f(x)$ over A has zero measure then $f(x)$ is measurable on A. In particular if $f(x)$ is continuous on A then $f(x)$ is measurable on A.*

The set $E = A - D$ is measurable by Theorem 2.12. By Theorem 2.21 there exists a sequence of closed sets $C_1, C_2, \ldots, C_n \subset E$, $|E - C_n| \to 0$ as $n \to \infty$. Let $E_a = E(f \geq a, x \in A)$, and let x_0 be a limit point of E_aC_n. Then, since C_n is closed, $x_0 \in C_n \subset E$. If $x_i \in E_aC_n$ then $f(x_i) \geq a$. Since f is continuous on E, $x_0 \in E$, $x_i \in E$, it follows that $f(x_i) \to f(x_0)$ and consequently $f(x_0) \geq a$. Then $x_0 \in E_aC_n$ which makes this set E_aC_n closed, and, by Theorem 2.10, measurable. By Theorem 2.14, $\sum E_a C_n$ is measurable, and $E_a = F + \sum E_a C_n$, where F is a null set. It then follows that E_a is measurable. Also $E^a = E(f < a) = A - E_a$. Consequently this set is measurable and f is measurable on A. In case $f(x)$ is continuous on A, the set D is empty and the set E in the foregoing can be taken as the set A. Hence if f is continuous on A it is measurable on A.

THEOREM 3.9. *Let the function $f(x)$ be measurable on the measurable set A with $|A|$ finite. Corresponding to $\epsilon > 0$ there exists a closed set $C \subset A$ with $|A - C| < \epsilon$ and with $f(x)$ continuous on C* (Lusin's Theorem).

For a given n let $\ldots < a_{-k} < a_{-k+1} < \ldots < a_0 = 0 < a_1 \ldots < a_k < \ldots$ be a subdivision of $(-\infty, \infty)$ with $a_i - a_{i-1} < 1/n$. If $e_i = E(a_{i-1} \leq f < a_i)$ it follows from Theorem 2.21 that for any n we may choose closed sets $c_i \subset e_i$ such that if k is sufficiently great and

$$C_n = c_{-k} + c_{-k+1} + \ldots + c_k,$$

then $|A - C_n| < \epsilon/2^n$. If $x \in C_n$, then $x \in c_p$ for p with some one of the values $-k, -k+1, \ldots, k$. Since $c_i c_j = 0$, $i \neq j$, and the sets c_i are closed, it follows that no point of c_i can be a limit point of c_j, $i \neq j$. Hence there is an interval δ with $x \in c_p$ as centre such that $C_n \delta = c_p \delta$. Then for $x' \in C_n \delta = c_p \delta$,

$$|f(x') - f(x)| < \frac{1}{n}.$$

Let $C = C_1 C_2 \ldots$. Then C is closed and $|A - C| < \epsilon/2 + \epsilon/2^2 + \ldots = \epsilon$. If $x \in C$ then $x \in C_n$ for every n. Let $\eta > 0$ be given. Fix n so that $1/n < \eta$. Then if $x \in C$, $x \in C_n$ and $x \in c_p \in C_n$. Hence there is an interval $\delta \ni x$ such that $C_n \delta = c_p \delta$. Then if $x' \in C\delta$ it follows that $x' \in C_n\delta$, $x' \in c_p \delta$ and

$$|f(x') - f(x)| < \frac{1}{n} < \eta.$$

Hence $f(x)$ is continuous on C. Since C is closed, and $|A - C| < \epsilon$, the theorem is established.

Let the set A be on the interval (a, b). Let $C \subset A$ be the closed set of Theorem 3.9. Let (a_i, b_i) be the intervals of $\tilde{C}(a, b)$.

Let $\varphi(x)$ be a function such that $\varphi(a) = \varphi(b) = 0$, $\varphi(x) = f(x)$, $x \in C$, and on (a_i, b_i) the ordinate of φ is the ordinate of a linear segment joining the points $[a_i, \varphi(a_i)]$, $[b_i, \varphi(b_i)]$. Then $\varphi(x)$ is continuous on $[a, b]$. Let $\varphi(x) = 0$ for x outside of $[a, b]$. We have thus established

THEOREM 3.10. *If $f(x)$ is measurable on the bounded and measurable set A, then for $\epsilon > 0$ there exists a function $\varphi(x)$ continuous on the whole space and equal to $f(x)$ on a closed set $C \subset A$, with $|A - C| < \epsilon$.*

Again let C_n be a sequence of the sets C of Theorem 3.9 with $|A - C_n| < \epsilon/2^n$, and φ_n the corresponding function of Theorem 3.10. If $E_k = C_k C_{k+1} \ldots$, then for $x \in E_k$, $\varphi_n(x) = f(x)$, $n \geq k$. But $|A - E_k| < \epsilon/2^k + \epsilon/2^{k+1} + \ldots = \epsilon/2^{k-1}$. Hence for all $x \in A$, except possibly for a null set, there exists k such that $\varphi_n(x) = f(x)$, $n > k$. This establishes

THEOREM 3.11. *If the function $f(x)$ is measurable on the bounded and measurable set A, there exists a sequence of functions $\varphi_n(x)$, continuous on the whole space, and such that $\varphi_n(x) \to f(x)$ almost everywhere on A.*

Problems

3.1. For $0 \leq x \leq 1$ let $f(x) = 1/q$ when x is rational and equal to p/q, and when x is irrational let $f(x) = 0$. Show that $f(x)$ is continuous at the irrational numbers on $(0, 1)$. Show that $R(f, 0, 1)$ exists, and determine its value.

3.2. Let $f(x)$ be bounded on the interval $[a, b]$ and let $(x_{n,i-1}, x_{ni})$ be a consecutive sequence of subdivisions of this interval. Let M_{ni}, m_{ni} be respectively the supremum and infimum of $f(x)$ on $x_{n,i-1} \leq x \leq x_{ni}$. Show that

$$S_n = \sum_{i=1}^{n} M_{ni}(x_{ni} - x_{n,i-1})$$

does not increase as n increases. Show that as $\max(x_{ni} - x_{n,i-1}) \to 0$, S_n tends to a limit $\bar{I}$, and that if $\epsilon > 0$ is given, there exists $\delta > 0$ such that if

$$S = \sum_{i=1}^{n} M_i(x_i - x_{i-1}),$$

M_i the supremum of $f(x)$ on $x_{i-1} \leq x \leq x_i$, then $| \bar{I} - S | < \epsilon$ whenever $x_i - x_{i-1} < \delta$.

3.3. Show that $S_n = \sum m_{ni}(x_{ni} - x_{n,\, i-1})$ tends to a limit $\underline{I}$ and that a necessary and sufficient condition for the existence of $R(f, a, b)$ is that $\bar{I} = \underline{I}$.

3.4. Let $\phi_n(x) = M_{ni}$ on $x_{n,\, i-1} \leq x \leq x_{ni}$, M_{ni} defined in 3.2. Show that for each x, $\phi_n(x)$ does not increase as n increases. Hence show that $\phi_n(x)$ tends to a limit $\phi(x)$. Construct an example to show that $R(\phi, a, b)$ does not necessarily exist. If $R(\phi, a, b)$ does exist, show that $R(\phi, a, b) = \bar{I}$.

3.5. Construct a function $f(x)$ such that for the corresponding function $\phi(x)$ of Problem 3.4, $f(x) < \phi(x)$ for every x.

3.6. If a positive integer n is given, show that the set E_n for which $f(x) > \phi(x) - 1/n$ is everywhere dense on $[a, b]$.

3.7. Show that for $\epsilon > 0$ there is a number $\delta > 0$ such that when $x_i - x_{i-1} < \delta$ there is a point ξ_i on $[x_{i-1}, x_i]$ for which $\sum f(\xi_i)(x_i - x_{i-1}) > \bar{I} - \epsilon$, $f(x)$ being bounded.

3.8. Let E be an everywhere dense set on $[a, b]$ such that if $\xi_i \in E$, $\sum f(\xi_i)\,(x_i - x_{i-1}) \rightarrow U$ as $x_i - x_{i-1} \rightarrow 0$. Let E' be a second everywhere dense set such that for $\xi'_i \in E'$, $\sum f(\xi'_i)(x_i - x_{i-1}) \rightarrow L < U$, as $x_i - x_{i-1} \rightarrow 0$. Show that if λ is a number with $L < \lambda < U$, then it is possible to choose ξ_i on $x_{i-1} \leq x \leq x_i$ so that $\sum f(\xi_i)(x_i - x_{i-1}) \rightarrow \lambda$ as $x_i - x_{i-1} \rightarrow 0$.

3.9. Show that if λ is a number with $\underline{I} < \lambda < \bar{I}$, then it is possible to choose ξ_i on $x_{i-1} \leq x \leq x_i$ in such a way that $\sum f(\xi_i)\,(x_i - x_{i-1}) \rightarrow \lambda$ as $x_i - x_{i-1} \rightarrow 0$.

3.10. Let the function $f(x)$ be continuous on $[a, b]$. Show that $f(x)$ assumes every value between its supremum and infimum for at least one value of x. Hence show that for some value ξ on $[a, b]$, $R(f, a, b) = (b - a)f(\xi)$, the first law of the mean for integrals.

3.11. If $f(x)$ is continuous on $[a, b]$ and $F(x) = R(f, a, x)$, show that

$$F'(x) = \lim_{h \rightarrow 0} \frac{F(x+h) - F(x)}{h} = f(x).$$

3.12. If a function $f(x)$ is non-decreasing and bounded on $[a, b]$ then $R(f, a, b)$ exists [22, p. 148].

3.13. Let the functions $f(x)$ and $\phi(x)$ be continuous on $[a, b]$, $\phi(x)$ positive and non-increasing. Show that for some ξ on $[a, b]$

$$\int_a^b f(x)\phi(x)dx = \phi(a)\int_a^\xi f(x)dx + \phi(b)\int_\xi^b f(x)dx,$$

the second law of the mean for integrals. [22, p. 153.]

3.14. Let the function $f(x)$ be continuous on the closed and bounded set C. Let $[a, b]$ be an interval containing C, $x_0 = a < x_1 < \ldots < x_n = b$, a subdivision of $[a, b]$. Let $x_k \leq x \leq x'_k$ be the intervals of this subdivision which contain at least one point ξ_k of C. Show that

$$\sum f(\xi_k)(x'_k - x_k), \ \xi_k \in C,$$

tends to a limit as $x_i - x_{i-1} \rightarrow 0$.

3.15. (Egoroff's theorem). If a sequence of measurable functions $s_1(x), s_2(x), \ldots$ converges on a measurable set A to a function $s(x)$ then, if $\epsilon > 0$ is given, there is a measurable set $E \subset A$ with $|A - E| < \epsilon$ on which $s_n(x)$ converges uniformly to $s(x)$ [62, p. 339].

CHAPTER IV

PROPERTIES OF THE LEBESGUE INTEGRAL

Introduction: In this chapter we set forth the principal properties of the Lebesgue integral, and give an elementary proof of the ergodic theorem.

4.1. Notation and conventions. Let $f(x)$ be bounded and measurable on the bounded and measurable set A. Let m, M be two real numbers such that for $x \in A$, $m < f(x) < M$. We shall speak of (m, M) as a range including $f(x)$. We shall call $a_0 = m < a_1 < \ldots < a_n = M$ a subdivision of a range including $f(x)$ on A. When no misunderstanding can arise we shall use (a_{i-1}, a_i) to denote such a subdivision. If $e_i = E(a_{i-1} \leq f < a_i)$, $x \in A$, then from the definition of and subsequent discussion of the Lebesgue integral for a bounded function, it follows that $\sum a_i |e_i|$ and $\sum a_{i-1} |e_i|$ both tend to $L(f, A)$ as the maximum of $a_i - a_{i-1}$ tends to zero. When we speak of sums such as these tending to a limit, we shall understand that it is under the condition that the maximum of $a_i - a_{i-1}$ tends to zero, without making explicit mention of this condition.

The statement that $f(x)$ is summable on A implies that the set A is measurable. We shall use B to denote a measurable sub-set of A over which $f(x)$ is bounded. It follows from Theorem 3.1 that $f(x)$ is measurable on B. Then, since $f(x)$ is bounded and measurable on B it follows from Definition 3.2 that $L(f, B)$ exists.

4.2. Properties of the Lebesgue integral. In this section we shall use the conventions and notation introduced in Section 4.1 without mentioning them explicitly. In particular, the sets A on which $f(x)$ is defined are bounded sets.

In Section 4.3 the results of this section will be extended to unbounded sets.

THEOREM 4.1. *If the function $f(x)$ is summable on A then $-f(x)$ is summable on A and $L(-f, A) = -L(f, A)$.*

By Theorem 3.2, $-f$ is measurable on A. For $B \subset A$, let (a_{i-1}, a_i) be a subdivision of a range including $-f$ on B. Then if $e_i = E(a_{i-1} \leq -f < a_i, x \in B)$ it follows that $e_i = E(-a_i < f \leq -a_{i-1}, x \in B)$ and $(-a_i, -a_{i-1})$ is a subdivision of a range including f on B. Consequently $\sum -a_i |e_i| = -\sum a_i |e_i| \to L(f, B)$. But $\sum a_i |e_i| \to L(-f, B)$. From these two relations it results that $L(-f, B) = -L(f, B)$. The theorem is completed by letting $|B| \to |A|$.

THEOREM 4.2. *If $f(x)$ is summable on A, and c is any real number then $cf(x)$ is summable on A and $L(cf, A) = cL(f, A)$.*

If $c = 0$ the theorem is obvious. Suppose that $c > 0$. For $B \subset A$, cf is bounded on B, and by Theorem 3.2, measurable on B. Hence $L(cf, B)$ exists.

Let (a_{i-1}, a_i) be a subdivision of a range including cf on B. Then if $e_i = E(a_{i-1} \leq cf < a_i, x \in B)$, it follows that $e_i = E(a_{i-1}/c \leq f < a_i/c, x \in B)$, and consequently $(a_{i-1}/c, a_i/c)$ constitutes a subdivision of a range including f on B. Hence

$$\sum \frac{a_i}{c} |e_i| = \frac{1}{c} \sum a_i |e_i| \to L(f, B).$$

But $\sum a_i |e_i| \to L(cf, B)$. From these relations it follows that $L(cf, B) = cL(f, B)$. The theorem may be completed for $c > 0$ by letting $|B| \to |A|$. If $c < 0$, let $c' = -c > 0$. Then $cf = c'(-f)$. But by what we have just proved, and Theorem 4.1, it follows that

$L(cf, A) = L(c'(-f), A) = c'L(-f, A) = -c'L(f, A) = cL(f, A)$.

This completes the proof.

THEOREM 4.3. *If $f(x)$ is summable on each of the sets, A_1, A_2, where $A_1A_2 = 0$, then $f(x)$ is summable on the set $A = A_1 + A_2$ and $L(f, A_1 + A_2) = L(f, A_1) + L(f, A_2)$. If $f_1(x), f_2(x)$ are each summable on a set A then $f_1(x) + f_2(x)$ is summable on A and $L(f_1 + f_2, A) = L(f_1, A) + L(f_2, A)$.*

If a is any real number the set $E(f < a)$ is measurable; for it is the sum of two measurable sets $E(f < a, x \in A_1)$ and $E(f < a, x \in A_2)$. Hence for $B \subset A$, $L(f, B)$ exists. If (a_{i-1}, a_i) is a subdivision of a range including f on B, it is at the same time a subdivision of the range of f on $B_1 = BA_1$, and of f on $B_2 = BA_2$. If $e_i = E(a_{i-1} \leq f < a_i, x \in B)$ then $e_i = e_{i1} + e_{i2}$ where $e_{ij} = E(a_{i-1} \leq f < a_i, x \in B_j)$, $j = 1, 2$. Consequently $e_{i1}e_{i2} = 0$, and by Theorem 2.12 it follows that

$$(4.1) \quad \sum a_i |e_i| = \sum a_i |e_{i1} + e_{i2}| = \sum a_i |e_{i1}| + \sum a_i |e_{i2}| .$$

By letting $a_i - a_{i-1} \to 0$ it follows that (4.1) becomes

$$(4.2) \qquad \int_B f(x)dx = \int_{B_1} f(x)dx + \int_{B_2} f(x)dx.$$

If, now, $|B| \to |A|$ it follows that $|B_1| \to |A_1|$ and $|B_2| \to |A_2|$. Hence the right-hand side of (4.2) tends to $L(f, A_1) + L(f, A_2)$. From this it follows that $L(f, B)$ tends to a limit which is, by definition, $L(f, A)$ and this limit is equal to $L(f, A_1) + L(f, A_2)$. This completes the first part of the theorem and it is obvious that the result can be extended to three or more sets.

To prove the second part of the theorem, first let f_1 and f_2 be bounded and let (m, M) be an interval such that for $x \in A$ the values of f_1, f_2 and $f_1 + f_2$ lie on this interval. By Theorem 3.2 the function $f_1 + f_2$ is measurable, and since it is bounded on A, it is summable on this set. Let (a_{i-1}, a_i) be a subdivision of (m, M) and let

$$e_j = E(a_{j-1} \leq f_1 < a_j), \; e'_k = E(a_{k-1} \leq f_2 < a_k).$$

Then on $e_je'_k$

$$a_{j-1} + a_{k-1} \leq f_1 + f_2 < a_j + a_k.$$

Consequently

$$(a_{j-1} + a_{k-1})|e_je'_k| \leq \int_{e_je_k} (f_1 + f_2)dx < (a_j + a_k)|e_je'_k| .$$

By summing first over j and then over k, rearranging terms and using the first part of Theorem 4.3 on the sum arising from the middle term, we get

$$\sum a_{j-1}|e_j| + \sum a_{k-1}|e'_k| \leq \int_A (f_1 + f_2)dx < \sum a_j|e_j| + \sum a_k|e'k|.$$

From this relation it follows that

$$\int_A (f_1 + f_2)\, dx = \int_A f_1 dx + \int_A f_2 dx.$$

This establishes the theorem when the functions f_1 and f_2 are bounded.

If one at least of the functions f_1 and f_2 is not bounded, let $B \subset A$ be a measurable set on which $f_1 + f_2$ is bounded. It may not follow that both f_1 and f_2 are bounded on B. Let $B_1 \subset B$ be a set on which both f_1 and f_2 are bounded. Then $f_1 + f_2$ is bounded on B_1 and from what has just been proved

$$\int_{B_1} (f_1 + f_2) dx = \int_{B_1} f_1 dx + \int_{B_1} f_2 dx.$$

By letting $|B_1| \to |B|$, and using the fact that $f_1 + f_2$ is summable over B and bounded on B, we get

$$\int_B (f_1 + f_2) dx = \int_B f_1 dx + \int_B f_2 dx.$$

To complete the theorem let $|B|$ tend to $|A|$ and use Definition 3.4.

THEOREM 4.4. *If the function $f(x)$ is summable over the set A and $E \subset A$ is measurable, then $f(x)$ is summable over E.*

Let $B_i \subset E$ be a sequence of sets B_i with $|B_i| \to |E|$, and $B'_j \subset A - E$ a sequence with $|B'_j| \to |A - E|$. Then $|B_i + B'_j| \to |A|$, as $i, j \to \infty$. Hence for $\epsilon > 0$, there exists k with

$$|L(f, A) - L(f, B_i + B'_j)| < \epsilon, \quad i, j \geq k.$$

But $B_i B'_j = 0$. Hence by Theorem 4.3

$$L(f, B_i + B'_j) = L(f, B_i) + L(f, B'_j).$$

From these two relations it follows that

$$|L(f, A) - L(f, B_i) - L(f, B'_k)| < \epsilon, \quad i > k,$$
$$|L(f, A) - L(f, B_p) - L(f, B'_k)| < \epsilon, \quad p > k.$$

Subtracting, there is obtained

$$|L(f, B_i) - L(f, B_p)| < 2\epsilon, \quad i, p > k.$$

which shows that $L(f, B_i)$ is a Cauchy sequence, and consequently has a limit. That this limit is independent of the particular sequence B_i can be shown by keeping the sequence B'_j and replacing B_i in the foregoing by any other sequence B_i with $|B_i| \to |E|$. By definition, the limit of $L(f, B_i)$ is $L(f, E)$.

THEOREM 4.5. *If $f(x)$ is summable on A then so is $|f(x)|$, the numerical value of $f(x)$, and $|L(f, A)| \leq L(|f|, A)$.*

Let $e^+ = E(f \geq 0)$, $e^- = E(f < 0)$. By Theorem 4.4, f is summable over e^+ and e^-, and $L(f, A) = L(f, e^+) + L(f, e^-)$. Therefore $L(|f|, A)$ exists by Theorem 4.3. Moreover,

$$\begin{aligned} L(|f|, A) &= L(f, e^+) + L(-f, e^-) \\ &= L(f, e^+) - L(f, e^-) \geq |L(f, e^+) + L(f, e^-)|, \\ &\geq |L(f, A)|, \end{aligned}$$

which is the theorem.

The property that $|f(x)|$ is summable when $f(x)$ is summable is described by the statement: *The Lebesgue integral is absolutely summable or absolutely convergent.* We call attention to the fact that the converse of this is not necessarily true. Let A be a non-measurable set on (a, b). Let $f(x) = 1$ on A, $f(x) = -1$ on $\tilde{A}(a, b)$. Then $f(x)$ is not summable on (a, b), since it is not measurable, but $|f(x)| = 1$ on (a, b) and is, therefore, summable.

THEOREM 4.6. *If $f(x)$ is summable on A and $E \subset A$ is measurable, then $L(f, E)$ exists and tends to zero as $|E| \to 0$.*

Let $\epsilon > 0$ be given, and let the set $B \subset A$ be such that $L(|f|, A - B) < \epsilon$. Now let $M = \sup f$, $x \in B$, and let E be a measurable set with $E \subset A$ and $M|E| < \epsilon$. Then

$$\begin{aligned} |L(f, E)| &\leq L(|f|, BE) + L[|f|, (A - B)E] \\ &\leq M|E| + L(|f|, A - B) < 2\epsilon. \end{aligned}$$

Since ϵ is arbitrary the theorem follows.

THEOREM 4.7. *If $f(x)$ is summable over A and $E \subset A$ is measurable, then $L(f, E) \to L(f, A)$* as $|E| \to |A|$.

By Theorem 4.3

$$L(f, E) = L(f, A) - L(f, A - E).$$

By Theorem 4.6 the second term on the right tends to zero as $|E| \to |A|$. Hence the theorem.

THEOREM 4. 8. *If the function $f(x)$ is summable on the set A and $e_n = E(f \geq n\lambda)$, n a positive integer and $\lambda > 0$, then $n|e_n| \to 0$ as $n \to \infty$, and $\sum |e_n|$ converges.*

Since f is defined for each point of A, $|e_n| \to 0$ as $n \to \infty$.

It then follows from Theorem 4.6 that $L(f, e_n) \to 0$. But $L(f, e_n) \geq n\lambda |e_n|$. From these relations it follows that $n|e_n| \to 0$.

To prove the second part of the theorem, let

$$A_n = (e_1 - e_2) + (e_2 - e_3) + \ldots + (e_{n-1} - e_n).$$

The sets forming the terms of the sum on the right are mutually exclusive and measurable, and on $e_{n-1} - e_n$ the relation $f \geq (n-1)\lambda$ holds. Hence

$$\int_{A_n} f dx \geq \lambda[|e_1 - e_2| + 2|e_2 - e_3| + \ldots + (n-1)|e_{n-1} - e_n|].$$

Again, since $e_{n-1} \supset e_n$, it follows from Theorem 2.12 that $|e_{n-1} - e_n| = |e_{n-1}| - |e_n|$. It then follows that

$$\int_{A_n} f dx \geq \lambda[|e_1| + |e_2| + \ldots + |e_{n-1}| - (n-1)|e_n|].$$

Furthermore, $(n-1)|e_n| < n|e_n|$ which, by the first part of the theorem, tends to zero as $n \to \infty$. Then, since the right-hand side is positive for n sufficiently great, and since by Theorem 4.5

$$L(f, A_n) \leq L[|f|, A_n] \leq L(|f|, A),$$

it follows that $|e_1| + \ldots + |e_{n-1}|$ is bounded. Consequently $\sum |e_n|$ converges, which is the second part of the theorem.

In Example 3.1 we saw that a function could be integrable in the sense of Lebesgue without being integrable in the sense of Riemann. The converse of this is not true, as we shall now show by proving

THEOREM 4.9. *If the function $f(x)$ defined on the interval $[a, b]$ is Riemann integrable on this interval then it is Lebesgue integrable and the two integrals are equal.*

The fact that f is Riemann integrable implies that it is bounded. Furthermore it follows from Theorems 3.5 and 3.9 that $f(x)$ is measurable on $[a, b]$. It then follows from the definition of the Lebesgue integral that f is summable on every subinterval of $[a, b]$. Clearly

$$m_i(x_i - x_{i-1}) \leq L(f, x_{i-1}, x_i) \leq M_i(x_i - x_{i-1}),$$

where, as before, $m_i = \inf f$, $M_i = \sup f$, $x_{i-1} \leq x \leq x_i$. By Theorem 4.3, $\sum L(f, x_{i-1}, x_i) = L(f, a, b)$. Hence

$$s \leq L(f, a, b) \leq S.$$

Then, since both s and S tend to $R(f, a, b)$ as $x_i - x_{i-1} \to 0$, it follows that $R(f, a, b) = L(f, a, b)$.

We complete this section with a theorem on the summability of functions over sequences of sets.

THEOREM 4.10. *Let the function $f(x)$ be summable on each set of the sequence of mutually exclusive sets $A_1, A_2, \ldots$, and let $\sum L(|f|, A_i)$ converge. Then $f(x)$ is summable on $A = \sum A_i$, and $L(f, A) = \sum L(f, A_i)$. If $f(x)$ is summable on a set A and $E_1, E_2, \ldots$ is a sequence of mutually exclusive measurable sets with $E_i \subset A$, then $\sum L(f, E_i) = L(f, \sum E_i)$.*

If a is any real number then the set $E(f<a) = \sum A_i E(f<a)$, which is measurable by Theorem 2.14. Hence f is measurable on A. First let f be non-negative, and let $B \subset A$ be any measurable set on which f is bounded. Then $L(f, B)$ exists and

$$L(f, B) = L[f, B(A_1 + \ldots + A_n)] + L[f, B(A_{n+1} + \ldots)].$$

If A is a bounded set then $|B(A_{n+1} + \ldots)| \to 0$ as $n \to \infty$, and since f is summable over B it follows from Theorem 4.6 that the last term on the right tends to zero. It then follows that as $n \to \infty$

$$L[f, B(A_1 + \ldots + A_n)] \to L(f, B),$$

and, since $L(f, BA_i) \leq L(f, A_i)$, that

$$L(f, B) \leq \sum L(f, A_i). \tag{4.3}$$

For an arbitrary positive number ϵ, fix n so that

$$\sum_{n+1}^{\infty} L(f, A_i) < \epsilon,$$

and take B with $|B|$ so close to $|A|$ that

$$\sum_{i=1}^{n} L(f, BA_i) > \sum_{i=1}^{n} L(f, A_i) - \epsilon.$$

Then

$$L(f, B) > \sum_{i=1}^{n} L(f, BA_i) > \sum_{i=1}^{n} L(f, A_i) - 2\epsilon.$$

Since ϵ is arbitrary this, with (4.3), shows that as $|B| \to |A|$, $L(f, B) \to \sum L(f, A_i)$, which, with Definition 3.4, completes the proof when $f \geq 0$.

Now let f be any function satisfying the conditions of the theorem. From what has been proved for $f \geq 0$, it follows that $|f|$ is summable on A. Consequently, since f is measurable on A, it follows as in Theorem 4.5 that $L(f, A)$ exists. Then, by Theorem 4.3, $L(f, A) = L(f, e^+) + L(f, e^-)$, and again by what has been proved when $f \geq 0$,

$$L(f, e^+) = \sum L(f, A_i e^+),\ L(f, e^-) = \sum L(f, A_i e^-).$$

From these relations we get $L(f, A) = \sum L(f, A_i)$, which completes the proof of the first part of the theorem.

To prove the second part of the theorem it is sufficient to note that $\sum L(|f|, E_i) \leq L(|f|, A)$, and the desired result then follows from the first part of the theorem.

4.3. Definitions of summability and their extension to unbounded sets. In Section 3.4 two definitions of summability of unbounded functions were considered, and the question was raised as to whether or not they were equivalent. We now prove

THEOREM 4.11. *Definitions* 3.4 *and* 3.5 *are equivalent.*

Suppose a function f is summable under Definition 3.4. First let f be non-negative, and for $\epsilon > 0$ fix n so that if $E_n = E(0 \leq f < n)$ then

$$|L(f, A) - L(f, E_n)| < \epsilon.$$

Now fix $\eta > 0$ and such that if $a_i - a_{i-1} < \eta$, then

$$\Big| \sum_{a_i < n} a_i |e_i| - L(f, E_n)\Big| < \epsilon.$$

Let a'_i be the point of the set a_i next below n, and let $e' = E(a'_i \leq f < n)$. For a'_i sufficiently close to n, $|e'|$ is arbitrarily small. Hence if η is sufficiently small and $a_i - a_{i-1} < \eta$, then $n|e'| < \epsilon$. We then have for values of i for which $a_i \geq n$,

$$\sum_{a_i \geq n} a_{i-1}|e_i| \leq \sum_{a_i \geq n} \int_{e_i} f dx \leq \int_{A-E_n} f dx + n|e'| < 2\epsilon,$$

and

$$\sum_{a_i \geq n} a_i|e_i| - \sum_{a_i \geq n} a_{i-1}|e_i| \leq \eta \sum |e_i| < \eta |A|.$$

These relations now combine to give

$$\left| \sum a_i | e_i | - L(f, A) \right| < 4\epsilon + \eta | A |.$$

Since ϵ and η are arbitrarily small it follows that $\sum a_i | e_i | \to L(f, A)$ as $a_i - a_{i-1} \to 0$.

Now suppose that $f \geq 0$ is summable under Definition 3.5. Then $\sum a_i | e_i |$ tends to a limit as $a_i - a_{i-1} \to 0$. But f is bounded on e_i and consequently summable over this set according to Definition 3.4. Since $f < a_i$ for $x \in e_i$, it follows that $L(f, e_i) < a_i | e_i |$, and consequently the convergence of $\sum L(f, e_i)$ follows from the convergence of $\sum a_i | e_i |$. It then follows from Theorem 4.10 that $\sum L(f, e_i) = L(f, A)$, where $L(f, A)$ exists in accordance with Definition 3.4. It now follows from what we have already proved that $\sum a_i | e_i | \to L(f, A)$, and the theorem is established for $f \geq 0$.

If the function f is not restricted to be positive, let (a_{i-1}, a_i) be a subdivision of the range $(-\infty, \infty)$ and let a_i^0 be the point of the set a_i which is next below zero. Then, from what has been proved it follows that

$$\sum_{a_i > a_i^0} a_i | e_i | \to L(f, e^+), \quad \sum_{a_i \leq a_i^0} a_i | e_i | \to L(f, e^-),$$

as $a_i - a_{i-1} \to 0$. The theorem then follows from these relations and Theorem 4.3.

The definitions of summability and the theorems of Section 4.2 will now be extended to include the case in which the functions are defined on unbounded sets.

DEFINITION 4.1. *Let A be any set, and let the function $f(x)$ be measurable on A. Let (a_n, b_n) be a sequence of intervals with $a_n \to -\infty$, $b_n \to \infty$. Let $f(x)$ be summable on the set $A(a_n, b_n)$ for every value of n. If*

$$\lim_{n \to \infty} L[| f |, A(a_n, b_n)]$$

exists, and is finite, the function $f(x)$ is summable on the set A. This limit is evidently independent of the sequence (a_n, b_n), and it easily follows that

$$\lim_{n \to \infty} L[f, A(a_n, b_n)]$$

exists, is finite, and is independent of the sequence (a_n, b_n)*. The second limit is the integral of* $f(x)$ *over* A, $L(f, A)$.

For some functions the second limit in Definition 4.1 depends on the sequence (a_n, b_n), for example, $f(x) = \sin x$. There is also an important class of functions for which the second limit exists but for which the first limit is infinite.

EXAMPLE 4.1. Let $f(x) = (-1)^{n-1}/n$ on $(n-1, n)$, $n = 1, 2, \ldots$, and let $f(x) = 0$ elsewhere on $A = (-\infty, \infty)$. Clearly, for any choice of (a_n, b_n), $L[f, A(a_n, b_n)] \to \log 2$, and $L[|f|, A(a_n, b_n)] \to \infty$.

Functions such as that in Example 4.1 are said to have a non-absolutely convergent integral, or to be non-absolutely integrable. In Chapter VI further consideration will be given to such integrals, but for the present we shall study only functions for which the first limit is finite, and shall speak of such functions as being summable on A.

The extension of the results of Section 4.2 to include functions summable under Definition 4.1 will now be considered. If $f(x)$ is summable under this definition on any set A and $E = A - A(a_n, b_n)$, then $L(|f|, E)$ is arbitrarily small if n is sufficiently great. From this it follows at once that Theorems 4.1—4.6 hold with integration in the sense of Definition 4.1. If E is any measurable subset of A then $L[|f|, E - E(a_n, b_n)]$ is arbitrarily small if n is sufficiently great. But for n fixed it follows from Theorem 4.6 as it stands that $L[|f|, E(a_n, b_n)]$ is arbitrarily small, if $|E|$ is sufficiently small. These considerations allow us to conclude that Theorem 4.7 holds with integration in the sense of Definition 4.1. It then follows that Theorem 4.8 holds without change. Coming to Theorem 4.9, Riemann integrals are defined for finite intervals only. Consequently this theorem is not concerned with Lebesgue integrals in the sense of Definition 4.1.

From Theorem 4.10 as it stands, it follows that for each interval (a_n, b_n),

$$L[|f|, A(a_n, b_n)] = \sum_i L[|f|, A_i(a_n, b_n)].$$

It is therefore sufficient to show that $L[|f|, A(a_n, b_n)] \to \sum L(|f|, A_i)$ as $n \to \infty$. Now

$$L[|f|, A(a_n, b_n)] = L[|f|, (A_1 + \ldots + A_k)(a_n, b_n)] + L[|f|, (A_{k+1} + \ldots)(a_n, b_n)] .$$

The second term on the right is not greater in numerical value than

$$\sum_{k+1}^{\infty} (|f|, A_i)$$

which is close to zero if k is sufficiently great. With k fixed, the first term on the right is close to

$$\sum_{i=1}^{k} L(|f|, A_i)$$

if n is sufficiently great. These relations combine to show that $L[|f|, A(a_n, b_n)] \to \sum (|f|, A_i)$. Then since $L[|f|, A(a_n, b_n)]$ tends to a limit, f is summable under Definition 4.1.

It has now been shown that the results of Section 4.2 hold when the set A is unbounded and integration is in the sense of Definition 4.1. We conclude this section with a theorem on measure preserving transformations which we shall use in the proof of the ergodic theorem.

THEOREM 4.12. *If the function $f(x)$ is summable on the measurable set A, and if T is a measure preserving transformation according to Definition 2.7 for which $TA = A$, then $f(Tx)$ is summable over A and $L[f(x), A] = L[f(Tx), A]$. If $E \subset A$ is measurable, then $L[f(Tx), E] = L[f(x), TE]$.*

If $x' = Tx$, $E' = E(f(x') < a)$, $E^a = E(f(x) < a)$, then $E' = TE^a$, and therefore E' is measurable. Consequently $f(x') = f(Tx)$ is measurable on A. Let (a_{i-1}, a_i) be a subdivision of $(-\infty, \infty)$ and let $e_i = E[a_{i-1} \leq f(x) < a_i, x \in A]$, $e'_i = E[a_{i-1} \leq f(x') < a_i, x' = Tx \in A]$. Then $e'_i = Te_i$, and since T is measure preserving, $|e'_i| = |e_i|$. Hence

$$\sum a_i |e'_i| = \sum a_i |e_i| .$$

The first of these sums tends to $L[f(x'), A] = L[f(Tx), A]$ and the second to $L[f(x), A]$. Consequently $L[f(Tx), A] = L(f(x), A]$. This completes the proof of the first part of the theorem. The second part follows immediately from the fact that T is one to one and measure preserving.

4.4. The integrability of sequences. We now consider the behaviour of sequences with respect to integration. If $s_1(x), s_2(x), \ldots$ is a sequence of functions each summable over A and $s_n(x)$ tends to a function $f(x)$ summable over A, under what conditions does $L(s_n, A)$ tend to $L(f, A)$? That the answer is not always in the affirmative is shown by the following.

EXAMPLE 4.2. On the set $A = (0 \leq x \leq 1)$, let $s_n(x) = n(1 - nx)$, $0 < x \leq 1/n$, $s_n(x) = 0$, $1/n < x \leq 1$, $s_n(0) = 0$. Then $s_n(x) \rightarrow f(x) = 0$ on $[0, 1]$. Hence $L(f, A) = 0$. But $L(s_n, A) = 1/2$ for every n, and conseq ently $L(s_n, A)$ does not tend to $L(f, A)$.

The problem of the integrability of sequences arose early in the study of Riemann integrals, but even for sequences which are bounded in x and n the complete answer was not obtained until the Lebesgue integral became available. An important but easily proved result which involves Riemann integration is:

THEOREM 4.13. *Let the sequence of functions $s_1(x)$, $s_2(x)$, ... be defined on $[a, b]$, where $s_n(x)$ is Riemann integrable on this interval. If $s_n(x)$ tends uniformly to $f(x)$, then $f(x)$ is Riemann integrable on $[a, b]$ and $R(s_n, a, b)$ tends to $R(f, a, b)$.*

To show that $R(f, a, b)$ exists, set $f(x) = s_n(x) + \eta(x)$, and for $\epsilon > 0$ but otherwise arbitrary, fix n_ϵ so that $|\eta(x)| < \epsilon$ when $n > n_\epsilon$. For $n > n_\epsilon$, form the upper and lower sums of Theorem 3.3. for $f(x)$, $s_n(x)$, and $\eta(x)$. Then

$$\sum(M_i - m_i)(x_i - x_{i-1}) \leq \sum(M_{ni} - m_{ni})(x_i - x_{i-1}) + \sum(M_{\eta i} - m_{\eta i})(x_i - x_{i-1}).$$

Since $s_n(x)$ is Riemann integrable it follows from Theorem 3.3 that the first term on the right tends to zero as $x_i - x_{i-1} \rightarrow 0$. The second term on the right is not greater in numerical value than $2\epsilon(b - a)$. Hence the left side is not greater than 2ϵ

$(b - a) + \epsilon$ if $x_i - x_{i-1}$ is sufficiently small, and it follows from Theorem 3.3 that $R(f, a, b)$ exists.

Now consider

$$\left| \int_a^b f(x)dx - \int_a^b s_n(x)dx \right| \leq \int_a^b |f(x) - s_n(x)|\, dx$$
$$< \int_a^b |\eta(x)|\, dx < \epsilon(b - a),$$

where the integration is in the sense of Riemann. Since ϵ is arbitrary it follows that $R(s_n, a, b) \to R(f, a, b)$.

That uniform convergence is not necessary, however, is shown by an examination of Example 1.4. In this example there is only one point of non-uniform convergence. The result can easily be proved when the points of non-uniform convergence are finite in number. But these points need not be finite in number, nor even denumerably infinite. For let G be a Cantor ternary set on $(0, 4)$. On each interval of the set complementary to G define a sequence $s_{ni}(x)$ of functions similar to that of Example 1.1, with both ends of the interval points of non-uniform convergence. Every point of G is then a point of non-uniform convergence of the sequence, and it has been shown that G is non-denumerable. Furthermore, the set G could be any non-dense closed set and consequently the set of points of non-uniform convergence of the sequence could have measure greater than zero. It is this last situation for which Theorem 4.13 is difficult to prove without recourse to the Lebesgue theory.

THEOREM 4.14 (BOUNDED CONVERGENCE THEOREM). *Let $s_i(x)$, $s_2(x)$, . . . be a sequence of functions summable over A, bounded in x and n, and for which $s_n(x)$ tends to a limit function $f(x)$ which is measurable by Theorem* 3.7. *Then $L(f, A)$ exists and $L(s_n, A)$ tends to $L(f, A)$.*

Let $M > 0$ be such that $|s_n| < M$. Then $|f(x)| \leq M$. For suppose that for $x = x_1$, $f(x_1) > M$. This with $|s_n| < M$ contradicts the hypothesis that $s_n(x_1) \to f(x_1)$. Then since f is measurable, $L(f, A)$ exists. Let $\epsilon > 0$ be given, and let $e_l = E(|f - s_n| < \epsilon, n \geq l)$. The set e_l is measurable and $e_l \subset e_{l+1}$. For let

$E_0 = E(|f - s_l| < \epsilon)$, $E_1 = E(|f - s_{l+1}| < \epsilon)$, ... Then $e_l = E_0E_1 \ldots$, which is measurable by Theorem 2.16. Furthermore, $|e_l| \to |A|$ as $l \to \infty$. Consequently, $|\tilde{e}_l| \to 0$, and we have for $n \geq l$

$$\int_A |f - s_n|\, dx = \int_{e_l} |f - s_n|\, dx + \int_{\tilde{e}_l} |f - s_n|\, dx,$$
$$\leq \epsilon|A| + 2M|\tilde{e}_l|.$$

Since ϵ is arbitrary and $|\tilde{e}_l| \to 0$ as $l \to \infty$, it follows that $L(s_n, A) \to L(f, A)$. ✓

Let the function $f(x)$ of Theorem 3.11 be summable over the set A. We modify the function φ_n of this theorem in the following way. Let (a_i, b_i) be an interval of the set complementary to the closed set C_n on (a, b). Let (a'_i, b'_i) be an interval with $a_i < a'_i < b'_i < b_i$. Let $\varphi_n = 0$ on (a'_i, b'_i), and on (a_i, a'_i), (b'_i, b_i) let φ_n be linear in such a way that it is continuous on the closed intervals $[a_i, a'_i]$ $[b_i, b'_i]$. It is obvious that the intervals (a'_i, b'_i) can be so chosen that for an arbitrary $\eta > 0$, $L(|\varphi_n|, \tilde{C}_n) < \eta$, $\tilde{C}_n$ the complement on (a, b) of the closed set C_n. We then have

$$\int_A |\varphi_n - f|\, dx = \int_{C_n} |\varphi_n - f| dx + \int_{A-C_n} |\varphi_n - f|\, dx.$$

Since $\varphi_n = f$ on C_n, the first integral on the right is zero. For the second integral we have

$$\int_{A-C_n} |\varphi_n - f|\, dx \leq \int_{\tilde{C}_n} |\varphi_n|\, dx + \int_{A-C_n} |f|\, dx. \tag{4.4}$$

The first integral on the right of (4.4) is less than η where η is arbitrary, and since $|A - C_n| \to 0$ the second integral of (4.6) tends to zero as $n \to \infty$. We conclude, therefore, that $L(|\varphi_n - f|, A) \to 0$ as $n \to \infty$. We have thus proved

THEOREM 4.15. *If $f(x)$ is summable on the bounded and measurable set A, there exists a sequence of functions $\varphi_n(x)$ with $\varphi_n(x)$ continuous on the whole space, summable on A, such that $\varphi_n(x) \to f(x)$ almost everywhere on A and such that*

$$\int_A |\varphi_n - f|\, dx \to 0.$$

4.5. Integrals Containing a parameter. Consider the function $F(y)$ defined by the relation

$$F(y) = \int_a^b f(x, y)dx, \; a \leq x \leq b, \; c \leq y \leq d.$$

This implies that $f(x, y)$ is summable in x for each y. A question of frequent occurrence is that of the continuity of $F(y)$. In particular, if $f(x, y)$ is bounded and continuous in y at y_0 for each x, is $F(y)$ continuous at y_0?

In some cases, this question can be answered in the following way. Let $\delta_1 > \delta_2 > \ldots$ be a sequence of numbers with $\delta_n \to 0$. Let $\epsilon > 0$ be given and let E_n be the set of values of x for which

$$|f(x, y_0+\Delta y) - f(x, y_0)| < \epsilon,$$

when $|\Delta y| < \delta_n$. Clearly $E_{n+1} \supset E_n$ and $E_1+E_2+\ldots$ is the interval (a, b). *Hence if E_n is measurable,* it follows from Theorem 2.13 that $|E_n| \to b-a$. We then write

$$\begin{aligned} |F(y_0+\Delta y) - F(y_0)| &\leq \int_a^b |f(x, y_0+\Delta y) - f(x, y_0)|\, dx, \\ &\leq \int_{E_n} |f(x, y_0+\Delta y) - f(x, y_0)|\, dx + \\ &\quad \int_{\tilde{E}_n} |f(x, y_0+\Delta y) - f(x, y_0)|\, dx, \\ &\leq \epsilon(b-a) + 2M|\tilde{E}_n|, \end{aligned}$$

where M is such that $|f(x, y)| \leq M$ on (a, b). Since ϵ is arbitrary, and since $|\tilde{E}_n| \to 0$, it follows that $F(y)$ is continuous in y at y_0 according to Definition 1.21.

This result was obtained on the assumption that the sets E_n are measurable. This is, indeed, the case for many functions $f(x, y)$ which are summable in x for each y, and continuous in y at y_0 for each x, and it is with surprise that we learn that it is not the case for all such functions.

EXAMPLE 4.3. In constructing the non-measurable set of Section 2.7 a single point was selected from each set $B(x)$. The set $B(x)$ is dense on $(0, 1)$. Consequently if (a, b) is a subinterval of $(0, 1)$ the point selected from each set $B(x)$ could be taken from (a, b). The set thus obtained on (a, b) would be non-measurable.

Let $(1/(n + 1), 1/n)$, $n = 1, 2, \ldots$ be a sequence of open intervals on $(0, 1)$, and let E_n be a non-measurable set on $(1/(n + 1), 1/n)$. Since E_i, $E_j (i \neq j)$ are on intervals which have no points in common, it follows that, for each n, the set $E_n + E_{n+1} + \ldots$ is non-measurable.

Let $f(x, y)$ be defined on the rectangle $0 \leq x \leq 1$, $0 \leq y \leq 1$ as follows. On the line $y = x$, let $f(x, y) = 1$ if $x \in E_1 + E_2 + \ldots$. For other points (x, y) on the rectangle let $f(x, y) = 0$. For each $y, f(x, y) \neq 0$ for at most a single point. Hence $f(x, y)$ is summable in x for each y. Also, for each x the function $f(x, y)$ is continuous in y at $y = 0$. If $\epsilon < 1$ and $\delta_n = 1/(n + 1)$, the set A_n for which

$$|f(x, 0 + \Delta y) - f(x, 0)| < \epsilon, \quad 0 \leq \Delta y < \delta_n,$$

is the complement of $E_{n+1} + E_{n+2} + \ldots$, which is non-measurable by Theorem 2.8. Hence for functions such as this, the proof of the continuity of $F(y)$ given above is meaningless. We cannot talk about the integral of $|f(x, y_0 + \Delta y) - f(x, y_0)|$ over a non-measurable set.

Let us now return to the general case and show how this difficulty, arising from the possible existence of non-measurable sets, can be overcome.

THEOREM 4.16. *Let $f(x, y)$ be a bounded function on $a \leq x \leq b$, $c \leq y \leq d$, which is summable in x for each y and, for each x, continuous in y at y_0. Then*

$$F(y) = \int_a^b f(x, y)dx$$

is continuous at y_0.

Let $y_1 > y_2 > \ldots$ be a sequence of values of y with $y_n \to y_0$. Let E_l be the set for which

$$|f(x, y_n) - f(x, y_0)| < \epsilon, \quad n \geq l.$$

To show that E_l is measurable let A_n be the set of values of x for which

$$|f(x, y_n) - f(x, y_0)| < \epsilon.$$

Then A_n is measurable by Theorem 3.2 and it follows from

Theorem 2.13 that $E_l = A_l + A_{l+1} + \ldots$ is measurable. Also $E_l \subset E_{l+1}$, and $E_1 + E_2 + \ldots$ is the interval (a, b). Hence by Theorem 2.13, $|E_l| \to b - a$. We thus have, as in Theorem 4.14,

$$\begin{aligned} |F(y_n) - F(y_0)| &\leq \int_a^b |f(x, y_n) - f(x, y_0)|\, dx; \\ &\leq \int_{E_l} |f(x, y_n) - f(x, y_0)|\, dx + \\ &\quad \int_{\tilde{E}_l} |f(x, y_n) - f(x, y_0)|\, dx, \\ &< \epsilon(b - a) + 2M|\tilde{E}_l|, \end{aligned}$$

where $|f(x, y)| < M$ on $[a, b]$. Again, since ϵ is arbitrary and $|\tilde{E}_l| \to 0$, it follows that $F(y_n) \to F(y_0)$.

It has thus been shown that if $y_1, y_2, \ldots$ is a sequence of values tending to y_0 monotonically then $F(y_n) \to F(y_0)$. It then follows that if $y_1, y_2, \ldots$ is any sequence whatever with $y_n \to y_0$ then $F(y_n) \to F(y_0)$. For if this were not the case, a monotone sequence could be selected from the arbitrary sequence for which $F(y_n)$ failed to tend to $F(y_0)$. Consequently we have proved $F(y)$ continuous at y_0 according to Definition 1.21. In attempting to prove $F(y)$ continuous under Definition 1.20 we encountered non-measurable sets. The change to Definition 1.21 overcame the difficulty, for in Note 1.4 the two definitions were shown to be equivalent. It is to be noted, however, that the difficulty was not overcome without recourse to the Zermelo axiom, for this axiom was used in the equivalence proof.

4.6. Further theorems on sequences of functions.

THEOREM 4.17 (FATOU'S THEOREM). *If $s_1(x), s_2(x), \ldots$ is a sequence of summable functions defined on the measurable set A; if $s_n(x) \geq 0$ and $s_n(x) \to s(x)$ as $n \to \infty$, then*

$$\int_A s(x)dx \leq \liminf_{n \to \infty} \int_A s_n(x)dx$$

if $s(x)$ is summable. Otherwise

$$\lim_{n \to \infty} \int_A s_n(x)dx = \infty.$$

The function $s(x)$ is measurable by Theorem 3.7. Let $k_n(x) = s_n(x)$ if $s_n(x) < k$, otherwise let $k_n(x) = 0$; let $k(x) = s(x)$ if $s(x) < k$, otherwise $k(x) = 0$. If k is a fixed positive number it is evident that $k_n(x) \to k(x)$. Then, using Theorem 4.14 (bounded convergence theorem) and the fact that $s_n \geq k_n$ it follows that

$$\lim_{n \to \infty} \int_A k_n dx = \int_A k dx,$$

and

$$\int_A s_n dx \geq \int_A k_n dx.$$

Hence

$$\liminf_{n \to \infty} \int_A s_n dx \geq \int_A k(x) dx.$$

The theorem then follows by letting $k \to \infty$.

THEOREM 4.18 (MEAN CONVERGENCE THEOREM). Let $s_1(x)$, $s_2(x)$, . . . *be a sequence of summable functions defined on the measurable set* A, *and let the sequence be such that*

$$\lim_{m, n \to \infty} \int_A | s_m(x) - s_n(x)| \, dx = 0.$$

There then exists on A *a summable function* $s(x)$ *which is such that*

$$\lim_{n \to \infty} \int_A |s_n(x) - s(x)| dx = 0,$$

and a subsequence $s_{n_1}(x)$, $s_{n_2}(x)$, . . . *of the sequence* $s_1(x)$, $s_2(x)$, . . . *which is such that*

$$\lim_{\nu \to \infty} s_{n_\nu}(x) = s(x)$$

for almost all x *in* A.

Let n_ν be the smallest integer for which

$$\int_A |s_m - s_n| dx < \frac{1}{3^\nu}, \quad m, n \geq n_\nu.$$

Let A_ν be the set for which $|s_{n_{\nu+1}} - s_{n_\nu}| > 1/2^\nu$. It then follows that $|A_\nu| < (2/3)^\nu$, and consequently, by comparison with the series $\sum 1/2^\nu$, the series

$$\sum_\nu |s_{n_{\nu+1}}(x) - s_{n_\nu}(x)|$$

converges for every x which does not belong to the set $A_{\nu+1} + A_{\nu+2} + \ldots$ for some value of ν. However, since $|A_\nu| < (2/3)^\nu$, the measure of this set tends to zero as $\nu \to \infty$, and it follows that this series converges for almost all x in A. Consequently the series

$$\sum_{\nu=1}^{\infty} \{s_{n_{\nu+1}}(x) - s_{n_\nu}(x)\}$$

converges for almost all x in A, and it follows from this that $|s_{n_\mu} - s_{n_\nu}| \to 0$ as $\mu,\ \nu \to \infty$ for almost all x in A. This in turn implies that for almost all x in A the sequence $s_{n_1}(x)$, $s_{n_2}(x)$, $\ldots$ is a Cauchy sequence and, therefore, converges to a function $s(x)$ for almost all x in A. The function $s(x)$ is measurable by Theorem 3.7. Furthermore, since $\int_A |s_{n_\mu} - s_{n_\mu}| dx \to 0$ as $\mu,\ \nu \to \infty$, there exists an integer ν_0 which is such that for $\epsilon > 0$

$$\int_A |s_{n_\mu} - s_{n_\nu}| dx < \epsilon$$

when $\mu,\ \nu > \nu_0$. Then, for μ fixed, by Theorem 4.17 (Fatou's theorem), the relation

$$\epsilon \geq \liminf_{\nu \to 0} \int_A |s_{n_\mu} - s_{n_\nu}| dx \geq \int_A |s_{n_\mu} - s| dx$$

holds, and it follows from this that the function s is summable. Since ϵ is arbitrary it then follows that

$$\lim_{\nu \to \infty} \int_A |s_{n_\nu} - s| dx = 0.$$

Again

$$\int_A |s_n - s| dx \leq \int_A |s_n - s_{n_\nu}| dx + \int_A |s_{n_\nu} - s| dx.$$

By the conditions of the theorem and what we have already proved both integrals on the right tend to zero as n and n_ν tend to infinity. Hence

$$\lim_{n \to \infty} \int_A |s_n - s| dx = 0,$$

and the sequence $s_1(x)$, $s_2(x)$, . . . is said to converge in the mean to the function $s(x)$.

4.7. The ergodic theorem.

We conclude this chapter with a proof of the ergodic theorem of G. D. Birkhoff [6, 7, 8]. This theorem is of recent origin but has, nevertheless, become famous. The ergodic theory, on which there is now an extensive literature, had its source in the problems of dynamics and statistical mechanics. Among those who have made contributions to its development are von Neumann [48], Koopman [38, 39], Hopf [30], Weiner [64, 65], Hurewicz [32] and Garrett Birkhoff [9]. It soon came to be recognized as a problem in the abstract theory of Lebesgue integration. The earlier results gave information on the behaviour of the average value of the integrals of the functions $f_0(x)$, $f_0(Tx)$, . . . , $f_0(T^n x)$ where $f_0(x)$ is a function which is summable on a set A and T is a measure preserving transformation which carries A into itself. G. D. Birkhoff's theorem is a result of the behaviour of the average value of the functions $f_0(x)$, $f_0(Tx)$, . . . , $f_0(T^n x)$. We give the proof of this theorem, first because we wish to pay tribute to one of the great mathematicians of all time, and secondly because we know no other single theorem which calls for the use of so many of the principles set forth in the preceding pages. The proof which we give is elementary. If it appears long it is because it is written for fourth year honour students or first year graduate students rather than for mature mathematicians. The proof can be given in shorter space.

THEOREM 4.19 (THE ERGODIC THEOREM). *Let $f_0(x)$ be summable over the measurable set A. Let T be a measure preserving transformation which carries A into itself. Let*

$$f_n(x) = \frac{f_0(x) + f_0(Tx) + \dots + f_0(T^n x)}{n+1}.$$

Then, for almost all $x \in A$, $f_n(x)$ tends to a limit $f(x)$ which is measurable on A. If E is any measurable subset of A with $TE = E$, and $|E|$ finite, then $f(x)$ is summable on E and $L[f(x), E] = L[f_0(x), E]$.

It will first be shown that for almost all $x \in A$

$$\lim_{n \to \infty} [f_n(Tx) - f_n(x)] = 0. \tag{4.5}$$

Expanding $f_n(Tx)$ and $f_n(x)$ and taking their difference we find that

$$f_n(Tx) - f_n(x) = \frac{f_0(T^{n+1}x) - f_0(x)}{n+1}.$$

Since for each x, $f_0(x)/(n+1) \to 0$ as $n \to \infty$, it is, therefore, sufficient to show that for almost all $x \in A$, $f_0(T^{n+1}x)/(n+1) \to 0$ as $n \to \infty$. For $\lambda > 0$ let

$$E_\lambda = E\left[\limsup_{n \to \infty} \frac{f_0(T^{n+1}x)}{n+1} > \lambda \right]. \tag{4.6}$$

Then E_λ is measurable by Theorems 3.7 and 3.1, and it will be shown that $|E_\lambda| = 0$. Let

$$E_n = E[f_0(T^{n+1}x) > \lambda(n+1)].$$

The set E_n is measurable by Theorems 4.12 and 3.1 and $E_\lambda \subset E_n + E_{n+1} + \ldots$ for every n. Let $G_n = T^{n+1}E_n$. Since T is measure preserving, the set G_n is measurable, and $|G_n| = |E_n|$. For $x \in G_n$, $f_0(x) > (n+1)\lambda$. Hence if $e_n = E[f_0(x) > (n+1)\lambda]$, it follows that $G_n \subset e_n$, and consequently $|G_n| \leq |e_n|$. By Theorem 4.8 $\sum |e_n|$ converges. Then, since $|E_n| = |G_n| \leq |e_n|$, it follows that $|E_n| + |E_{n+1}| + \ldots$ tends to zero as n increases. But $E_\lambda \subset E_n + E_{n+1} + \ldots$ for every n, from which it follows that $|E_\lambda| = 0$. If $\lambda_1 > \lambda_2 > \ldots$ is a sequence of values of λ with $\lambda_n \to 0$ then $E = E_{\lambda_1} + E_{\lambda_2} + \ldots$ is the set for which

$$\limsup_{n \to \infty} \frac{f_0(T^{n+1}x)}{n+1} > 0.$$

Since $|E_{\lambda_n}| = 0$ for each n, it follows that $|E| = 0$. In a similar way it can be shown that the set for which

$$\liminf_{n \to \infty} \frac{f_0(T^{n+1}x)}{n+1} < 0$$

has measure zero. From these considerations it follows that (4.5) holds for almost all points of the set A.

With (4.5) established, we let h and k be two rational numbers with $h > k$, and let

$$E_{hk} = E\,[\limsup_{n\to\infty} f_n(x) > h,\ \liminf_{n\to\infty} f_n(x) < k].$$

This set is measurable by Theorems 3.7 and 3.2, and $\sum_{hk} E_{hk}$ is the set for which

$$\limsup_{n\to\infty} f_n(x) > \liminf_{n\to\infty} f_n(x).$$

Hence, if it is shown that $|E_{hk}| = 0$, it follows that the measure of this set is zero, and that $f_n(x)$ tends to a limit $f(x)$ almost everywhere on A.

To show that $|E_{hk}| = 0$ we first show that

$$h|E_{hk}| \leq \int_{E_{hk}} f_0 dx \leq k|E_{hk}|, \tag{4.7}$$

which, since $h > k$, can hold only if $|E_{hk}| = 0$. To prove (4.7) we first note that, except for a null set, $TE_{hk} = E_{hk}$. For it follows from (4.5) that, except for a null set, $f_n(Tx)$ behaves like $f_n(x)$. Let E be the part of E_{hk} which is carried into itself by the transformation T. For $x \in E$

$$\limsup_{n\to\infty} f_n(x) > h.$$

Let E_n be the part of E for which $f_n > h$, $n = 0, 1, 2, \ldots$, and let

$$G_0 = E_0,\ G_1 = E_1 - G_0,\ G_2 = E_2 - (G_0 + G_1), \ldots.$$

We first suppose that $h > 0$ and prove

$$\int_{G_0+\ldots+G_n} f_0(x)dx \geq h|G_0 + \ldots + G_n| \tag{4.8}$$

the equality holding only when $|G_0 + \ldots + G_n| = 0$.

Let $A_n = G_n$, and define the sets $A_{n-1}, A_{n-2}, \ldots, A_0$ successively by the relations

$$\begin{aligned} A_k = G_k - G_k\,(TA_n + T^2A_n + \ldots + T^nA_n + \\ \ldots + T^{n-1}A_{n-1} + \ldots + TA_{k+1} + \ldots + T^{k+1}A_{k+1}). \end{aligned} \tag{4.9}$$

If a point x is in G_k then

$$T^r x \in E_{k-r} = G_{k-r} + \ldots + G_0. \tag{4.10}$$

For we have $f_0(x) + f_0(Tx) + \ldots + f_0(T^kx) > (k+1)h$, and if $r > 0$ then $f_0(x) + \ldots + f_0(T^{r-1}x) \leq rh$, from which it follows that $f(T^rx) + \ldots + f(T^kx) > (k - r + 1)h$ and consequently T^rx is in E_{k-r}. If $r = 0$ then (4.10) is trivial.

An important fact for us will be that the sets $T^r A_k$, $r = 0, 1, \ldots, n$, $k \geq r$, are mutually exclusive. Suppose that x is a common point of $T^{r_1}A_{k_1}$ and $T^{r_2}A_{k_2}$. Then we show that $r_1 = r_2$, $k_1 = k_2$.

If $r_1 < r_2$ then $x' = T^{-r_1}x$ is in A_{k_1} and in $T^{r_2 - r_1}A_{k_2}$. Hence it is sufficient to take $r_1 = 0$ and show that A_{k_1} and $T^{r_2}A_{k_2}$, $0 \leq r_2 \leq n$, are mutually exclusive. If $r_2 = 0$ then A_{k_1} and A_{k_2} are mutually exclusive by definition, unless $k_1 = k_2$. Suppose $r_2 > 0$ and $k_1 < k_2$. Then A_{k_1} and $T^{r_2}A_{k_2}$ are mutually exclusive by definition. If $k_1 \geq k_2$ then $T^{r_2}A_{k_2}$ is, by (4.10), mutually exclusive with $G_{k_2} + \ldots + G_n$ and *a fortiori* with $A_{k_1} \subset G_{k_1}$.

We next prove (4.8). From (4.9), $G_0 + \ldots + G_n = A_0 + \ldots + A_n + \sum_{r,k} T^r A_k(G_0 + \ldots + G_{k-1})$, $r = 1, 2, \ldots, n$, $k \geq r$. By (4.10) $T^r A_k \in G_0 + \ldots + G_{k-r}$. Therefore $G_0 + \ldots + G_n = A_0 + (A_1 + TA_1) + \ldots + (A_n + \ldots + T^n A_n)$, where all sets on the right are mutually exclusive. Hence by Theorem 4.12

$$\begin{aligned}\int_{G_0 + \cdots + G_n} f_0(x)dx &= \int_{A_0} f_0(x)dx + \int_{A_1 + TA_1} f_0(x)dx + \ldots \\ &\quad + \int_{A_n + TA_n + \cdots + T^n A_n} f_0(x)dx \\ &= \int_{A_0} f_0(x)dx + \int_{A_1} [f_0(x) + f_0(Tx)]dx + \ldots \\ &\quad + \int_{A_n} [f_0(x) + f_0(Tx) + \ldots + f_0(T^n x)]dx \\ &\geq h|A_0| + 2h|A_1| + \ldots + n + 1h|A_n|,\end{aligned}$$

and there is equality only if all sets are of zero measure. Then because $|E| = |T^k E|$ it follows that

$$\begin{aligned}\int_{G_0 + \cdots + G_n} f_0(x)dx &\geq h|A_0| + h|A_1 + TA_1| + \ldots \\ &\quad + h|A_n + \ldots + T^n A_n| \\ &\geq h|G_0 + \ldots + G_n|.\end{aligned}$$

This establishes 4.8 when $h > 0$. Then, since $f_0(x)$ is summable on $E = G_0 + G_1 + \ldots$ it follows that $|E|$ is finite and

$$\int_E f_0(x)dx \geq h|E| = h|E_{hk}|.$$

It can be shown in a similar way that

$$\int_E f_0(x) \leq k|E| = k|E_{hk}|.$$

It follows from these relations and the summability of $f_0(x)$ that if $h > 0$ then $|E_{hk}| = 0$. If $h \leq 0$, $h > k$ it is possible to arrive at the same result by first proving that $L[f_0(x), E_{hk}] \leq k|E_{hk}|$. This completes the proof of the first part of the ergodic theorem, and we remark that the proof has been obtained without requiring that $|A|$ be finite. For example, if $A = (-\infty, \infty)$, $f_0(x) = 1/(x^2 + 1)$ and $Tx = x + 1$, then $f_n(x) \rightarrow f(x) \equiv 0$.

In order to prove the second part of the theorem we consider any measurable set $e \subset A$ with $|e|$ finite. The function $f_n(x)$ is summable on e by Theorems 3.2, 4.3 and 4.12, and $f(x)$ is measurable on e by Theorem 3.7. We then have

$$(n + 1) \int_e f_n(x)dx = \int_e f_0(x)dx + \int_e f_0(Tx)dx + \ldots + \int_e f_0(T^n x)dx.$$

By making use of Theorem (4.12) and the fact that $|Te| = |e|$ it follows that

$$\left|\int_e f_n(x)dx\right| \leq \sup \int_E |f_0(x)|dx,$$

where E is measurable, $E \subset A$ and $|E| \leq |e|$. Then since e is any measurable set contained in A it follows that

$$\int_E |f_n(x)|dx \rightarrow 0 \tag{4.12}$$

uniformly in n as $|e| \rightarrow 0$. Since $|e|$ is finite it now follows that $f(x)$ is summable on e. For otherwise if $G > 0$ is given there is a measurable set $B \subset e$ with $|B|$ arbitrarily near zero and $L(|f|, B) > G$. Then since $f_n(x) \rightarrow f(x)$ almost everywhere on B it follows that $L(|f_n(x)|, B) > G$, which contradicts (4.12). Thus $f(x)$ is summable on E. Let $\epsilon > 0$ be given and let $e = E(|f - f_n| < \epsilon), n > l$. As in Theorem 4.14, $|e - e_l| \to 0$ as $l \to \infty$. Also

$$\int_e |f - f_n|dx = \int_{e_l} |f - f_n|dx + \int_{e-e_l} |f - f_n|dx.$$

Since $|e - e_l| \to 0$ as $l \to \infty$ and since ϵ is arbitrary it follows that

$$\int_e f_n(x)dx \to \int_e f(x)dx. \tag{4.13}$$

Now suppose that $E \subset A$ is measurable with $|E|$ finite, and E is also such that $TE = E$. Then, by Theorem 4.12,

$$\begin{aligned}(n + 1)\int_E f_n(x)dx &= \int_E [f_0(x) + f_0(Tx) + \ldots + f_0(T^n x)]dx \\ &= \int_E f_0(x)dx + \int_{TE} f_0(x)dx + \ldots \\ &\qquad + \int_{T^n E} f_0(x)dx \\ &= (n + 1)\int_E f_0(x)dx,\end{aligned}$$

which gives $L[f_n(x), E] = L[f_0(x), E]$. It now follows from this and (4.13) that $L[f(x), E] = L[f_0(x), E]$.

The proof of the ergodic theorem is now complete. Another proof of the last part of the theorem will be given, which is due to Hurewicz [32].

We let $E \subset A$ be such that E is measurable, $|E|$ finite, and $TE = E$. Let $E_k = E[k\epsilon \leq f < (k + 1)\epsilon]$, $x \in E$, ϵ arbitrary, $k = 0, \pm 1, \pm 2, \ldots$. It follows from (4.5) that $TE_k = E_k$. Furthermore, since for $x \in E_k$, $f(x) < (k + 1)\epsilon$, it follows that for some integer n, $f_n(x) < (k + 1)\epsilon$. It then follows as in the proof of (4.13) that

$$\int_{E_k} f_0(x)dx \leq \epsilon(k + 1)|E_k|. \tag{4.14}$$

Also if $x \in E_k$, $f(x) > k\epsilon - \delta$ for every real $\delta > 0$. Hence

$f_n(x) > k\epsilon - \delta$ for some integer n and it follows as in the proof of (4.12) that

$$(4.15) \qquad \int_{E_k} f_0(x)dx > (k\epsilon - \delta)|E_k|\,.$$

Then, since δ is arbitrary, we conclude that

$$\int_{E_k} f_0(x)dx \geq \epsilon k|E_k|\,.$$

Relations (4.13) and (4.15) now give

$$(4.16) \qquad \epsilon k|E_k| \leq \int_{E_k} f_0(x)dx \leq \epsilon(k+1)|E_k|\,.$$

From the definition of E_k it follows that

$$(4.17) \qquad \epsilon k|E_k| \leq \int_{E_k} f(x)dx \leq \epsilon(k+1)|E_k|\,.$$

Subtracting (4.17) from (4.16) we get

$$(4.18) \qquad -\epsilon|E_k| \leq \int_{E_k} f_0(x)dx - \int_{E_k} f(x)dx < \epsilon|E_k|\,,$$

and it follows from this, since $|E|$ is finite, that

$$\sum_{-\infty}^{\infty} \int_{E_k} f(x)dx$$

converges. It then follows as in Theorem 4.10 and the fact that $|E|$ is finite, that f is summable over E. Also, from (4.18) it follows that

$$-\epsilon|E| \leq \int_E f_0(x)dx - \int_E f(x)dx < \epsilon|E|,$$

which shows that

$$\int_E f(x)dx = \int_E f_0(x)dx,$$

and this completes the proof of the second part of theorem.

Problems

4.1. If $f_1(x)$ and $f_2(x)$ are summable on the set A and $f_1(x) > f_2(x)$, show that $L(f_1, A) > L(f_2, A)$.

4.2. If $f_1(x)$ and $f_2(x)$ are summable on A, $f_1(x) \leq f_2(x)$ and $L(f_1, A) = L(f_2, A)$, then $f_1(x) = f_2(x)$ almost everywhere on A.

4.3. If the sequence $f_n(x)$ of measurable functions defined on the set A tends uniformly to the summable function $f(x)$ then $L(f_n, A) \to L(f, A)$, $|A| < \infty$.

4.4. If the sequence of summable functions $f_n(x)$ defined on the set A are such that $L(|f_n|, e) \to 0$ uniformly in n as $|e| \to 0$ and such that $f_n(x) \to f(x)$, then $f(x)$ is summable on A and $L(f_n, A) \to L(f, A)$.

4.5. Construct an example to show that $f_1(x)$ and $f_2(x)$ can each be summable on a set A, and be such that the product $f_1(x)f_2(x)$ fails to be summable on A. Show that if one of the functions is bounded the product is summable.

4.6. (Schwarz's inequality). If $[f(x)]^2$ is summable on a set A and $f(x)$ is summable on A, then $f(x)$ is said to belong to class L^2 on A. If $f(x)$ and $g(x)$ are of class L^2 on (a, b) then

$$\left| \int_a^b f(x)g(x)dx \right| \overline{<} \left\{ \int_a^b |f(x)|^2 dx \int_a^b |g(x)|^2 dx \right\}^{\frac{1}{2}}.$$

[62, p. 381.]

4.7. If $f(x)$ is in class L^2 on (α, β) and $[a, b]$ is an interval with $\alpha < a < b < \beta$, then

$$\lim_{x \to 0} \int_a^b [f(t + x) - f(t)]^2 dt = 0.$$

[62, p. 397.]

4.8. If $f_n(x)$ is in class L^2 on A for every n, and if as $m, n \to \infty$

$$\int_A [f_m(x) - f_n(x)]^2 dx \to 0,$$

there is a subsequence $f_{n_i}(x)$, of the functions $f_n(x)$, which tends to a summable function $f(x)$ almost everywhere on A, and such that

$$\lim_{n \to \infty} \int_A [f(x) - f_n(x)]^2 dx = 0.$$

[62, p. 386].

4.9. Let $f(x)$ be summable on the set $A \subset (a, b)$. By Theorem 3.9 there is a sequence of closed sets $C_n \subset A$ such that $f(x)$ is continuous on C_n, and such that $|C_n| \rightarrow |A|$. Let (x_{i-1}, x_i) be a subdivision of (a, b), and (x_k, x'_k) the intervals of this subdivision which have points of C_n on their interior. Let ξ_k be a point of C_n on (x_k, x'_k). Show that as $x'_k - x_k \rightarrow 0$,

$$\sum_k f(\xi_k)(x'_k - x_k)$$

tends to a limit L_n (Problem 3.14). Show that $L_n \rightarrow L(f, A)$.

4.10 (The second mean value theorem for Lebesgue integrals). Let $f(x)$ be summable on $[a, b]$, $\phi(x)$ monotonic on $[a, b]$. Then there is a number ξ with $a < \xi < b$, such that

$$\int_a^b f(x)\phi(x)dx = \phi(a+)\int_a^\xi f(x)dx + \phi(b-)\int_\xi^b f(x)dx.$$

[62, p. 379.]

4.11. If $f(x)$ is summable on (a, b) and (x_{i-1}, x_i) is a subdivision of (a, b), show that it is possible to choose ξ_i on (x_{i-1}, x_i) so that

$$\sum f(\xi_i)(x_i - x_{i-1}) \rightarrow \int_a^b f(x)dx$$

as $x_i - x_{i-1} \rightarrow 0$.

4.12. If the sequence of summable functions $f_n(x)$ defined on the set A is such that $f_n(x) \rightarrow f(x)$ and such that there is a summable function $\varphi(x) \geq 0$ with $|f_n(x)| \leq \varphi(x)$ then $f(x)$ is summable on A and $L(f_n, A) \rightarrow L(f, A)$. [62, p. 345.]

4.13. Let $f_1(x), f_2(x), \ldots$ be a sequence of non-negative functions which are such that $f_n(x)$ is summable on A, $f_{n-1}(x) \leq f_n(x)$, and such that $L(f_n, A)$ tends to a finite limit. Then for almost all of A, $f_n(x)$ tends to a finite limit $f(x)$. Also $L(f, A)$ exists and $L(f_n, A)$ tends to $L(f, A)$.

4.14. Let $f_1(x), f_2(x), \ldots$ be a sequence of non-negative functions summable on A, and such that $f_{n-1}(x) \leq f_n(x)$, $f_n(x)$ tends to $f(x)$ and $L(f, A)$ exists. Then $L(f_n, A) \rightarrow L(f, A)$.

4.15. Let $f_n(x) = nxe^{-nx^2}$. Show that $f_n(x) \rightarrow 0$, $0 \leq x \leq 1$, but that $L(f_n, 0, 1) \rightarrow 1/2$. Show that at $x = 0$ the measure of non-uniform convergence (Problem 1.18) of the function $f_n(x)$ is infinite.

4.16. Let $f_n(x)$ be a sequence of functions defined on $0 \leq x \leq 2$ in the following way: $f_n(1) = 0$.

$$0 \leq x < \frac{n-1}{n},\ f_n(x) = 0, \qquad \frac{n-1}{n} \leq x < 1,\ f_n(x) = n,$$

$$1 < x < \frac{n+1}{n},\ f_n(x) = -n, \qquad \frac{n+1}{n} \leq x \leq 2,\ f_n(x) = 0.$$

Show that (1) $f_n(x) \to 0$; (2) $L(f_n, 0, 2) \to L(f, 0, 2)$; (3) $L(f_n, 0, 1)$ does not tend to $L(f, 0, 1)$. Also show that if $\epsilon > 0$ is given, there exists a measurable set e with $|e| < \epsilon$, and an integer n_ϵ, such that

$$\int_e f_n dx > 1 - \epsilon,\ n > n_\epsilon.$$

4.17. Let $f_1(x), f_2(x), \ldots$ be a sequence of measurable functions defined on the measurable set A. Let the sequence be such that if $\epsilon > 0$ is given, there exists $\delta > 0$ such that if e is any measurable set on A with $|e| < \delta$, then $|L(f_n, e)| < \epsilon$, $n = 1, 2, \ldots$. Show that if $f_n(x)$ tends to a summable function $f(x)$, then $L(f_n, E) \to L(f, E)$ where E is any measurable subset of A. [29, p. 292.]

4.18. If the sequence $f_1(x), f_2(x), \ldots$ of summable functions defined on the set A is such that $f_n(x)$ tends to a summable function $f(x)$, and if there are no points x at which the measure of non-uniform convergence (Problem 1.18) of $f_n(x)$ is infinite, then $L(f_n, A) \to L(f, A)$.

CHAPTER V

METRIC DENSITY AND FUNCTIONS OF BOUNDED VARIATION

Introduction: In this chapter the Vitali covering theorem is first proved and then used in a study of the density properties of sets and the properties of functions of bounded variation.

5.1. The Vitali covering theorem.

DEFINITION 5.1. *Let A be an arbitrary set. Let V be a family of closed intervals. The family V is said to cover A in the Vitali sense if each $x \in A$ is on some sequence $v_1, v_2, \ldots$ of the intervals of V with $|v_n| \to 0$.*

THEOREM 5.1. *If the set A is bounded and the family of closed intervals V covers A in the Vitali sense, then corresponding to an arbitrary $\epsilon > 0$ there exists a finite, mutually exclusive set $v_1, v_2, \ldots, v_n$ of the family V for which*

$$\left|\sum_{i=1}^{n} Av_i\right|^{\circ} > |A|^{\circ} - \epsilon, \qquad \sum_{i=1}^{n} |v_i| < |A|^{\circ} + \epsilon.$$

Let $\epsilon > 0$ be given and let $a \supset A$ with $|a| < |A|^{\circ} + \epsilon$. Delete from V all intervals which are not on a. The remaining set V is a Vitali family covering A. Choose $v_1 \in V$ and let

$$l_1 = \sup |v|,\ v \in V - v_1.$$

Choose $v_2 \in V - v_1$ with $|v_2| > l_1/2$, and let

$$l_2 = \sup |v|,\ v \in V - (v_1 + v_2).$$

Choose v_3 with $|v_3| > l_2/2$. Continuing this process there is obtained a sequence of intervals $v_1, v_2, \ldots$ with $v_i \in V$, $v_iv_j = 0$, $i \neq j$. Then since $v_i \subset a$, $\sum |v_i| \leq |a| < |A|^{\circ} + \epsilon$, and the theorem is established if it can be shown that $\sum v_i$ contains almost all of A. Let

$$E_n = v_1 + v_2 + \ldots + v_n, \quad E = v_1 + v_2 + \ldots$$

Then since $v_i v_j = 0$, $i \neq j$, and $E \subset \alpha$, we have

$$\Sigma |v_i| = |E| \leq |\alpha|. \tag{5.1}$$

It then follows that for $\epsilon' > 0$ there exists N with

$$\sum_{i=N}^{\infty} |v_i| < \epsilon'. \tag{5.2}$$

Now consider $P \in A\tilde{E}_N$. Since $\tilde{E}_N$ is open there exists $v' \in V$ with $P \in v' \subset \tilde{E}_N$. But it cannot be that $v' \subset \tilde{E}_n$ for all $n > N$. For if $v' \subset \tilde{E}_n$ then $v' \subset \tilde{E}_{n-1}$ and consequently

$$|v'| \leq l_{n-1} = \sup |v|, \; v \in V\text{-}(v_1 + v_2 + \ldots + v_{n-1}).$$

But since $|v_n| > l_{n-1}/2$, it follows from (5.1) that $l_n \to 0$. This contradicts $|v'| \leq l_n$ for every n, and precludes the possibility of $v' \subset \tilde{E}_n$ for every $n > N$. Consequently there is a first integer $m > N$ with

$$v' E_{m-1} = 0, \quad v' v_m \neq 0.$$

Since $v' \subset \tilde{E}_{m-1}$, $|v'| \leq l_{m-1} < 2|v_m|$. Hence if w_m is an interval concentric with v_m and $|w_m| = 5|v_m|$ then $w_m \supset v' \ni P \in A\tilde{E}_N$. Such an interval w_m exists for each point $P \in A\tilde{E}_N$, and consequently, using (5.2),

$$|A\tilde{E}_N|^\circ \leq \Sigma |w_m| < 5 \Sigma |v_m| \leq 5 \sum_{i=N}^{\infty} |v_i| < 5\epsilon'.$$

Since ϵ' is arbitrary it follows that $|A\tilde{E}|^\circ = 0$, $|\Sigma A v_i|^\circ = |A|^\circ$, and $\Sigma |v_i| \leq |\alpha| < |A|^\circ + \epsilon$. If n is sufficiently great the set $v_1 + \cdots + v_n$ satisfies the conditions of the theorem.

NOTE 5.1. It has been shown that there is a denumerable set of mutually exclusive intervals $v_1, v_2, \ldots$ of the family V which contains almost all of A with $\Sigma |v_i| < |A|^\circ + \epsilon$. This is more than the theorem calls for. The theorem is stated as it is because it is in this form that it is usually used. Theorem 5.1 is not valid in two dimensions, intervals being replaced by rectangles with greatest diameter tending to zero. The further condition must be added that the ratio of the short side to the long side of the rectangles be bounded from zero, the bound depending on the points of A. We give an example to illustrate this.

EXAMPLE 5.1 (CARATHÉODORY [15, p. 689]). Denote the rectangle $0 < x < a$, $0 < y < b$ by I. On $(0, a/n)$, $(0, 2a/n)$, $\ldots$, $(0, a)$ construct rectangles with altitudes $b, b/2, \ldots, b/n$ respectively. The area of each rectangle I_p, $p = 1, 2, \ldots, n$, is ab/n. The area of the set A_1 covered by these rectangles is given by

$$|A_1| = \frac{ab}{n}\left(1 + \tfrac{1}{2} + \ldots + \frac{1}{n}\right) = |I_p|\left(1 + \tfrac{1}{2} + \ldots + \frac{1}{n}\right).$$

Given $\eta > 0$, n can be so fixed that

$$1 + \tfrac{1}{2} + \ldots + \frac{1}{n} > \frac{1}{\eta}, \quad |I_p| < \eta\,|A_1|.$$

Through the points a/n, $2a/n$, $\ldots$, $(n - 1)\,a/n$ draw lines parallel to the y-axis. These lines divide $I - A_1$ into $n - 1$ rectangles $J_2, J_3, \ldots, J_n$. On each of these rectangles determine sets $A_2, A_3, \ldots, A_n$ by the operation used in determining the set A_1, the rectangle J_i replacing I, $i = 2, 3, \ldots, n$. Then $A_iA_j = 0$, $i \neq j$. Set

$$\frac{1}{n}\left(1 + \tfrac{1}{2} + \cdots + \frac{1}{n}\right) = 1 - \theta_\eta.$$

Then

$$|A_1| = (1 - \theta_\eta)\,|I|, \; |I - A_1| = \theta_\eta\,|I|.$$

Also

$$|J_2 - A_2| = \theta_\eta\,|J_2|, \ldots, |J_n - A_n| = \theta_\eta\,|J_n|.$$

The set $R = (J_2 - A_2) + \ldots + (J_n - A_n)$ is the part of I not covered by the sets $A_1, A_2, \ldots, A_n$. Hence

$$|R| = \theta_\eta\,|J_2 + \ldots + J_n| = \theta_\eta\,|I - A_1| = \theta^2_\eta\,|I|.$$

If the foregoing constructions are repeated $k - 1$ times there are obtained $1 + (n - 1) + (n - 1)^2 + \ldots + (n - 1)^{k-1}$ mutually exclusive sets A_l, and $(n - 1)^k$ rectangles J_m, where $\sum |J_m| < \theta_\eta^k\,|I|$. Any two rectangles of the set of rectangles whose points make up a set A_l have interior points in common. The closed rectangles of the set making up the set A_l together with the closed rectangles of the set J_m cover $\bar{I}$, the closure of I. If $\delta_1, \delta_2, \ldots, \delta_r$ is any set of rectangles chosen from these two sets and which have no points in common, then not more than one of these rectangles δ_l can come from a single set A_l and $|\delta_l| < \eta |A_l|$. If k is so great that $\theta_\eta^k < \eta$ then

(i) $|\delta_1 + \ldots + \delta_r| < \eta|I| + |J_m| < \eta|I| + \theta_\eta^k|I| < 2\eta|I|.$

Now let there be considered any finite set of these rectangles $\delta_1, \delta_2, \ldots, \delta_n$ which covers $\bar{I}$. If P is any point of $\bar{I}$, there is a first rectangle δ_p of this set which contains P. Let $\delta(P)$ be the smallest rectangle which has P as centre and which contains δ_p. Then

(ii) $$|\delta(P)| \leq 4|\delta_p|,$$

and the diameter of $\delta(P)$ is not more than twice the diameter of I.

If $\epsilon > 0$ is given and η is taken with $\eta < \epsilon/8$, it follows from (i) and (ii) that each point P of I can be made the centre of a rectangle $\delta(P)$ in such a way that if $\delta(P_1), \delta(P_2), \ldots$ is any finite set of these rectangles which do not overlap then

$$\sum |\delta(P_i)| \leq 4|\sum \delta_p| < \epsilon|I|.$$

Let I be a rectangle and let $\rho > 0$ be an arbitrary positive number. Divide I into K congruent rectangles I_k each with diameter less than $\rho/2$. On each I_k carry out the foregoing operations, and assign to each point P of $\bar{I}_k$ a rectangle $\delta(P)$. Then the diameter of $\delta(P)$ is less than ρ, and any finite set $\delta(P_1), \delta(P_2), \ldots$ of these rectangles which do not overlap is such that

$$\sum |\delta(P_i)| < \epsilon \sum |I_k| < \epsilon|I|.$$

If this construction is carried out with ρ taking on a sequence of values $1/2, 1/2^2, \ldots$, and ϵ is replaced by corresponding values $\epsilon/2, \epsilon/2^2, \ldots$ then the resulting sets of rectangles $\delta(P)$ constitute a Vitali family which covers $\bar{I}$. If $\delta(P_1), \delta(P_2), \ldots$ is any finite set of these rectangles which do not overlap then

$$\sum |\delta(P_i)| < \sum \frac{\epsilon}{2^i}|I| < \epsilon|I|.$$

It then follows that Vitali's theorem does not hold for plane sets. It is easily verified that for the rectangles of the set

$\delta(P)$ which covers $\bar{I}$ the ratio of the short side to the long side is not bounded from zero. For further information on this topic see Busemann and Feller [13] and Zygmund [70, p. 838].

5.2. Metric density of sets.

DEFINITION 5.2. *Let A be any set, x any point and ω an interval containing x. Then*

$$\limsup_{|\omega| \to 0} \frac{|A\omega|^{\circ}}{|\omega|}, \ \liminf_{|\omega| \to 0} \frac{|A\omega|^{\circ}}{|\omega|}$$

are respectively the upper and lower metric densities of A at the point x. If these limits are equal, their common value is the metric density of A at the point x, or the density of A at x.

It is obvious that the density values would be unchanged if the intervals ω were taken as closed or half closed. In what follows it is frequently necessary to consider intervals defining the densities at points of a set as a Vitali family covering the set. When this is the case they are taken as closed.

THEOREM 5.2. *At almost all points of a set A the density of A exists and is unity.*

It is evident from the relation

$$\frac{|A\omega|^{\circ}}{|\omega|} \leq 1$$

that the upper density is not greater than unity. Suppose that there exists a set $B \subset A$ with $|B|^{\circ} > 0$, and such that at each point $x \in B$

$$\liminf_{|\omega| \to 0} \frac{|A\omega|^{\circ}}{|\omega|} < \lambda < 1.$$

If $x \in B$ there is associated with x a sequence of closed intervals $v_i \ni x$ with $|v_i| \to 0$, and with

$$\frac{|Av_i|^{\circ}}{|v_i|} < \lambda.$$

Since $B \subset A$, it follows that for $x \in B$

$$\frac{|Bv_i|^{\circ}}{|v_i|} < \lambda. \tag{5.3}$$

These intervals v_i associated with the points $x \in B$ form a Vitali family covering B. Hence, for an arbitrary ϵ, by Theorem 5.1, there exists a finite mutually exclusive set of these intervals $v_1 + \ldots + v_n$ for which

$$(5.4) \qquad |\sum_{i=1}^{n} Bv_i|^\circ > |B|^\circ - \epsilon, \quad \sum_{i=1}^{n} |v_i| < |B|^\circ + \epsilon.$$

Since the intervals $v_1, \ldots, v_n$ are mutually exclusive

$$|\sum_{i=1}^{n} Bv_i|^\circ = \sum_{i=1}^{n} |Bv_i|^\circ.$$

Relations (5.3) and (5.4) now combine to give

$$|B|^\circ - \epsilon < \sum_{i=1}^{n} |Bv_i|^\circ < \lambda \sum_{i=1}^{n} |v_i| < \lambda[|B|^\circ + \epsilon].$$

Since $\lambda < 1$ this leads to a contradiction if ϵ is sufficiently small, and we conclude that $|B|^\circ = 0$. If $\lambda_1 < \lambda_2 < \cdots$ is a sequence of values of λ with $\lambda_n \to 1$ we have just shown that the set $B_n \subset A$ at which the lower density of A is less than λ_n is a null set. But the part of A at which the lower density of A is less than unity is the set

$$B = B_1 + B_2 + \cdots.$$

Then by theorem 2.7,

$$|B|^\circ \leq |B_1|^\circ + |B_2|^\circ + \cdots,$$

and since each $|B_n|^\circ = 0$ it follows that $|B|^\circ = 0$. Hence at almost all points of A the density exists and is equal to unity.

THEOREM 5.3. *If two sets A and B are metrically separated, then at almost all points of one set the density of the other set is zero.*

Let $\lambda_1 > \lambda_2 > \ldots$ be a sequence of positive numbers with $\lambda_n \to 0$. Let A_n be the points of A at which the upper density of B is greater than λ_n. For $\epsilon > 0$ and arbitrary, let $\alpha \supset A$, $\beta \supset B$ with $|\alpha\beta| < \epsilon$. Associated with each point $x \in A_n$ is a sequence of closed intervals $v_1, v_2, \ldots$ with $x \in v_i \subset \alpha$, and with

$$\frac{|Bv_i|^\circ}{|v_i|} > \lambda_n.$$

The intervals v_i constitute a Vitali family covering A_n. Consequently there is a finite mutually exclusive set $v_1, v_2, \ldots,$ v_n of these intervals with

$$|A_n|^\circ + \epsilon > \sum_{i=1}^{n} |v_i| \geq \sum_{i=1}^{n} |A_n\, v_i|^\circ > |A_n|^\circ - \epsilon.$$

Since $v_i \subset \alpha$, $B \subset \beta$, it follows that

$$\epsilon > |\alpha\beta| > \sum_{i=1}^{n} |Bv_i|^\circ > \lambda_n \sum_{i=1}^{n} |v_i| > \lambda_n[|A_n|^\circ - \epsilon].$$

Since ϵ is arbitrary, this leads to a contradiction unless $|A_n|^\circ = 0$. The part of A at which the upper density of B is greater than zero is the set

$$A_1 + A_2 + \cdots$$

which, since $|A_n|^\circ = 0$ for every n, is a null set. Then since the lower density of a set at any point is not greater than the upper density, we conclude that at almost all points of A the density of B is zero. In a similar way it can be shown that at almost all points of B the density of A is zero.

THEOREM 5.4. *If at almost all points of a set A the density of a set B is zero then the sets A and B are metrically separated.*

Let A_1 be the points of A at which the density of B is zero. Then $|A_1|^\circ = |A|^\circ$. Let $\epsilon > 0$ be given. Associated with each point $x \in A_1$ is a sequence of intervals $v_1, v_2, \ldots$ with $x \in v_i$, and with

$$\frac{|Bv_i|^\circ}{|v_i|} < \epsilon. \tag{5.5}$$

These intervals constitute a Vitali family covering A_1, and consequently there exists a finite mutually exclusive set $v_1, \ldots, v_n$ of these intervals with

$$\sum_{i=1}^{n} |A_1 v_i|^\circ > |A_1|^\circ - \epsilon, \quad \sum_{i=1}^{n} |v_i| < |A_1|^\circ + \epsilon. \tag{5.6}$$

Let α be the interior points of the set $v_1 + \ldots + v_n$. Since these intervals are mutually exclusive, it follows from the first part of (5.6), Theorem 2.7, and the fact that $|A_1|^\circ = |A|^\circ$ that $|A - \alpha A|^\circ < \epsilon$. Let $\alpha' \supset A - \alpha A$ with $|\alpha'| < \epsilon$. From (5.5) and the last part of (5.6)

$$\sum_{i=1}^{n} |Bv_i|^\circ < \epsilon \sum_{i=1}^{n} |v_i| < \epsilon\,[|A_1|^\circ + \epsilon].$$

Hence it is possible to put $B\alpha$ in a set $\beta \subset \alpha$ with $|\beta| < \epsilon\,[|A_1|^\circ + \epsilon]$, and $B - B\alpha$ in a set β' with $|\alpha\beta'| < \epsilon$. Then $\alpha + \alpha' \supset A$, $\beta + \beta' \supset B$ and

$$|(\alpha + \alpha')\ (\beta + \beta')| < \epsilon\,[|A_1|^\circ + \epsilon] + 3\epsilon.$$

Since ϵ is arbitrary it follows that A and B are metrically separated.

THEOREM 5.5. *A necessary and sufficient condition that two sets be metrically separated is that at almost all points of one set the density of the other set is zero.*

This follows from Theorems 5.3 and 5.4.

THEOREM 5.6. *If the set A is measurable, then at almost all points of A the density of $\tilde{A}$ is zero, and at almost all points of $\tilde{A}$ the density of A is zero.*

This follows from the definition of measurability and Theorem 5.5.

THEOREM 5.7. *If A and B are not metrically separated and A_B, B_A are the parts of A and B, respectively, at which the density of B, A is greater than zero, then $|A_B|^\circ = |B_A|^\circ > 0$.*

That the metric of each of these sets is greater than zero follows from Theorem 5.5. Suppose that $|A_B|^\circ < |B_A|^\circ$. Let $\alpha \supset A_B$ with $|\alpha| < |B_A|^\circ$. Then $|\tilde{\alpha}B_A|^\circ > 0$. Since α and $\tilde{\alpha}$ are metrically separated, the same is true of αA and $\tilde{\alpha}B_A$. Since $\alpha \supset A_B$, it follows that at all points of $\tilde{\alpha}A$ the density of B, and consequently of $\tilde{\alpha}B_A$, is zero. Hence, by Theorem 5.5, $\tilde{\alpha}A$ and $\tilde{\alpha}B_A$ are metrically separated. It then follows that $A = \alpha A + \tilde{\alpha}A$ is metrically separated from $\tilde{\alpha}B_A$, and it follows from Theorem 5.4 that at almost all points of $\tilde{\alpha}B_A$ the density of A is zero. But this contradicts the definition of B_A and the supposition that $|\tilde{\alpha}\, B_A|^\circ > 0$. We conclude, therefore, that $|A_B|^\circ \geq |B_A|^\circ$. In the same way it can be shown that $|B_A|^\circ \geq |A_B|^\circ$. Consequently $|A_B|^\circ = |B_A|^\circ = c > 0$. It is easily shown that $c = \inf |\alpha\beta|$ for all sets $\alpha \supset A$, $\beta \supset B$.

THEOREM 5.8. *At almost all points of A_B the density of B is unity, and at almost all points of B_A the density of A is unity.*

We omit the details of proof, for the reason that it is similar to the proofs of the preceding theorems. The supposition that there is a part E of A_B with $|E|^\circ > 0$ at which the density of B is less than unity, leads to the conclusion that $|B_A|^\circ < |A_B|^\circ$.

DEFINITION 5.3. *The point $x \in A$ is a point of density of the set A if at x the density of A is unity.*

5.3. Approximate continuity.

DEFINITION 5.4. *Let the function $f(x)$ be defined on the set A and let x be a point of density of A. If*

$$\lim_{\xi \to x} f(\xi) = f(x), \ \xi \in A$$

except for a set ξ of density zero at x, then $f(x)$ is approximately continuous on A at x.

THEOREM 5.9. *If the set A is measurable, and the function $f(x)$ is measurable on A, then $f(x)$ is approximately continuous at almost all points of A.*

By Theorem 3.10, for $\epsilon > 0$ there exists a closed set $C \in A$ with $|A - C| < \epsilon$ and such that $f(x)$ is continuous on C. By Theorems 5.2 and 5.6 at almost all points of C the density of C is unity and the density of $\tilde{C}$ is zero. Hence $f(x)$ is approximately continuous at almost all points of C. Since ϵ is arbitrary, the theorem follows.

5.4. Functions of bounded variation.

DEFINITION 5.5. *Let $f(x)$ be defined on the set A. Let (x_i, x'_i) be a set of non-overlapping intervals with x_i, x'_i points of A. If there exists a number $M > 0$ such that*

$$\Sigma\, |f(x'_i) - f(x_i)| < M \tag{5.7}$$

for every such set of intervals (x_i, x'_i), then $f(x)$ is of bounded variation (BV) on A.

THEOREM 5.10. *If the function $f(x)$ is BV on the set A then the set D of discontinuities of $f(x)$ on A is at most denumerable.*

Let D_n be the points of A at which the saltus of $f(x)$ exceeds $1/n$. The set D_n is made up of a finite number of distinct points. For suppose there are an infinite number of such points, $x_1, x_2, \ldots$. Take k so great that $k(1/n) > M$ where M is defined by (5.7). Since at x_i the saltus of $f(x)$ is greater than $1/n$, there are two points x'_i, x''_i arbitrarily near to x_i with $|f(x''_i) - f(x'_i)| > 1/n$. Since there are a finite number of the points x_i, $i = 1, 2, \ldots, k$, the intervals defined by the points x'_i, x''_i can be taken so that they do not overlap. Then

$$\sum |f(x''_i) - f(x'_i)| > k(1/n) > M.$$

This contradicts the definition of M. Hence the set D_n is finite and consequently denumerable. Then $D = D_1 + D_2 + \ldots$, which is denumerable by Theorem 0.2.

The set of discontinuities of a function of bounded variation can, however, be everywhere dense, as we shall show by an example. We first state two definitions.

DEFINITION 5.6. *Let $f(x)$ be defined on a set A and let x_0 be a limit point on the right of points of A. If $f(x)$ tends to a limit as $x \to x_0$, $x > x_0$, $x \in A$, this limit is denoted by*

$$\lim_{x \to x_0+} f(x) = f(x_0+).$$

The limit $f(x_0 -)$ is similarly defined.

DEFINITION 5.7. *If $f(x)$, defined on a set A, is such that $f(x_1) \geq f(x_2)$ when x_1 and x_2 are points of A with $x_1 > x_2$, then $f(x)$ is non-decreasing on A. There is a similar definition for non-increasing function. Functions which are non-increasing or non-decreasing are called monotone.*

EXAMPLE 5.2 [15, p. 159]. A function $\varphi(x)$ will be constructed on the interval $[0, 1]$ which is bounded and non-decreasing and consequently of bounded variation, but which has a discontinuity at each point of the everywhere dense set $x = p/2^n$, $p = 1, 2, \cdots, 2^n - 1$, $n = 1, 2, \cdots$.

First we describe an operation for defining a function $f(x)$ on an interval (a, b) with assigned values for $f(a)$, $f(a+)$, and $f(b)$. We shall call this operation $O(a, b)$.

Divide the interval $f(a+) \leq y \leq f(b)$ into thirds. Let $y = b_1$, $y = b_2$ be the lower and upper ends respectively, of the middle third. Join the points $[a, f(a+)]$, $[(a + b)/2, b_1]$

with a straight line, and join the points $[(a+b)/2, b_2]$, $[b, f(b)]$ with a straight line. For $a < x \leq (a+b)/2$, $(a+b)/2 < x \leq b$, $y = f(x)$ has the value of y on these straight line segments. At $x = (a+b)/2$, $f(x)$ has a saltus equal to

$$f\left(\frac{a+b}{2}+\right) - f\left(\frac{a+b}{2}\right) = \frac{1}{3}\left[f(b) - f(a+)\right].$$

Let $[a, b] = [0, 1]$. Let $\varphi_1(0) = 0, \varphi_1(0+) = 0, \varphi_1(1) = 1$. Elsewhere define $\varphi_1(x)$ by the operation $O[0, 1]$. This makes $\varphi_1(1/2) = 1/3$ and $\varphi_1(1/2+) = 2/3$. Let $\varphi_2(x) = \varphi_1(x)$ for $x = 0, 1/2, 1$ and let $\varphi_2(1/2+) = \varphi_1(1/2+)$. On $(0, 1/2)$, $(1/2, 1)$ define $\varphi_2(x)$ by the operations $O[0, 1/2]$, $O[1/2, 1]$ respectively. This makes $\varphi_2(1/4) = 1/9$, $\varphi_2(1/4+) = 2/9$, $\varphi_2(3/4) = 7/9$, $\varphi_2(3/4+) = 8/9$. At the points $1/2^2$, $3/2^2$, $\varphi_2(x)$ has a saltus equal to $1/3^2$. This process can now be repeated for each of the intervals $(0, 1/4)$, $(1/4, 1/2)$, $(1/2, 3/4)$, $(3/4, 1)$ to give a function $\varphi_3(x)$ which at the end-points of these intervals is equal to $\varphi_2(x)$ and which at the mid-points has a saltus $1/3^3$. If these functions are plotted, it will help to see how they are being built up.

Continuing the process there is obtained a sequence of non-decreasing functions $\varphi_1(x), \varphi_2(x), \ldots$, which are such that for any x on $[0, 1]$:

$$|\varphi_m(x) - \varphi_n(x)| < \frac{1}{3^k} + \frac{1}{3^{k+1}} + \cdots = \frac{1}{2}\frac{1}{3^{k-1}},$$

where k is the smaller of the numbers m, n. It then follows that $\varphi_n(x)$ is a Cauchy sequence and consequently tends to a limit $\varphi(x)$, Theorem 1.6. If $x_1 < x_2$ then $\varphi_n(x_1) \leq \varphi_n(x_2)$, $n = 1, 2, \ldots$. Hence $\varphi(x_1) \leq \varphi(x_2)$ and $\varphi(x)$ is non-decreasing. Then for any set of non-overlapping intervals (x_i, x'_i)

$$\sum |\varphi(x'_i) - \varphi(x_i)| \leq \varphi(1) - \varphi(0) = 1,$$

and consequently $\varphi(x)$ is BV on $(0, 1)$.

The function $\varphi(x)$ is discontinuous at every point of the everywhere dense set of points of the form $p/2^n$, $n = 1, 2, \ldots$;

$p = 1, 2, \ldots, 2^n - 1$, and these are its only points of discontinuity. For if x_0 is different from any of these points, then for every n there exist integers p and $p + 1$ such that

$$\frac{p}{2^n} < x_0 < \frac{p+1}{2^n}.$$

For x on this interval which contains x_0

$$|\varphi(x) - \varphi(x_0)| \leq \varphi\left(\frac{p+1}{2^n}\right) - \varphi\left(\frac{p}{2^n}+\right) \leq \frac{1}{3^n}.$$

This shows that $\varphi(x)$ is continuous at x_0.

THEOREM 5.11. *If A is measurable and $f(x)$, defined on A, is BV then $f(x)$ is measurable on A.*

By Theorem 5.10 the set of discontinuities of $f(x)$ is denumerable. Then by Theorems 2.11 and 3.8, f is measurable on A.

THEOREM 5.12. *If $f(x)$ is BV on a set A then for each limit point x_0 of A the limits $f(x_0+)$, $f(x_0-)$ exist.*

Let x_0 be a limit point of A on the right. Then $f(x_0+)$ exists. For, suppose that

$$\limsup_{x \to x_0+} f(x) - \liminf_{x \to x_0+} f(x) > \lambda > 0.$$

It is then possible to get a sequence of points $x_1 > x'_1 > x_2 > x'_2 > \ldots, x_n, x'_n \to x_0$ with $|f(x'_i) - f(x_i)| > \lambda$,

$$\sum_{i=1}^{n} |f(x'_i) - f(x_i)| > n\lambda,$$

where n may be taken arbitrarily great. Hence $f(x)$ is not BV on A. This is a contradiction, and the truth of the assertion follows. Similarly if x_0 is a limit point of A on the left, $f(x_0-)$ exists, and the proof is complete.

THEOREM 5.13. *If $f(x)$ is BV on the set A, then $f(x) = \varphi_1(x) - \varphi_2(x)$ where $\varphi_1(x)$ and $\varphi_2(x)$ are non-decreasing functions on A.*

Let a be a point of A. Let $x > a$ be a point of A. Let $a = x_0 < x_1 < \ldots < x_n = x$ be a subdivision of (a, x). Then

$$f(x) - f(a) = \sum [f(x_i) - f(x_{i-1})],\ x_2 \in A. \tag{5.8}$$

Let $P(x)$, $N(x)$ be, respectively, the sums of the positive and negative terms on the right of (5.8), and let $p(x) = \sup P(x)$, $n(x) = \inf N(x)$ for all possible subdivisions of $[a, x]$. We show that $f(x) - f(a) = p(x) + n(x)$.

For every $P(x)$ and $N(x)$, $f(x) - f(a) = P(x) + N(x)$. Let $x_0 < x_1 < \ldots < x_n$ be a subdivision of $[a, x]$ for which $P(x) > p(x) - \epsilon$, $\epsilon > 0$. Since always $N(x) \geq n(x)$, and $f(x) - f(a) = P(x) + N(x)$ we have

$$f(x) - f(a) > p(x) + n(x) - \epsilon. \tag{5.9}$$

Now let $x_0 < x_1 < \ldots < x_n$ be a subdivision for which $N(x) < n(x) + \epsilon$. Then for this subdivision $P(x) \leq p(x)$ and consequently

$$f(x) - f(a) < p(x) + n(x) + \epsilon. \tag{5.10}$$

Since ϵ is arbitrary it follows from (5.9) and (5.10) that

$$f(x) - f(a) = p(x) + n(x).$$

It is obvious that $p(x)$ is non-decreasing and $n(x)$ is non-increasing. If $\varphi_1(x) = p(x) + f(a)$, $\varphi_2(x) = -n(x)$, the theorem is established.

5.5. Upper and lower derivatives.

DEFINITION 5.8. *If $f(x)$ is defined on a set A, then for $x \in A$ the upper and lower derivatives of f over A, ${}_A\bar{D}f$ and ${}_A\underline{D}f$, are respectively*

$$\limsup_{h \to 0} \frac{f(x+h) - f(x)}{h}, \ \liminf_{h \to 0} \frac{f(x+h) - f(x)}{h}$$

where h is such that $x + h \in A$. If these limits are the same their common value is the derivative of $f(x)$ over A, ${}_ADf$. If the set A is an interval then ${}_ADf$ is written Df, and likewise for the other symbols.

THEOREM 5.14. *If $f(x)$ is BV on the set A then ${}_ADf$ exists and is finite at almost all points of A.*

It follows from Theorem 5.13 that it is sufficient to prove the theorem for non-decreasing functions. The derivatives are not defined for isolated points of A, but isolated points constitute at most a null set, since almost all points of A are points of density of A.

We first show that when f is BV on A then, except for a null set, ${}_A\bar{D}f$, ${}_A\underline{D}f$ are finite. Let $E \subset A$ be the set at which

$$\limsup_{h \to 0} \left| \frac{f(x+h) - f(x)}{h} \right| = \infty .$$

For $x \in E$ and N arbitrary there exists a sequence $x_i \in A$ with $|x - x_i| \to 0$, for which

$$\frac{|f(x_i) - f(x)|}{|x_i - x|} > N. \tag{5.11}$$

Let v_i be the closed interval determined by the points x, x_i. Then the intervals thus associated with $x \in E$ constitute a family covering the set E in the Vitali sense. Hence, for $\epsilon > 0$, there exists a finite, mutually exclusive set of these intervals, $v_1, \ldots, v_n$ for which $\sum |v_i| > |E|^\circ - \epsilon$. Then if x'_i is the point $x \in E$ which is associated with v_i, it follows from (5.11) that

$$0 \leq \sum |f(x_i) - f(x'_i)| > N[|E|^\circ - \epsilon].$$

Since ϵ and N are arbitrary, it follows that f cannot be BV on A unless $|E|^\circ = 0$. Hence ${}_A\bar{D}f$ and ${}_A\underline{D}f$ are finite except for a null set.

Now let f be non-decreasing and let h, k be rational numbers with $h < k$. Let $E_{h,k}$ be the set for which

$${}_A\underline{D}f < h < k < {}_A\bar{D}f.$$

Since f is non-decreasing ${}_A\underline{D}f \geq 0$. Hence for $x \in E_{hk}$ there is a sequence x_i associated with x with $|x_i - x| \to 0$ for which

$$\frac{|f(x_i) - f(x)|}{|x_i - x|} < h. \tag{5.12}$$

As in the foregoing argument, we arrive at a Vitali family covering E_{hk}, from which, for $\epsilon > 0$, we can select a finite set of non-overlapping intervals $v_1, \ldots, v_n$ with $|E_{hk}|^\circ - \epsilon \leq \sum |v_i E_{hk}|^\circ \leq \sum |v_i| < |E_{hk}|^\circ + \epsilon$. Then, if x'_i is the point $x \in E_{hk}$ associated with v_i, we have from (5.12)

$$\sum |f(x'_i) - f(x_i)| < h\,[|E_{hk}|^\circ + \epsilon]. \tag{5.13}$$

Since $\sum |v_i E_{hk}|^\circ > |E_{hk}|^\circ - \epsilon$ we can work in exactly the same way with the relation $\bar{D}f > k$, for $x \in E_{hk} \sum v_i$ and obtain a set of intervals $v'_1, \ldots, v'_p$ which are on the set $v_1, \ldots, v_n$ and for which

$$\sum |v'_i| > |E_{hk}|^\circ - 2\epsilon.$$

It then follows as before that if x_i, x'_i are end-points of v'_i we have

$$(5.14) \qquad \sum |f(x'_i) - f(x_i)| > k[|E_{hk}|^\circ - 2\epsilon].$$

Since f is non-decreasing and since each of the intervals $v'_1, \ldots, v'_p$ is on an interval of the set $v_1, \ldots, v_n$, it follows that

$$\sum_{v'_i} |f(x'_i) - f(x_i)| \leq \sum_{v_i} |f(x'_i) - f(x_i)|.$$

Since $h < k$, this is inconsistent with (5.13) and (5.14) unless $|E_{hk}|^\circ = 0$. If E is the set for which ${}_A\underline{D}f < \bar{D}f$, then $E = \sum_{hk} E_{hk}$. Since for every pair of rational numbers $|E_{hk}|^\circ = 0$, it follows that $|E| = 0$. It then follows that, except for a null set, ${}_ADf$ exists and is finite.

It has now been shown that if $f(x)$ is BV on a set A then ${}_ADf(x)$ exists almost everywhere and is finite. It will be further shown that ${}_ADf(x)$ is measurable on A.

THEOREM 5.15. *If the function $f(x)$ is measurable on the measurable set A and ${}_ADf$ exists on A, then ${}_ADf$ is measurable on A.*

First let the set A be the interval (a, b). Then, if $h_1, h_2, \ldots$ is a sequence of numbers with $h_n \to 0$, the function $f(x + h_n)$ is measurable by Theorem 2.25 and the function

$$\varphi_n(x) = \frac{f(x + h_n) - f(x)}{h_n}$$

is then measurable by Theorem 3.2. Furthermore

$$\lim_{n \to \infty} \varphi_n = {}_ADf.$$

Consequently ${}_ADf$ is measurable by Theorem 3.7. If f is defined only on a set A, the point $x + h_n$ is not necessarily a point of A, and consequently it cannot be asserted that $\varphi_n \to {}_ADf$. By Theorem 3.10 there is a closed set $C \subset A$ with $|A - C|$ arbitrarily small and a continuous function φ which is equal to f on C and linear on the intervals (a_i, b_i) of $\tilde{C}$. It then follows that for almost all of C the relation $D\varphi = {}_ADf$ holds. From the result just proved for functions defined on (a, b) it follows that $D\varphi = {}_ADf$ is measurable on C. It is then possible to obtain a sequence of closed sets $C_n \subset A$ with $|A - C_n| \to 0$ and with ${}_ADf$ measurable on C_n. If $\chi_n = {}_ADf$ on $C_1 + C_2 + \cdots + C_n$ and $\chi_n = 0$ elsewhere then χ_n is measurable on A and $\chi_n \to {}_ADf$ for almost all points of A. Again using Theorem 3.7 we can conclude that ${}_ADf$ is measurable on A, which is the desired result.

5.6. Functions of sets.

DEFINITION 5.9. *Let A be any set, e an element of a class of subsets of A. The function of sets $\varphi(e)$ is defined if for every set e there is a law which assigns a value to the function $\varphi(e)$.*

Thus the metric of e is a function which is defined for every set $e \subseteq A$, $\varphi(e) = |e|^\circ$. If A is measurable and e the measurable subsets of A then $\varphi(e) = |e|$ is a function defined on the measurable subsets of A. If $f(x)$ is a function which is summable on A, e the measurable subsets of A, then

$$\varphi(e) = \int_e f(x)dx$$

is a function defined on the measurable subsets $e \subseteq A$.

DEFINITION 5.10. *Let A be any set, $\varphi(e)$ defined for the sets $e \subseteq A$. If $x \in A$ and ω is an interval with $x \in \omega$, then the upper and lower derivatives of $\varphi(e)$ at the point x are respectively*

$$\limsup_{|\omega| \to 0} \frac{\varphi(A\omega)}{|\omega|}, \quad \liminf_{|\omega| \to 0} \frac{\varphi(A\omega)}{|\omega|}.$$

If for any point x these limits are equal, their common value is the derivative of $\varphi(e)$, $D\varphi(e)$, at the point x.

Thus while the function $\varphi(e)$ is defined for sets e, which can include the case for which e is a single point, the derivatives of $\varphi(e)$ are defined only for points.

THEOREM 5.16. *Let $f(x)$ be summable on the measurable set A. For e measurable and $e \subseteq A$, let*

$$\varphi(e) = \int_e f(x)dx.$$

Then for almost all points $x \in A$, $D\varphi(e) = f(x)$.

We wish to show that if $x \in \omega$ then

$$\lim_{|\omega| \to 0} \int_{A\omega} f(x)dx/|\omega| = f(x) \tag{5.15}$$

for almost all points $x \in A$. Let E be the points of A at which f is approximately continuous. Let x be a point of density of E, and for $x \in \omega$ let e be the points $\xi \in A$ which are such that $|f(\xi) - f(x)| < \epsilon$, and $e'\omega = (A - e)\omega$. By Theorems 3.1 and 2.12, e and e' are measurable. Then

$$\int_{A\omega} fdx = \int_{e\omega} fdx + \int_{e'\omega} fdx. \tag{5.16}$$

Also

$$[f(x) - \epsilon]\,|e\omega| < \int_{e\omega} fdx < [f(x) + \epsilon]|e\omega|.$$

Since the density of e at x is unity, $|e\omega|/|\omega| \to 1$ as $|\omega| \to 0$, and it follows that as $|\omega| \to 0$ the upper and lower limits of

$$\int_{e\omega} fdx/|\omega| \tag{5.17}$$

lie between $f(x) - \epsilon$ and $f(x) + \epsilon$, where ϵ is arbitrary. It then follows that the ratio in (5.17) tends to f as $|\omega| \to 0$. Consequently, (5.15) is established if it can be shown that

$$\lim_{|\omega| \to 0} \int_{e'\omega} fdx/|\omega| = 0 \tag{5.18}$$

for almost all points $x \in E$. In the ratio of (5.18) the open interval ω can be replaced by a closed interval v without changing the value of the numerator or the denominator. Let E_λ be the part of E for which the upper limit of the ratio in (5.18), with v replacing ω is greater than $\lambda > 0$. Since the density of e' at $x \in E$ is zero $|e'v|/|v| \to 0$ as $|v| \to 0$. Hence associated with each point $x \in E$ there is a sequence of intervals v_i, $x \in v_i$, with

$$\int_{e'v_i} |f|dx > \lambda|v_i|, \; |e'v_i| < \epsilon|v_i|. \tag{5.19}$$

From the Vitali family thus covering E_λ it is possible to select a finite set of non-overlapping intervals $v_1, \ldots, v_n$, satisfying (5.19), and such that $\sum|v_i| > |E_\lambda|^\circ - \epsilon$. Then from (5.19) it follows that

$$\int_{\Sigma e' v_i} |f| dx > \lambda[|E_\lambda|^\circ - \epsilon], \ |\sum e' v_i| < \epsilon[|E_\lambda|^\circ + \epsilon].$$

Since ϵ is arbitrary, there is a contradiction unless $|E_\lambda|^\circ = 0$, for by Theorem 4.6, $L(|f|, \sum e' v_i) \to 0$ as $|\sum e' v_i| \to 0$.

By taking a sequence of values of λ tending to zero, we are led to the conclusion that the part of E for which the upper limit of the ratio in (5.18) is greater than zero has zero measure. This is the desired result, and the proof of the theorem is complete.

5.7. The summability of the derivative of a function of bounded variation. In what follows we shall be dealing with the derivatives which are finite almost everywhere on measurable sets A. If E is the set for which Df is finite then $|E| = |A|$. If Df is summable over the set E we shall say that Df is summable over A. It may be understood that Df has been assigned an arbitrary value, zero for example, on the set $A - E$. We shall not again mention this circumstance explicitly.

THEOREM 5.17. *If the function $f(x)$ is BV on the measurable set A then ${}_ADf(x)$ exists and is finite at almost all points of A. Also ${}_ADf(x)$ is measurable on A and is summable over the set for which it is finite. If $f(x)$ is non-decreasing on the interval $[a, b]$ then*

$$\int_a^b Df(x)dx \leq f(b) - f(a). \tag{5.20}$$

The first part of the theorem follows from Theorem 5.14, and ${}_ADf$ is measurable by Theorem 5.15. To prove that ${}_ADf$ is summable let E be the points of A at which ${}_ADf$ is finite. Since ${}_ADf$ is measurable on E it is summable on E if $|{}_ADf|$ is summable on E. If $|{}_ADf|$ is not summable over E then it follows from the definition of summability that there exists $B \subset E$ with $L(|{}_ADf|, B)$ arbitrarily great, and $|B|$ arbitrarily near to $|E|$. By Theorem 5.16 for almost all points $x \in B$

there exists a sequence of intervals v_i, $x \in v_i$, in particular x can be a left-hand end-point of v_i, and such that

$$\lim_{|v_i| \to 0} \int_{Bv_i} |_A Df| dx / |v_i| = |_A Df|.$$

Hence if v_i is $[x, x_i]$ and ϵ is arbitrary there exists an infinite set of intervals v_i with v_i arbitrarily small such that

$$(5.21) \qquad \left| \int_{Bv_i} |_A Df| dx / |v_i| - \frac{|f(x_i) - f(x)|}{|x_i - x|} \right| < \epsilon.$$

It is then possible to select a finite set of these intervals $v_1, v_2, \ldots, v_n$ with

$$\sum |Bv_i| > |B| - \epsilon, \; \sum |v_i| < |B| + \epsilon.$$

We then get, if the point x on v_i is denoted by x'_i, $v_i = [x'_i, x_i]$,

$$(5.22) \quad \left| \sum \int_{Bv_i} |_A Df| dx - \sum |f(x_i) - f(x'_i)| \right| < \epsilon [|B| + \epsilon].$$

Since $B \subset E$ can be found so that $L(|_A Df|, B)$ is arbitrarily great, and since ϵ is arbitrary independently of the choice of B, it follows that the intervals v_i can be so chosen that the integral on the left side of (5.22) is arbitrarily great. This implies the possibility of making $\sum |f(x'_i) - f(x_i)|$ arbitrarily great, which contradicts the fact that f is BV. We can now conclude that $_A Df$ is summable on E.

With the knowledge that $_A Df$ is summable, we can return to (5.21), remove the absolute value sign from the numerator of the first ratio, and from both numerator and denominator of the second ratio, and arrive at

$$(5.23) \quad | \sum \int_{Bv_i} {_A Df} - \sum [f(x_i) - f(x'_i)]| < \epsilon [|B| + \epsilon].$$

Then, if f is non-decreasing on $A = [a, b]$, it follows, since $B \subset A$, that

$$(5.24) \qquad \sum \int_{Bv_i} Df \, dx < f(b) - f(a) + \epsilon (b - a + \epsilon).$$

The set B and the intervals v_i can be so chosen that the left side is arbitrarily near to $L({_A Df}, a, b)$. Since ϵ is arbitrary it then follows that

$$\int_a^b Dfdx \leq f(b) - f(a). \tag{5.25}$$

This completes the proof of the theorem. An example will now be given which shows that the equality sign in (5.25) does not always hold.

EXAMPLE 5.3. Using the notation of Example 0.1 a function $\varphi(x)$ will be constructed on $[0, 1]$ which is non-decreasing, and for which $\varphi(1) - \varphi(0) = 1$, $L(D\varphi, 0, 1) = 0$.

Let $\varphi_0(0) = 0$, $\varphi_0(1) = 1$. On α^0 let $\varphi_0(x) = 1/2$. On each of the intervals u_{11}, u_{12} let $\varphi_0(x)$ be a linear segment drawn in such a way that the function $\varphi_0(x)$ is continuous on $[0, 1]$.

On each of the intervals α_{11}, α_{12} let $\varphi_1(x)$ be constant, and be equal to the value of $\varphi_0(x)$ at the left end-point of the interval. Elsewhere on $[0, 1]$ except on the intervals u_{22}, u_{24} let $\varphi_1(x) = \varphi_0(x)$. On each of the intervals u_{22}, u_{24} let $\varphi_1(x)$ be a linear segment drawn in such a way that $\varphi_1(x)$ is continuous on $[0, 1]$.

This procedure can be continued to give a sequence of non-decreasing continuous functions defined on $[0, 1]$. Also for each x, $\varphi_{n-1}(x) \geq \varphi_n(x) \geq 0$. It then follows from Theorem 1.3 that $\varphi_n(x)$ tends to a limit $\varphi(x)$. If $0 \leq x_1 < x_2 \leq 1$, then $\varphi_n(x_1) \leq \varphi_n(x_2)$, and it easily follows from this that $\varphi(x_1) \leq \varphi(x_2)$. $\varphi(x)$ is constant on each of the intervals of the set α_{ij}. Hence $D\varphi = 0$ at each point of this set of intervals, which means that $D\varphi = 0$ almost everywhere on $[0.1]$. From this we get

$$\int_0^1 D\varphi dx = 0 < \varphi(1) - \varphi(0) = 1.$$

In elementary work we are accustomed to take it for granted that if Df exists on an interval $[a, b]$ then

$$f(b) - f(a) = \int_a^b Dfdx.$$

Example 5.3 shows that this is not always the case. As a matter of fact the relation can also fail for the reason that Df

is not summable. There are continuous functions $f(x)$ for which Df is finite everywhere but fails to be summable. In Chapter VI these questions will be given further consideration, and the necessary and sufficient conditions for the equality in (5.25) to hold will be obtained.

NOTE 5.2. This example completes what we shall say about functions of bounded variation. We have gone far enough to indicate how interesting and important is this class of functions. What we have said, however, is not more than an introduction. The complete story of the many fundamental ways functions of bounded variation enter into work in Analysis would fill volumes. We mention, in passing, the main lines of development: The idea of bounded variation enters into the determination of arc length. If $x = \varphi(t)$, $y = \psi(t)$ represents a curve in the plane a necessary and sufficient condition that the curve be rectifiable is that φ and ψ be of bounded variation. Carathéodory [16] generalized the concept of length of a curve to include sets of points in the plane which did not constitute a curve in the usual sense. Let A be a set of points in the plane. Let the points of A be covered by a finite or denumerably infinite set of convex regions $u_1, u_2, \ldots$ with greatest diameter d_i. Let $L_\rho = \inf \sum d_i$ for all such coverings with $d_i < \rho$. Clearly L_ρ does not decrease as ρ decreases. If L_ρ tends to a finite limit as $\rho \to 0$ this limit is the linear measure of the two dimensional set A. A. S. Besicovitch [4] studied the density properties of plane sets with finite linear measure and discovered many interesting and unexpected relations. Fundamental contributions have also been made to this development by A. P. Morse and J. F. Randolph [46, 47, 52].

Definitions of bounded variation for functions of two or more variables have also played an important role in Analysis. An exhaustive study of these definitions was carried out by Adams and Clarkson [1, 18], with a later contribution by Macphail [43]. Some of these definitions were applied to the theory of surface measure, first by Lebesgue, Geöcze and Tonelli, and later by Radó and his students, Morrey and

Reichelderfer. This whole fascinating story of surface measure is set forth by Radó in his recent book [51] in which the reader may find references to all the important contributions.

5.8. Functions of sets. We conclude this chapter with a further study of functions of sets, a topic which was introduced in Section 5.6, Definition 5.9. A comprehensive treatment of this subject is given by Hahn and Rosenthal [25].

DEFINITION 5.11. *Let A be any set and $\varphi(e)$ a function defined on the subsets e of A. $\varphi(e)$ is additive if for every two sets e_1, e_2 with $e_1e_2 = 0$, $\varphi(e_1 + e_2) = \varphi(e_1) + \varphi(e_2)$. The function $\varphi(e)$ is completely additive if for every sequence of sets $e_1, e_2 \ldots$ with $e_ie_j = 0$, $i \neq j$, $\varphi(\sum e_i) = \sum \varphi(e_i)$.*

DEFINITION 5.12. *The function $\varphi(e)$ defined on the subsets e of a set A is absolutely continuous on A if for $\epsilon > 0$ there exists $\delta > 0$ such that $\sum|\varphi(e_i)| < \epsilon$ for every sequence of sets $e_1, e_2, \ldots$ with $e_ie_j = 0$, $i \neq j$, and $\sum|e_i|^\circ < \delta$.*

EXAMPLE 5.4. Let A be a measurable set and e the measurable subsets of A. The function $\varphi(e) = |e|$ is completely additive and absolutely continuous. If $f(x)$ is a function which is summable on A then $\varphi(e) = L(f, e)$ is completely additive and absolutely continuous. The truth of these assertions easily follows from the properties of the measure function and of the Lebesgue integral.

EXAMPLE 5.5. Let A be any set and e the subsets of A. The function $\varphi(e) = |e|^\circ$ is not additive. Let A be the non-measurable set of Example 2.7. Since A is non-measurable, $|A|^\circ > 0$. The set $E_n(A)$ is a translation of the set A by means of $x' = x + r_n$, where r_n is a rational number on (0, 1). The method of proof used in Theorem 2.25 applies directly to show that $|E_n(A)|^\circ = |A|^\circ$. Furthermore it is shown in (v) of Example 2.7 that $E_m(A)E_n(A) = 0, m \neq n$. Since $A \subset (0, 1)$, $E_n(A) \subset (-1, 3)$ and consequently $|\sum E_n(A)|^\circ \leq 3$. But $|E_n(A)|^\circ = |A|^\circ > 0$ and it follows that $\sum|E_n(A)|^\circ = \infty$. Thus if $\varphi(e) = |e|^\circ$ on the subsets e of $A = (-1, 3)$, $\varphi(e)$ is not completely additive. Neither is it additive. For if n is fixed so that $n|A|^\circ > 3$, we have

$$\varphi\left[\sum_{i=1}^{n} E_i(A)\right] \leq 3, \quad \sum\varphi(E_i(A)) = n|A|^\circ > 3.$$

EXAMPLE 5.6. Let A be the interval (0, 1) and e the open subsets of A. Let $f_n(x) = n(n+1)$ on $1/(n+1) < x < 1/n$, $n = 1, 2, \ldots, f_n(x) = 0$ elsewhere on (0, 1). Let

$$\varphi(e) = \lim_{\lim n \to \infty} \int_e f_n dx$$

if this limit exists. Otherwise, $\varphi(e)$ is not defined. Let R be the set of subsets of A for which $\varphi(e)$ is defined. Then $R \supset A = (0, 1)$ and $\varphi(A) = 1$. Let $e_n = E(1/(n+1) \leq x < 1/n)$. Then $e_n \in R$ and $\varphi(e_n) = 0$. Also $\sum e_n = (0, 1) \subset R$. We have

$$\varphi(\sum e_n) = \varphi(0, 1) = 1, \sum\varphi(e_n) = 0,$$

and φ is not completely additive. If e_1, e_2 are any two sets in R with $e_1e_2 = 0$, that $\varphi(e_1 + e_2) = \varphi(e_1) + \varphi(e_2)$ follows from the definition of φ and the fact that

$$\int_{e_1+e_2} f_n dx = \int_{e_1} f_n dx + \int_{e_2} f_n dx.$$

Hence φ is additive on R.

EXAMPLE 5.7. Let the sets A and e and the function f_n be as in Example 5.6, and let

$$\varphi(e) = \limsup_{n \to \infty} \int_e f_n dx.$$

Then $\varphi(e)$ is defined for every open set $e \subset A$. But $\varphi(e)$ is not additive. For if

$$e_1 = \sum_n \left(\frac{1}{2n-1} < x < \frac{1}{2n-2}\right), \; e_2 = \sum_n \left(\frac{1}{2n} < x < \frac{1}{2n-1}\right),$$
$$n = 1, 2, \ldots,$$

then

$$\varphi(e_1 + e_2) = \varphi(e_1) = \varphi(e_2) = 1.$$

EXAMPLE 5.8. Let A be a denumerably infinite set of points, $x_1, x_2, \ldots, e$ the subsets of A. Let

$\varphi(e) = 0$ if e is finite.

$\varphi(e) = 1$ if $A - e$ is finite, or empty.

Otherwise $\varphi(e)$ is not defined. Let R be the subsets of A for which φ is defined. Then $A \subset R$ and $\varphi(A) = 1$. If e_1 and e_2 are in R and $e_1e_2 = 0$ then it is easily verified that $e_1 + e_2$ is in R, and that

$$\varphi(e_1 + e_2) = \varphi(e_1) + \varphi(e_2).$$

But if e_n is the single point x_n, then $\sum e_n = A \subset R$, and $\varphi(e_n) = 0$. Hence

$$\varphi(\sum e_n) = \varphi(A) = 1, \quad \sum \varphi(e_n) = 0,$$

which shows that φ is not completely additive on R.

DEFINITION 5.13. *The function $\varphi(e)$ defined on the subsets e of A is non-decreasing if for $e_1 \supset e_2$, $\varphi(e_1) \geq \varphi(e_2)$. $\varphi(e)$ is non-increasing if $\varphi(e_1) \leq \varphi(e_2)$. In either case $\varphi(e)$ is monotone.*

DEFINITION 5.14. *The function $\varphi(e)$ defined on the subsets e of A is of bounded variation on A if there exists $M > 0$ such that for every sequence of sets $e_1, e_2, \ldots$ with $e_ie_j = 0$, $i \neq j$, $\sum |\varphi(e_i)| < M$.*

THEOREM 5.18. *If the function $\varphi(e)$ defined on A is additive and of bounded variation then*

$$\varphi(e) = \varphi_1(e) - \varphi_2(e)$$

where $\varphi_1(e)$ and $\varphi_2(e)$ are positive or zero, additive and non-decreasing.

For e any set with $e \subseteq A$ let

$$e = e_1 + \cdots + e_k, \; e_ie_j = 0, \; i \neq j.$$

Then, since φ is additive,

$$\varphi(e) = \varphi(e_1) + \cdots + \varphi(e_k).$$

Let $e_p = e_{i_p}$ be the sets for which $\varphi(e_i) \geq 0$, $e_n = e_{i_n}$ the sets for which $\varphi(e_i) < 0$, $i = 1, 2, \ldots, k$. Then

$$\varphi(e) = \sum \varphi(e_p) + \sum \varphi(e_n).$$

Let

$$P(e) = \sup \sum \varphi(e_p), \; N(e) = \inf \sum \varphi(e_n)$$

for all possible subdivisions $e_1 + \cdots + e_k$ of e. Since the function φ is BV on A, both $P(e)$ and $N(e)$ are bounded. There then exists a subdivision of e, $e = e_1 + \cdots + e_r$, $e_ie_j = 0$, $i \neq j$, for which, if $\epsilon > 0$ is given,

$$P(e) \geq \sum \varphi(e_p) > P(e) - \epsilon.$$

For every subdivision $N(e) \leq \sum\varphi(e_n)$, and consequently for the subdivision $e = e_1 + \cdots + e_r$,

(5.26) $\varphi(e) = \sum\varphi(e_p) + \sum\varphi(e_n) > P(e) + N(e) - \epsilon.$

There also exists a subdivision of e, $e = e_1 + \cdots + e_s$, $e_i e_j = 0$, $i \neq j$, for which

$$N(e) \leq \sum\varphi(e_n) < N(e) + \epsilon.$$

This gives

(5.27) $\varphi(e) = \sum\varphi(e_p) + \sum\varphi(e_n) < P(e) + N(e) + \epsilon.$

Since ϵ is arbitrary, it follows from (5.26) and (5.27) that

$$\varphi(e) = P(e) + N(e).$$

It will next be shown that the functions $P(e)$ and $N(e)$ are additive. Let

$$e = e_1 + e_2, \quad e_1 e_2 = 0.$$

If $\epsilon > 0$ is given, there are subdivisions of e_1 and e_2

$$e_1 = e_{11} + \ldots + e_{1r},\ e_2 = e_{21} + \ldots + e_{2s}$$
$e_{ki}e_{kj} = 0$, $i \neq j$, $k = 1, 2$, for which

$$P(e_1) \geq \sum\varphi(e_{1p}) > P(e_1) - \frac{\epsilon}{2},$$

$$P(e_2) \geq \sum\varphi(e_{2p}) > P(e_2) - \frac{\epsilon}{2}.$$

For every such set of subdivisions

$$P(e) \geq \sum\varphi(e_{1p}) + \sum\varphi(e_{2p}) > P(e_1) + P(e_2) - \epsilon.$$

Since ϵ is arbitrary

(5.28) $P(e) \geq P(e_1) + P(e_2).$

Now let $e = e_1 + \ldots + e_k$ be a subdivision of e with

$$P(e) \geq \sum\varphi(e_p) > P(e) - \epsilon.$$

Let $e_p = e_{1p} + e_{2p}$. Then

$$P(e_1) \geq \sum\varphi(e_{1p}),\ P(e_2) \geq \sum\varphi(e_{2p}).$$

This gives, since φ is additive,

$$\begin{aligned} P(e_1) + P(e_2) &\geq \sum\varphi(e_{1p}) + \sum\varphi(e_{2p}) \\ &= \sum\varphi(e_{1p} + e_{2p}) > P(e) - \epsilon. \end{aligned}$$

Since ϵ is arbitrary, $P(e) \leq P(e_1) + P(e_2)$, and this with (5.28) shows that

$$P(e) = P(e_1 + e_2) = P(e_1) + P(e_2).$$

We conclude, therefore, that $P(e)$ is additive.

The function $P(e)$ is non-decreasing. Let $e_1 \supset e_2$. Then $e_1 = (e_1 - e_2) + e_2$, and, since $P(e)$ is additive,

$$P(e_1) = P(e_1 - e_2) + P(e_2).$$

But it is evident from the definition of $P(e)$ that $P(e) \geq 0$ for every e. Hence $P(e_1) \geq P(e_2)$, which shows that $P(e)$ is non-decreasing.

We have now shown that $\varphi(e) = P(e) + N(e)$ and that $P(e)$ is additive and non-decreasing. It can be shown in a similar way that $N(e)$ is additive and non-increasing. From the definitions of these functions it follows that $N(e) \leq 0 \leq P(e)$. Hence if

$$\varphi_1(e) = P(e), \quad \varphi_2(e) = -N(e)$$

then

$$P(e) = \varphi_1(e) - \varphi_2(e)$$

where the functions $\varphi_1(e)$, $\varphi_2(e)$ are positive or zero, additive and non-decreasing, which is the theorem.

THEOREM 5.19. *If the function $\varphi(e)$ defined on the set A is completely additive then it is of bounded variation on A.*

If $\varphi(e)$ is not BV then at least one of the relations $P(A) = \infty$, $N(A) = -\infty$ holds. Suppose $P(A) = \infty$. There then exists

$$E = e_1 + \cdots + e_n, \; e_i \in A$$

with

$$\sum \varphi(e_i) > |\varphi(A)| + 1.$$

Since $\varphi(e)$ is completely additive, it is additive. Hence, if $A_1 = A$, we get

$$\varphi(E) = \sum \varphi(e_i) > |\varphi(A_1)| + 1. \tag{5.29}$$

Since $P(A_1) = \infty$, then at least one of the relations

$$P(E) = \infty, \; P(A_1 - E) = \infty$$

holds. If $P(E) = \infty$; set $A_2 = E$, and it follows from (5.29) that

$$\varphi(A_2) = \varphi(E) > |\varphi(A_1)| + 1.$$

If $P(A_1 - E) = \infty$ set $A_1 - E = A_2$. Then, since $A_1 \supset E$ and $\varphi(e)$ is additive, we get

$$|\varphi(A_2)| = |\varphi(A_1 - E)| = |\varphi(A_1) - \varphi(E)|.$$

Again using (5.29) we get

$$|\varphi(A_2)| = \varphi(E) - |\varphi(A_1)| > 1.$$

Thus in both cases $|\varphi(A_2)| > 1$ and $P(A_2) = \infty$. There then exists

$$E = e_1 + \cdots + e_n,\ e_i \in A_2, \text{ with}$$
$$\varphi(E) = \sum \varphi(e_i) > |\varphi(A_2)| + 2.$$

As before at least one of the relations

$$P(E) = \infty,\ P(A_2 - E) = \infty$$

holds. If the first holds let $A_3 = E$. Then

$$\varphi(A_3) = \varphi(E) > |\varphi(A_2)| + 2. \tag{5.30}$$

If the second holds set $A_3 = A_2 - E$. Then since φ is additive and $A_2 \supset E$,

$$|\varphi(A_3)| = \varphi(A_2 - E) = |\varphi(A_2) - \varphi(E)|.$$

Now using (5.30) we get

$$|\varphi(A_3)| = \varphi(E) - |\varphi(A_2)| > 2.$$

In both cases $|\varphi(A_3)| > 2$, $P(A_3) = \infty$. This procedure can be continued to give a sequence of sets

$$A_1 \supset A_2 \supset \cdots$$

with $|\varphi(A_n)| > n - 1$. Set

$$B = (A_1 - A_2) + (A_2 - A_3) + \cdots.$$

Then since $\varphi(e)$ is completely additive

$$\varphi(B) = \sum_{n=1} \varphi(A_n - A_{n+1})$$

which implies that the series on the right converges to the finite number $\varphi(B)$. But the sum of the first n terms of the series on the right is

$$S_n = \varphi(A_1 - A_2) + \varphi(A_2 - A_3) + \ldots + \varphi(A_n - A_{n+1}),$$

since $A_n \supset A_{n+1}$ for every n, and since $\varphi(e)$ is additive, this is equal to

$$\varphi(A_1) - \varphi(A_2) + \varphi(A_2) - \varphi(A_3) + \ldots + \varphi(A_n) - \varphi(A_{n+1})$$

which becomes $\varphi(A_1) - \varphi(A_{n+1})$. But $\varphi(A_{n+1}) > n$, hence S_n cannot tend to the finite number $\varphi(B)$, and we conclude that $\varphi(e)$ is BV on A.

Problems

5.1. The total variation of the function $F(x)$ on the interval $[a, b]$ is

$$T[a, b] = \sup \sum |F(x_i) - F(x_{i-1})|$$

where (x_{i-1}, x_i) is a subdivision of $[a, b]$. If $F(x)$ is BV on $[a, b]$ show that

$$T[a, b] \geq \int_a^b |F'(x)| dx.$$

5.2. Let $F(x)$ be defined on (a, b) and let $[\alpha, \beta]$ be a closed interval on (a, b). The point x is a point of bounded variation of $F(x)$ if there is an interval (a', b') containing x on which $F(x)$ is BV. Show that if every point of $[\alpha, \beta]$ is a point of bounded variation of $F(x)$, then $F(x)$ is BV on $[\alpha, \beta]$. Also show that the points of bounded variation of $F(x)$ form an open set.

5.3. Let $F(x)$ be defined on $[a, b]$ and let $T[a, x]$ be the total variation of $F(x)$ on $[a, x]$. If $T[a, x]$ is bounded on $[a, b)$ then $F(x)$ is BV on $[a, b]$.

5.4. If the function $F(x)$ is such that $F'(x) \geq 0$ on $[a, b]$, then $F(x)$ is non-decreasing on $[a, b]$.

5.5. Let $F(x)$ be continuous on $[a, b]$ and let $A_1, A_2, \ldots$ be a sequence of closed sets covering $[a, b]$, on each of which $F(x)$ is BV. Let M_n be the number M of Definition 5.5 which is associated with the set A_n. If $\sum M_n$ converges show that $F(x)$ is BV on $[a, b]$.

5.6. Let $F(x)$ be non-decreasing on $[a, b]$. Let $s(x) = F(x + 0) - F(x - 0)$, and let

$$\varphi(x) = \sum_{(a, x)} s(x_i),$$

where x_i are the points of discontinuity of $F(x)$ on $[a, x)$. Show that $\varphi(x)$ is continuous except at the discontinuities of $F(x)$, and that $F(x) - \varphi(x)$ is continuous. Hence show that if

$F(x)$ is BV then, except possibly at the discontinuities of $F(x)$, $F(x) = \psi(x) + \varphi(x)$ where $\psi(x)$ is continuous and $\varphi(x)$ has the same points of discontinuity as $F(x)$. Also show that $\varphi'(x) = 0$ almost everywhere.

5.7. Let $x_1, x_2, \ldots$ be an everywhere dense denumerable set on (a, b). Let a function $u(x_i) > 0$ be assigned to each point x_i of this set in such a way that $\sum u(x_i)$ converges. Let E be a measurable set on (a, b), and let

$$\varphi(x) = |E(a, x)| + \sum_{(a, x)} u(x_i).$$

Show that $\varphi(x)$ is non-decreasing on $[a, b]$, and that the discontinuities of $\varphi(x)$ are everywhere dense on $[a, b]$. Also show that $\varphi'(x) = 1$ at almost all points of E, and $\varphi'(x) = 0$ at almost all points of $\tilde{E}$.

5.8. Let E be a non-dense closed set on $[a, b]$. Let (a_i, b_i) be the intervals of $\tilde{E}[a, b]$. Let $F(x)$ be BV on E, and be such that $\sum w_i$ converges where $w_i = \sup \sum |F(x'_j) - F(x_j)| (x_j, x'_j)$ intervals on $[a_i, b_i]$. Show that $F(x)$ is BV on $[a, b]$.

5.9. Let E be a non-dense closed set on $[a, b]$, and let α_i be the intervals of the set $\tilde{E}[a, b]$. Let $\varphi(\alpha_i) > 0$ be a function of the interval α_i where $\sum \varphi(\alpha_i)$ converges. If

$$\psi(x, x + h) = \sum_{(x,\, x + h)} \varphi(\alpha_i),\ h > 0,$$

where only whole intervals α_i on $(x, x + h)$ are considered, show that

$$\lim_{h \to 0} \frac{\psi(x, x + h)}{h} = 0$$

for almost all $x \in E$, $x + h \in E$.

5.10. Let $F(x)$ be defined on A and be such that at each point of the set A, ${}_ADf$ is finite. Show that $A = A_1 + A_2 + \ldots$, where $F(x)$ is BV on A_n.

5.11. Let $F(x)$ be such that $F'(x) = 0$ at each point of the interval $[a, b]$. If $\epsilon > 0$ be given, then for each point x on $[a, b]$ there is an interval ω with x as centre such that if x' is any other point on ω,

$$-\epsilon < \frac{F(x') - F(x)}{x' - x} < \epsilon.$$

Use this and the Heine-Borel theorem to show that $F(x)$ is constant on $[a, b]$.

5.12. Let $\varphi(x)$ be non-decreasing on $[a, b]$, and let $E_n = E(\bar{D}\varphi > n)$. If (a', b') contains E_n show that $\varphi(b') - \varphi(a') > n|E_n|/2$.

5.13. Let the functions $f(x)$ and $g(x)$ be defined on $[a, b]$, where $f(x)$ is continuous and $g(x)$ is BV. Let (x_{i-1}, x_i) be a subdivision of $[a, b]$ and ξ_i any point on an interval (x_{i-1}, x_i). Show that if the maximum of $x_i - x_{i-1}$ tends to zero as $n \to \infty$, then

$$\lim_{n \to \infty} \sum_{i=1}^{n} f(\xi_i) \{g(x_i) - g(x_{i-1})\}$$

exists.

5.14. Construct an example to show that if $f(x)$ has a single point of discontinuity the limit in problem 5.13 may fail to exist.

5.15. On the interval $[a, b]$ let $f(x)$ be summable and $g(x)$ be BV. Show that $f(x)\, g(x)$ is summable on $[a, b]$.

CHAPTER VI

THE INVERSION OF DERIVATIVES

Introduction: The main topic of this chapter is the relation between functions and their derivatives. The functions will be denoted by $F(x)$ and their derivatives by $F'(x)$. It was shown in the preceding chapter that if $F(x)$ is BV on $[a, b]$ then $F'(x)$ exists and is finite almost everywhere on $[a, b]$ and is summable over the set on which it is finite, or as we have agreed to say, summable on $[a, b]$. It has also been shown that the relation $F(x) - F(a) = L(F', a, x)$ does not hold for every such function $F(x)$. Necessary and sufficient conditions will be determined for the validity of this relation. Some consideration will also be given to the problem of determining $F(x) - F(a)$ when $F'(x)$ is given and is finite at each point of $[a, b]$, but is not summable.

6.1. Functions defined by integrals, $\mathbf{F(x) = L(f, a, x)}$.

THEOREM 6.1. *Let the function $f(x)$ be summable on $[a, b]$, and let*

$$F(x) = \int_a^x f(x)dx.$$

Then $F'(x) = f(x)$ for almost all points x on $[a, b]$.

Let u represent the closed intervals on $[a, b]$ and let $\varphi(u) = L(f, u)$. It was shown in Theorem 5.16 that if $x \in u$ the ratio $\varphi(u)/|u|$ tends to $f(x)$ for almost all x on $[a, b]$. There was nothing in the proof of Theorem 5.16 to preclude the restriction that x be an end-point of u. If $h > 0$ and $u = [x, x+h]$ then $[F(x+h) - F(x)]/h = \varphi(u)/|u|$. If $u = [x-h, x]$ then $[F(x+h) - F(x)]/(-h) = [F(x) - F(x-h)]/h = \varphi(u)/|u|$. Hence when the sign of h is not restricted,

$$F'(x) = \lim_{h \to 0} \frac{F(x+h) - F(x)}{h} = \lim_{|u| \to 0} \frac{\varphi(u)}{|u|} = f(x)$$

for almost all points x on $[a, b]$.

DEFINITION 6.1. *Let the function $F(x)$ be defined on a set*

A. The function $F(x)$ is absolutely continuous (AC) on A if for a given number $\epsilon > 0$ there exists a number $\delta > 0$ such that if (x_i, x'_i) is any set of non-overlapping intervals with x_i, x'_i points of A and $\sum(x'_i - x_i) < \delta$, then $\sum |F(x'_i) - F(x_i)| < \epsilon$.

NOTE 6.1. If a function $F(x)$ is AC on an interval $[a, b]$ it is continuous on this interval. The converse is not necessarily true, however. The function $\varphi(x)$ of Example 5.3 is continuous by Theorem 1.11. For φ_n is continuous for each n and $\varphi_n(x) \to \varphi(x)$ uniformly. But if (x_i, x'_i) is any set of non-overlapping intervals containing the set G then $\sum |\varphi(x'_i) - \varphi(x_i)| = 1$. Since G is closed and $|G| = 0$ the set (x_i, x'_i) can be so taken that $\sum (x'_i - x_i)$ is arbitrarily small. Hence $\varphi(x)$ is not AC on $[0, 1]$.

THEOREM 6.2. *If the function $f(x)$ is summable on the interval $[a, b]$ then $F(x) = L(f, a, x)$ is AC on $[a, b]$.*

Let $\epsilon > 0$ be given. Fix $\delta > 0$ and such that if e is any measurable set on $[a, b]$ with $|e| < \delta$ then $L(|f|, e) < \epsilon$. Let (x_i, x'_i) be any non-overlapping set of intervals on $[a, b]$ with $\sum (x'_i - x_i) < \delta$. Then

$$\sum |F(x'_i) - F(x_i)| \leq \sum \int_{x_i}^{x'_i} |f| dx < \epsilon.$$

Hence F is AC on $[a, b]$ according to Definition 6.1.

THEOREM 6.3. *If the function $F(x)$ is any function which is AC on a bounded set A then $F(x)$ is BV on A.*

Let $M > 0$ be given, and fix $\delta > 0$ and such that if (x_i, x'_i) is any set of non-overlapping intervals with $\sum (x'_i - x_i) < \delta$ then $\sum |F(x'_i) - F(x_i)| < M$. Let $(a, b) \supset A$, and let (a, b) be divided in halves. If $F(x)$ is not BV on A it is not BV on the part of A on at least one of the closed halves $[a_1, b_1]$ of (a, b). Similarly F is not BV on the part of A on at least one of the closed halves $[a_2, b_2]$ of $[a_1, b_1]$. Continuing, we get F not BV on the part of A on a closed interval $[a_n, b_n]$ with $b_n - a_n < \delta$. But if F is not BV on the part of A on this interval then there exists a set of non-overlapping intervals (x_i, x'_i) on $[a_n, b_n]$, x_i, x'_i points of A, for which

$$\sum |F(x'_i) - F(x_i)| > M.$$

Since $\sum (x'_i - x_i) \leq b_n - a_n < \delta$ this is a contradiction and we conclude that F is BV on A.

THEOREM 6.4. *If the function $f(x)$ is summable on the interval $[a, b]$ then $F(x) = L(f, a, x)$ is BV on $[a, b]$.*

This follows from Theorems 6.2 and 6.3. It can easily be proved by using the method of Theorem 6.2.

THEOREM 6.5. *Let the function $F(x)$ be continuous on $[a, b]$, and be such that $F'(x)$ is finite almost everywhere and summable. It is then necessary and sufficient for the validity of*

$$F(x) - F(a) = \int_a^x F'(x)\,dx \tag{6.1}$$

that $F(x)$ be AC on $[a, b]$.

The necessity of the condition follows from Theorem 6.2. Suppose F is AC. Then F is BV by Theorem 6.4 and consequently that F' is finite almost everywhere and summable follows from Theorem 5.17. To show that (6.1) holds, let $\epsilon > 0$ be given. Fix $\delta > 0$ and such that if $(x_i\, x'_i)$ is any set of non-overlapping intervals on $[a, b]$ with $\sum (x'_i - x_i) < \delta$ then

$$\sum [F(x'_i) - F(x_i)] < \epsilon,\ \sum \int_{x_i}^{x'_i} |F'|dx < \epsilon. \tag{6.2}$$

Since $F'(x)$ is summable on $[a, b]$ it follows from Theorem 5.16 that

$$\lim_{h \to 0} \int_x^{x+h} F'dx/h = F'(x)$$

for x contained in a set E with $|E| = b - a$. Hence for each x there is a sequence of intervals (x, x'_i) with $x'_i - x \to 0$ such that for each interval of the sequence

$$\left| \int_x^{x'_i} F'dx/(x'_i - x) - \frac{F(x'_i) - F(x)}{x'_i - x} \right| < \epsilon. \tag{6.3}$$

This set of intervals thus associated with the points x of the set E constitute a Vitali family covering E. Consequently, since $|E| = b - a$, there exists a finite set $v_1, \ldots, v_n$ of these intervals with

$$\sum |v_k| > b - a - \delta. \tag{6.4}$$

Let x_k be the point x with which the interval v_k is associated, $v_k = [x_k, x'_k]$. Then from (6.3) we get

$$\left|\sum \int_{x_k}^{x'_k} F'dx - \sum [F(x'_k) - F(x_k)]\right| < \epsilon\,(b - a). \tag{6.5}$$

If (x_j, x'_j) are the intervals complementary to the set $[x_k, x'_k]$ on $[a, b]$ it follows from the first part of (6.2), combined with (6.4), that $\sum |F(x'_j) - F(x_j)| < \epsilon$. Hence the second term on the left of (6.5) differs from $F(b) - F(a)$ by not more than ϵ. It follows from the second part of (6.2), combined with (6.4), that the first term on the left of (6.5) differs from $L(F', a, b)$ by not more than ϵ. Since ϵ is arbitrary we may conclude that

$$F(b) - F(a) = \int_a^b F'dx.$$

It is clear that in the foregoing reasoning any point x on $a < x < b$ can be substituted for the point b. Hence

$$F(x) - F(a) = \int_a^x F'dx,$$

and (6.1) is established. We conclude, therefore, that the condition of the theorem is sufficient.

The conditions of Theorem 6.5 are on $F(x)$. Conditions on $F'(x)$ will now be determined which insure the validity of (6.1).

THEOREM 6.6. *If the function $F(x)$ is continuous on the interval $[a, b]$ and if $F'(x)$ is finite, except for at most a denumerable set, and summable on $[a, b]$, then*

$$F(x) - F(a) = \int_a^x F'(x)\,dx.$$

Let $D = d_1, d_2, \ldots$ be the exceptional set. Let $\epsilon > 0$ be given, and choose a sequence of positive numbers $\eta_1 > \eta_2 > \ldots$, such that $\sum \eta_i < \epsilon$. Let d_i be the centre of an interval ω_i with

$$|F(x) - F(d_i)| < \eta_i, \quad x \in \omega_i. \tag{6.6}$$

That this can be done follows from the continuity of F. If $D \ni a$ the corresponding interval ω_i is half open. A similar statement applies to b. Let (a_{i-1}, a_i) be a subdivision of the range $(0, \infty)$, let $e_i = E(a_{i-1} \leq |F'| < a_i)$ where $a_i - a_{i-1}$ is sufficiently small to insure that

$$(6.7) \qquad \left| \int_a^b |F'|\,dx - \sum a_i |e_i| \right| < \epsilon.$$

Let $\epsilon_1 > \epsilon_2 > \ldots$ be a sequence of positive numbers with $\sum \epsilon_i a_i < \epsilon$, and let $\alpha_i \supset e_i$ with $|\alpha_i - e_i| < \epsilon_i$. There will next be determined a subdivision

$$(6.8) \qquad a = x_0 < x_1 \ldots < x_n = b,$$

of the interval $[a, b]$ such that

$$(6.9) \quad |F(x_i) - F(x_{i-1})| < \eta_j, \text{ or } \frac{|F(x_i) - F(x_{i-1})|}{x_i - x_{i-1}} < a_k,$$

where in the first relation x_i is the point d_j of the set D, and in the second x_i is a point of the set e_k.

If the point a is a point of the set D there is a point $x_1 > a$ with $|F(x) - F(a)| < \eta_j$, $a < x \leq x_1$. If a is not a point of D then $a \in e_k$ for some integer k. Hence a is contained in an interval ω of the set α_k, and since $F'(a) < a_k$ there exists $x_1 > a$ with $x_1 \in \omega$, and

$$\frac{|F(x_1) - F(x)|}{|x_1 - x|} < a_k, \quad a < x \leq x_1.$$

The same reasoning can be repeated with x_1 replacing a to get a value x_2 of x, $x_2 > x_1$, satisfying one or the other of the relations (6.9), and this procedure can be continued. It is possible for some choice $x_1, x_2, \ldots$ to include b in a finite number of steps. For let $\xi \leq b$ be the supremum of all points that can be included for all possible choices of $x_1, x_2, \ldots, x_n$. There exists $\delta > 0$ such that if $\xi - \delta < x < \xi$

$$(6.10) \quad |F(\xi) - F(x)| < \eta_j \text{ or } |F(\xi) - F(x)| < (\xi - x)\, a_k.$$

From the definition of ξ it follows that there is a sequence $x_1 < x_2 < \ldots < x_n$ with $\xi - \delta < x_n < \xi$. If $x_{n+1} = \xi$, the sequence

$$x_0 = a < x_1 < \ldots < x_n < x_{n+1} = \xi$$

satisfies (6.9). If $\xi = b$ the objective is attained. If $\xi < b$ the process can be continued, and the definition of ξ is denied. Thus there is a sequence

$$x_0 = a < x_1 < \ldots < x_n = b$$

satisfying (6.9). Consequently for this sequence

$$\begin{aligned} |F(b) - F(a)| &\leq \sum |F(x_i) - F(x_{i-1})|, \\ &< \sum \eta_j + \sum a_k | a_k |, \\ &< \epsilon + \sum a_k | e_k | + \sum a_k \epsilon_k, \\ &< 3\epsilon + \int_a^b | F' | dx. \end{aligned}$$

Since ϵ is arbitrary we conclude that

$$|F(b) - F(a)| \leq \int_a^b |F'| dx.$$

It is evident that this relation holds for any interval (x_i, x'_i) as well as for the interval (a, b). Hence if (x_i, x'_i) is any set of non-overlapping intervals on $[a, b]$

$$\sum |F(x_i) - F(x_i)| < \sum \int_{x_i}^{x'_i} |F'| dx.$$

Since $F'(x)$ is summable the right side is close to zero if $\sum (x'_i - x_i)$ is sufficiently small. Consequently the function F is AC. Theorem 6.6 now follows from Theorem 6.5.

THEOREM 6.7. *If the function $F(x)$ is defined on $[a, b]$ and $F'(x)$ exists and is bounded, then*

$$F(x) - F(a) = \int_a^x F'(x)\, dx.$$

If $F'(x)$ exists and is finite $F(x)$ is continuous. Also, since $F'(x)$ is bounded, and measurable by Theorem 5.15, it is summable. Hence the conditions of Theorem 6.6 are satisfied and Theorem 6.7 follows.

THEOREM 6.8. *If $F(x)$ is defined on $[a, b]$ and $F'(x)$ is finite then the ratio $[F(x + h) - F(x)]/h$ and $F'(x)$ have the same bounds.*

Since for every x there exists h with $[F(x + h) - F(x)]/h$ arbitrarily near to $F'(x)$, the supremum of this ratio cannot be less than $\sup F'(x)$ If the latter is infinite so is the former, and the equality holds. Suppose $\sup F'(x)$ is finite and suppose there is a number M with

$$\sup F'(x) < M < \sup \frac{F(x + h) - F(x)}{h}, \; M > 0.$$

There then exists a', b' on $[a\ b]$ with $a' < b'$ and with

$$F(b') - F(a') > M(b' - a'). \tag{6.11}$$

Also, since $F' < M$, there exists $x_1 > a'$ with $F(x_1) - F(a) < M(x_1 - a)$, $x_2 > x_1$ with $F(x_2) - F(x_1) < M(x_2 - x_1)$, and so on. It is possible to include b' in a finite number of such steps. For let $\xi \leq b'$ be the supremum of points that can be reached for all possible choices of $x_1 > x_2 > \ldots > x_n$. There exists $\delta > 0$ such that if $\xi - \delta < x < \xi$

$$\frac{F(x) - F(\xi)}{x - \xi} = \frac{F(\xi) - F(x)}{\xi - x} < M.$$

The proof now continues as in the corresponding situation in the proof of Theorem 6.6 to give the sequence

$$a' = x_0 < x_1 < \ldots < x_n = b',$$

with $F(x_i) - F(x_{i-1}) < M(x_i - x_{i-1})$. Hence $F(b') - F(a') < M(b' - a')$ which contradicts (6.11). The truth of the theorem follows when $M > 0$. If $M \leq 0$ the proof is similar. There is also a similar proof when infimum replaces supremum.

6.2. The inversion of derivatives which are not summable. So far we have considered derivatives which were finite everywhere or almost everywhere, and summable. It may happen that a continuous function $F(x)$ has a finite derivative at each point of an interval $[a, b]$ and this derivative is not summable. The classical example of this phenomenon is

EXAMPLE 6.1.

$$F(x) = x^2 \sin\frac{1}{x^2},\ x \neq 0,\ F(0) = 0.$$

By ordinary differentiation

$$F'(x) = 2x \sin\frac{1}{x^2} - \frac{2}{x}\cos\frac{1}{x^2},\ x \neq 0.$$

When $x = 0$,

$$\frac{F(0 + h) - F(0)}{h} = h \sin\frac{1}{h^2}$$

which tends to zero as h tends to zero. Hence $F'(0) = 0$ and $F'(x)$ is finite at each point x on $[0, 1]$, and is bounded on every closed interval which does not contain the origin. It will be shown that F' is not summable. If for $n \geq 1$

$$x'_n = \sqrt{\frac{2}{(4n-3)\pi}} \quad \text{then } \sin \frac{1}{x'^2_n} = 1.$$

There is a first point to the left of x'_n such that $F(x_n) = 0$, and $x_n > x'_{n+1}$. Also, on the interval $[x_n, x'_n]$, $F'(x)$ is bounded, and consequently by Theorem 6.7

$$\int_{x_n}^{x'_n} F'dx = F(x'_n) - F(x_n) = \frac{2}{(4n-3)\pi}.$$

Then

$$\int_{x_n}^{1} |F'|\, dx \geq \sum_{i=1}^{n} \frac{2}{(4i-3)\pi}.$$

As n increases the right-hand side increases without limit, and it follows that $|F'|$, and consequently F', is not summable on $[0, 1]$. Hence it is not possible to determine $F(1) - F(0)$ as $L(F', 0, 1)$. In this case we proceed as follows: For $h > 0$

$$F(1) - F(h) = \int_h^1 F'\, dx$$

by Theorem 6.7. Since $F(x)$ is continuous

$$F(1) - F(0) = \lim_{h \to 0} \int_h^1 F'\, dx.$$

For the function $F(x)$ of this example no difficulty arises on an interval which does not contain the origin. The points which cause difficulty are described by

DEFINITION 6.2. *If $f(x)$ is a function which is measurable on a set A then x is a point of non-summability of $f(x)$ over A if for every interval ω containing x, the function $f(x)$ is not summable over $A\omega$.*

In Example 6.1 there was a single point of non-summability. If $F(x)$ has a finite derivative at every point of an interval $[a, b]$, and $F'(x)$ has not more than a finite number of points of non-summability then $F(b) - F(a)$ can be determined by a suitable modification of the limiting process used in that example.

The question now is: Can a function $F(x)$ have a derivative which is finite at every point of an interval $[a, b]$ and be such that the set of points of non-summability of $F'(x)$ is infinite? The answer is in the affirmative. An example will now be given for which the points of non-summability have positive measure.

EXAMPLE 6.2. Let E be any non-dense closed set on $[0, 1]$ which includes the points zero and unity. Let (a_i, b_i) be the intervals of the set $\tilde{E}$. Let

$$F(x) = (x - a_i)^2 \sin \frac{1}{(x - a_i)^2}, \quad F(x) = (b_i - x)^2 \sin \frac{1}{(b_i - x)^2}$$

accordingly as $a_i < x \leq (a_i + b_i)/2$, $(a_i + b_i)/2 < x < b_i$. For $x \in E$ let $F(x) = 0$. That $F'(x)$ is finite at each point of (a_i, b_i) except $(a_i + b_i)/2$, and that the right-hand derivative at a_i and the left-hand derivative at b_i are zero can be shown as in Example 6.1. At the points $(a_i + b_i)/2$ the right-hand and left-hand derivatives exist and are finite. This can be shown by ordinary differentiation. At this point the right- and left-hand derivatives are not equal, however, and consequently we cannot say that F' exists at every point of (a_i, b_i). Before considering this point further we study the ratio

$$\frac{F(x + h) - F(x)}{h},$$

for $x \in E$. If $x + h$ is a point of E this ratio is zero. If $x + h$ is a point of an interval (a_i, b_i) this ratio becomes

$$\frac{(x + h - a_i)^2 \sin [1/(x + h - a_i)^2]}{h},$$

$$\frac{(b_i - x - h)^2 \sin [1/(b_i - x - h)^2]}{h}$$

accordingly as $x + h$ is less than, equal to, or greater than $(a_i + b_i)/2$. It is easily verified that in both cases the ratio tends to zero as $h \to 0$. Hence $F'(x)$ exists and is finite at every point of $[0, 1]$ except the mid-points of the intervals (a_i, b_i). That a_i and b_i are points of non-summability of F' can be shown as in Example 6.1. Consequently the points of

E which are limit points of the intervals (a_i, b_i) are points of non-summability of F'. Then since E is non-dense on $[0, 1]$ every interval ω containing $x \in E$ also contains points of the set a_i, b_i and it follows that the points of E are points of non-summability of F'. The set E is any non-dense closed set and can, therefore, be such that $|E| > 0$.

The function $F(x)$ can be modified in such a way that $F'(x)$ exists and is finite at every point. Let x_i be the mid-point of (a_i, b_i). It is easily verified by direct substitution that if $0 < h < (b_i - a_i)/2$ then $F(x_i - h) = F(x_i + h)$ and that $F'(x_i - h) = - F'(x_i + h)$. Hence an arc of a circle can be drawn which is tangent to the graph of $F(x)$ at the points for which $x = x_i - h$ and $x_i + h$. On $x_i - h < x < x_i + h$ let the ordinate of $F(x)$ be the ordinate of the corresponding point on this circle. The modified function then has a derivative at every point of $[0, 1]$.

In this example it is possible to determine $F(b_i) - F(a_i)$ from F by the limiting process used in Example 6.1, for every interval of the set (a_i, b_i) complementary to the set E.

$$F(b_i) - F(a_i) = \lim_{h \to 0} \int_{a_i+h}^{b_i-h} F' \, dx.$$

A theorem will now be proved which permits the determination of $F(1) - F(0)$.

THEOREM 6.9. *Let E be a closed set on the interval $[a, b]$, and let (a_i, b_i) be the intervals of the set $\tilde{E}$. If the continuous function $F(x)$ is such that $F'(x)$ is finite at all points of E except possibly a denumerable set and summable over E, and if $\sum |F(b_i) - F(a_i)|$ converges then*

$$F(b) - F(a) = \int_E F'(x)dx + \sum [F(b_i) - F(a_i)].$$

Let $G(x) = F(x)$ on E, and on (a_i, b_i) let the ordinate of $G(x)$ be the ordinate of a linear segment drawn in such a way that G is continuous on $[a, b]$. For $x \in E$, $F'(x)$ finite, x not an end-point of (a_i, b_i), ${}_E DG = F'$. For in the ratio

$$\frac{G(x + h) - G(x)}{h}$$

if the point $x + h$ is on an interval (a_i, b_i) then $G(x + h)$ is on the closed interval defined by the points $F(a_i)$, $F(b_i)$. Hence at $x \in E$ and x not an end-point of an interval (a_i, b_i) it follows that G' exists and is equal to F'. On an interval (a_i, b_i), G' is constant and the following two relations hold:

$$L(G', a_i, b_i) = G(b_i) - G(a_i) = F(b_i) - F(a_i);$$
$$L(|G'|, a_i, b_i) = |G(b_i) - G(a_i)| = |F(b_i) - F(a_i)|.$$

Consequently $\sum L(|G'|, a_i, b_i)$ converges, and from Theorem 4.10 it follows that $L[G', \sum(a_i, b_i)] = L(G', \tilde{E})$ exists. Hence G' is summable on $[a, b]$, at all of E except the end-points of the intervals (a_i, b_i) G' is finite, and $G' = F'$ where F' is finite. It then follows that G' satisfies the conditions of Theorem 6.6. Consequently

$$\begin{aligned} F(b) - F(a) = G(b) - G(a) &= \int_a^b G'dx \\ &= \int_E G'dx + \int_{\tilde{E}} G'dx \\ &= \int_E F'dx + \sum \int_{a_i}^{b_i} G'dx \\ & \int_E F'dx + \sum[F(b_i) - F(a_i)], \end{aligned}$$

which is the theorem.

In Example 6.2 after $F(b_i) - F(a_i)$ has been determined by the limiting process of that example, $F(1) - F(0)$ can be obtained by using Theorem 6.9. For, since $F(x) = 0$, $x \in E$, $\sum |F(b_i) - F(a_i)| = 0$, and F' is summable on E. Hence the conditions of Theorem 6.9 are satisfied and

$$F(1) - F(0) = \int_E F'dx + \sum[F(b_i) - F(a_i)].$$

We have thus shown how to handle the situation when F' is summable over the set E which is the set of points of non-summability of F' on $[a, b]$, and $\sum|F(b_i) - F(a_i)|$ converges where (a_i, b_i) are the intervals complementary to E. There are, however, functions for which at least one of these conditions fails to hold. Two theorems which help to overcome this difficulty will now be proved.

THEOREM 6.10. *If the continuous function $F(x)$ has a derivative which is finite at each point of a closed set E then there exists an interval ω containing points of E such that $F'(x)$ is summable on $E\omega$.*

It is sufficient to show that there is an interval ω such that F' is bounded on $E\omega$. If the closed set E contains isolated points the theorem is obvious, for an interval ω can be taken which contains a single point of E. Suppose E is perfect and the theorem fails to hold. Let ω be an interval containing points of E. Since F' is supposed to be unbounded on $E\omega$, there exists $x_1 \in E\omega$ and a closed interval $u_1 \subset \omega$ with x_1 on the interior of u_1, with $|u_1|$ arbitrarily small, and with

$$\frac{|F(x) - F(x_1)|}{|x - x_1|} > 1$$

for all $x \in u_1$. Since E is perfect there are points of E other than x_1 on ω_1 the interior of u_1. By supposition F' is unbounded on $E\omega_1$, and consequently there is a point $x_2 \in E\omega_1$ and a closed interval u_2 with x_2 on the interior of $u_2 \subset \omega_1$, with $|u_2|$ arbitrarily small and with

$$\frac{|F(x) - F(x_2)|}{|x - x_2|} > 2$$

for $x \in u_2$. This process can be continued in such a way that $|u_n| \to 0$, giving

$$\frac{|F(x) - F(x_n)|}{|x - x_n|} > n,$$

$x \in u_n \subset u_{n-1}$. It then follows from Theorem 2.22 and the fact that $|u_n| \to 0$ that $u_1 u_2 \ldots$ is a single point ξ. Since there are points of E on each u_n and E is closed, $\xi \in E$. Thus

$$\frac{|F(\xi) - F(x_n)|}{\xi - x_n} > n$$

for every n and $x_n \to \xi$. It follows from this that $F'(\xi)$ is infinite or does not exist, which contradicts the fact that F' exists and is finite at each point of E. Hence the theorem.

There will next be proved a theorem which gives some information about the behaviour of the sum $\sum|F(b_i) - F(a_i)|$.

THEOREM 6.11. *Let the continuous function $F(x)$ defined on $[a, b]$ be such that $F'(x)$ is finite at each point of a closed set E. If (a_i, b_i) are the intervals complementary to E then there exists an interval ω containing points of E such that*

$$\sum_\omega|F(b_i) - F(a_i)|$$

converges, where the sum is taken over the intervals and partial intervals of the set (a_i, b_i) which are on ω.

The theorem is obviously true if E contains isolated points, for there is then an interval ω which contains a single point of E. Suppose that E is perfect and that the theorem is false. Let ω be an interval containing points of E. By supposition

$$\sum_\omega|F(b_i) - F(a_i)|$$

diverges, and from this it readily follows that

$$\limsup_{n \to \infty} \frac{|F(b_n) - F(a_n)|}{b_n - a_n} = \infty.$$

For if this limit were finite $\sum|F(b_i) - F(a_i)|$ summed over the intervals on ω would converge. Hence there exists an interval (a_1, b_1) on ω with

$$\frac{|F(b_1) - F(a_1)|}{b_1 - a_1} > 1.$$

Then, since $F(x)$ is continuous there exists a closed interval $u_1 \subset \omega$, $b_1 \in \omega_1$, the interior of u_1, such that for $x \in u_1$

$$\frac{|F(x) - F(a_1)|}{x - a_1} > 1.$$

Since E is perfect and $b_1 \in E$ there are points of E on ω_1 other than b_1. By supposition

$$\sum_{\omega_1}|F(b_i) - F(a_i)|$$

diverges. Hence there exists (a_2, b_2) on ω_1 with $b_2 - a_2$ arbitrarily small, and

$$\frac{|F(b_2) - F(a_2)|}{b_2 - a_2} > 2.$$

Again, using the continuity of F, there is a closed interval u_2 containing b_2 on its interior ω_2 and with

$$\frac{|F(x) - F(a_2)|}{x - a_2} > 2$$

for $x \in u_2 \subset u_1$. This can be continued in such a way that $b_n - a_n$ and $|u_n|$ tend to zero. Then $\xi = u_1 u_2 \ldots$ is such that $\xi \in E$, and for every n

$$\frac{|F(\xi) - F(a_n)|}{|\xi - a_n|} > n.$$

Since $b_n \in u_n$, $b_n - a_n$ and $|u_n|$ tend to zero it follows that $a_n \to \xi$ and consequently $F'(\xi)$ is infinite or does not exist. This is a contradiction, and we conclude that there exists an interval ω such that

$$\sum_\omega |F(b_i) - F(a_i)|$$

converges.

DEFINITION 6.3. *Let $F(x)$ be defined on an interval $[a, b]$, E a closed set on $[a, b]$, (a_i, b_i) the intervals on $[a, b]$ complementary to E. Let x be a point of E. If for every interval ω which contains x,*

$$\sum_\omega |F(b_i) - F(a_i)|$$

diverges then x is a point of divergence of the sum $\sum |F(b_i) - F(a_i)|$.

NOTE 6.2. The statements of Theorems 6.10 and 6.11 are equivalent to the following: Let $F(x)$ be continuous on the interval $[a, b]$, and let E be any closed set on $[a, b]$, (a_i, b_i) the intervals on $[a, b]$ complementary to E. If $F'(x)$ is finite at each point of E then the set $E' \subset E$ which consists of the points of non-summability of $F'(x)$ over E and the points of divergence of $\sum |F(b_i) - F(a_i)|$, are non-dense on E. For, by these theorems, if ω is an interval containing points of E there is an interval $\omega' \subset \omega$, ω' containing points of E, such that $F'(x)$ is summable on $E\omega'$ and

$$\sum_{\omega'} |F(b_i) - F(a_i)|$$

converges. Then by Definition 0.1 the set E' is non-dense on E.

It will now be shown that the foregoing results can be used to obtain $F(b) - F(a)$ from $F'(x)$ when the latter is finite at every point of an interval $[a, b]$.

THEOREM 6.12. *If the derivative $F'(x)$ of a continuous function is finite at every point of an interval $[a, b]$ then $F(x) - F(a)$ can be determined by at most a denumerable set of operations on $F'(x)$.*

Let E_1 be the points of non-summability of $F'(x)$ on $[a\ b]$. The set E_1 is closed and, by Theorem 6.9, or Note 6.1, is non-dense on $[a, b]$. In this case the interval $[a, b]$ is the set E of Theorem 6.9. Let (a_{1i}, b_{1i}) be the intervals of the set $\tilde{E}_1$. If (a', b') is an interval with $a_{1i} < a' < b' < b_{1i}$ then $F'(x)$ is summable on $[a', b']$ and by Theorem 6.6

$$F(b') - F(a') = \int_{a'}^{b'} F'dx.$$

Then, since $F(x)$ is continuous as $a' \to a_{1i}$, $b' \to b_{1i}$

$$\int_{a'}^{b'} F'dx \to F(b_{1i}) - F(a_{1i}).$$

Thus, $F(b_{1i}) - F(a_{1i})$ can be determined for every interval (a_{1i}, b_{1i}) of the set $\tilde{E}_1$.

Let E_2 be the points of non-summability of F' over E_1 and the points of E_1 which are points of divergence of $\sum|F(b_{1i}) - F(a_{1i})|$. By note 6.1 the set E_2 is non-dense on E_1. Also the set E_2 is closed. Let (a_{2i}, b_{2i}) be the intervals of the set $\tilde{E}_2$. Since E_2 is non-dense on E_1 there are intervals of the set (a_{2i}, b_{2i}) which contain points of E_1. Let (a', b') be an interval with $a_{2i} < a' < b' < b_{2i}$. Then F' is summable over $E_1(a', b')$ and

$$\left|\sum_{(a', b')} F(b_{1i}) - F(a_{1i})\right|$$

converges, since all the points of divergence of this sum are in E_2. Hence by Theorem 6.8

$$F(b') - F(a') = \int_{E_1(a', b')} F'dx + \sum_{(a', b')} [F(b_{1i}) - F(a_{1i})].$$

Then, from the continuity of $F(x)$, $F(b_{2i}) - F(a_{2i})$ is determined by letting $a' \to a_{2i}$, $b' \to b_{2i}$. Thus it is possible to determine $F(b_{2i}) - F(a_{2i})$ for all the intervals (a_{2i}, b_{2i}) of the set $\tilde{E}_2$.

The next step is to denote by E_3 the points of E_2 which are points of non-summability of F' over E_2 and the points of E_2 which are points of divergence of $\sum |F(b_{2i}) - F(a_{2i})|$. The set E_3 is, as in the previous cases, non-dense on E_2, and the same procedure can be used to determine $F(b_{3i}) - F(a_{3i})$ for all the intervals (a_{3i}, b_{3i}) complementary to E_3. If for some n the set E_{n+1} is empty then

$$F(b) - F(a) = \int_{E_n} F'dx - \sum_{(a,\, b)} \{F(b_{ni}) - F(a_{ni})\}.$$

If for every n the set E_n is not empty, and the foregoing process is continued, there arises the sequence of closed sets $E_1, E_2, \ldots$ where E_n contains E_{n+1}. It then follows from Theorem 2.22 that the set $E_1E_2 \ldots$ is not empty and is closed. Denote this set by E_ω, and let $(a_{\omega i}, b_{\omega i})$ be the intervals of the set $\tilde{E}_\omega$. If (a', b') is an interval with $a_{\omega i} < a' < b' < b_{\omega i}$, then, since there are no points of E_ω on the closed interval $[a', b']$, in the process of obtaining the sets $E_1, E_2, \ldots$ a stage is reached at which $E_{n+1} [a', b']$ is empty. At this stage F' is summable over $E_n[a', b']$ and

$$\sum_{(a',\, b')} |F(b_{ni}) - F(a_{ni})|$$

converges. Hence by Theorem 6.8

$$F(b') - F(a') = \int_{E_n(a',\, b')} F'dx + \sum_{(a',\, b')} [F(b_{ni}) - F(a_{ni})],$$

and $F(b_{\omega i}) - F(a_{\omega i})$ can be determined by letting $a' \to a_{\omega i}$, $b' \to b_{\omega i}$.

This brings us to exactly the same place in relation to the set E_ω as we were at the beginning with the set E_1. Consequently we can proceed to operate on the set E_ω as we did on the set E_1 and obtain the sequence of sets $E_{\omega+1}, E_{\omega+2}, \ldots$. These sets are closed and each contains the succeeding set. Consequently by Theorem 2.22 the set $E_\omega E_{\omega+1} \ldots$ is not empty and is closed. Denote this set by $E_{2\omega}$. We are now in the same position relatively to $E_{2\omega}$ as we were relatively to E_ω

when we started to determine $F(b_{\omega i}) - F(a_{\omega i})$ and the sets $E_{\omega+1}, E_{\omega+2}, \ldots$. We can therefore proceed to determine the corresponding sets $E_{2\omega+1}, E_{2\omega+2}, \ldots$, and by Theorem 2.22 the set $E_{2\omega} E_{2\omega+1} \ldots$ is not empty and is closed.

It appears that the set of operations we are using involves a process for which there is no satisfactory stopping place. This is, however, not in fact the case. It is true that every sequence of the form $E_\gamma, E_{\gamma+1}, \ldots$ leads to a non-empty closed set $E_\xi = E_\gamma, E_{\gamma+1} \ldots$. Consequently if the process ever comes to an end a set of the form $E_{\gamma+n}$ must be reached for which $E_{\gamma+n+1}$, n zero or a positive integer, is empty. When such a set is reached it follows from Theorem 6.10 that

$$(6.12) \qquad F(b) - F(a) = \int_{E_{\gamma+n}} F' dx + \sum [F(b_{\gamma+n,\, i}) - F(a_{\gamma+n,\, i})].$$

It will be shown that a set of the form $E_{\gamma+n}$ is reached for which (6.12) holds. Let

$$(6.13) \qquad E_1, E_2, \ldots, E_\omega, E_{\omega+1}, \ldots, E_{2\omega}, \ldots$$

be the sets which are the result of carrying the set of operations through all possible stages. It can be shown that this set of sets is denumerable. For any two of the sets are such that one contains the other and they are not identical. Given any set E_1 and a set E_2 contained in E_1 then E_2 is closed and there is a point ξ_1 of $E_1 - E_2$ which is on $\tilde{E}_2$. Hence there is a rational interval α_1 containing ξ_1 with $E_2\alpha_1$ empty. Similarly, if E_3 is a set contained in E_2 there is a rational interval α_2 containing a point ξ_2 of E_2 with $E_3\alpha_2$ empty. Since $E_2\alpha_1$ is empty and α_2 contains a point of E_2, the intervals α_1 and α_2 cannot be identical. Hence it may be said that to each set in (6.13) there corresponds a single rational interval. Then, since the rational intervals are denumerable, it follows that the set of sets in (6.13) is denumerable.

Let the set of sets in (6.13) be arranged in the denumerable sequence

$$(6.14) \qquad A_1, A_2, \ldots,$$

and suppose that there is no set in (6.13) of the form $E_{\lambda+n}$, n zero or a positive integer, for which $E_{\lambda+n+1}$ is empty.

It will be shown that this supposition leads to the existence of a closed set E_c which is contained in all the sets of (6.13) and which is such that $F(b_{ci}) - F(a_{ci})$ can be determined for all the intervals (a_{ci}, b_{ci}) complementary to E_c. The set of operations can then be applied to the set E_c to obtain further sets of the type that are in (6.13). This contradicts the fact that (6.13) contains all possible sets of this type.

If there is no set of the type $E_{\lambda+n}$ for which $E_{\lambda+n+1}$ is empty then corresponding to any set in (6.13) there is another set which is contained in it. Let

(6.15) $$A_{n_1}, A_{n_2}, \ldots$$

be a subsequence of (6.14) chosen as follows: $A_{n_1} = A_1$, A_{n_2} is the first set in (6.14) which is contained in A_{n_1}, A_{n_3} is the first set that is contained in A_{n_2}, and so on. Since it is true of every two sets in (6.13) that one contains the other, it follows that every set in (6.14) which lies between $A_{n_{i-1}}$ and A_{n_i} contains A_{n_i}. Since the sets A_{n_i} are closed and $A_{n_{i-1}} \supset A_{n_i}$ it follows from Theorem 2.22 that

$$E_c = A_{n_1} A_{n_2} \ldots$$

is non-empty, and is closed. Since E_c is the set common to a subset of (6.14) it contains the set which is common to all the sets of (6.14). Since $A_{n_i} \supset E_c$ for every i, and since every set A_k in (6.13) which lies between $A_{n_{i-1}}$ and A_{n_i} contains A_{n_i}, it follows that $A_k \supset E_c$. Hence E_c is the set common to all the sets of (6.13).

Now let (a_{ci}, b_{ci}) be an interval of the set $\tilde{E}_c$, (a', b') an interval with $a_{ci} < a' < b' < b_{ci}$. There are no points of E_c on the closed interval $[a', b']$. Hence there must be some set of the form $E_{\lambda+n}$, n equal to zero or a positive integer, which is such that $(a', b')E_{\lambda+n+1}$ is empty. Theorem 6.10 can then be used to give

$$F(b') - F(a') = \int_E F'dx + \Sigma_{(a', b')} [F(b_{ci}) - F(a_{ci})]$$

where $E = (a', b')E_{\lambda+n}$. $F(b_{ci}) - F(a_{ci})$ can then be determined by letting $a' \to a_{ci}$ and $b' \to b_{ci}$. The set of operations which gave rise to (6.13) can now be applied to E_c to give further sets $E_{c+1}, E_{c+2}, \ldots$ not contained in (6.13), since none of them contains E_c all of whose points are in every set of (6.13). This contradicts the supposition that (6.13) contains all possible sets arising from the operations. We conclude, therefore that there is some set of the form $E_{\lambda+n}$ in (6.13) which is such that $E_{\lambda+n+1}$ is empty. At this stage (6.12) holds.

It has been shown that the set of sets in (6.13) is denumerable, and each set is the result of a finite or denumerable set of operations. $E_{\lambda+k+1}$ is the result of a finite set of operations on $E_{\lambda+k}$ and

$$E_{2\lambda} = E_\lambda E_{\lambda+1} \ldots$$

is the result of denumerable set of operations used in obtaining the sets $E_\lambda, E_{\lambda+1}, \ldots$. Theorem 6.12 now follows from Theorem 0.2.

6.3. The integrals of Denjoy and other generalized integrals. The work of Theorems 6.9 – 6.12 has its origin in three remarkably penetrating papers by Denjoy. The problem which Denjoy studied was that of determining $F(x) - F(a)$ when $F'(x)$ is given. The methods of these three papers have been abbreviated and generalized by Denjoy himself, and by others, notably Lebesgue, W. H. Young, and Khintchine. A complete bibliography of this work may be found in Saks [58, 59] and in Hobson [28]. It is clear that the operations of Theorem 6.12 can be applied to functions $f(x)$ which are not necessarily the finite derivatives of continuous functions $F(x)$. Such functions $f(x)$ must have special properties which are as follows:

(I) If E is any closed set of $[a, b]$ there exists an interval ω containing points of E such that $f(x)$ is summable on $E\omega$.

(II) If (a_i, b_i) is an interval of the set E and the operations can be performed on $f(x)$ on every interval (a', b') with $a_i < a' < b' < b_i$ to give a result $T(a', b')$ then $T(a', b')$ tends to a limit denoted by $T(a_i, b_i)$ as $a' \to a_i$, $b' \to b_i$.

(III) If $T(a_i, b_i)$ has been determined for all the intervals

(a_i, b_i) complementary to E then there exists an interval ω containing points of E such that $\Sigma_\omega |T(a_i, b_i)|$ converges.

For such a function $f(x)$ the operations of Theorem 6.12 would determine $T(a, b)$ in a denumerable number of stages. The result is the Young integral of $f(x)$ over $[a, b]$. If the operations are carried out for an interval $[a, x]$ the result is a function $T(a, x)$ which need not be continuous. But if this function is continuous it is the Denjoy—Khintchine—Young integral of $f(x)$, or the generalized Denjoy integral of $f(x)$.

In the first work of Denjoy condition (III) was less general. The condition that $\sum_\omega |T(a_i, b_i)|$ converge was replaced by the condition that $\sum_\omega w_i$ converge where w_i is the supremum of $|T(a', b')|$ for all intervals (a', b') with $a_i \leq a' < b' \leq b_i$. The result of the operations of Theorem 6.12 on functions satisfying this modification of (III) is called the special Denjoy integral. Denjoy showed that if $F'(x)$ is the derivative of a continuous function $F(x)$ and is finite at every point of $[a, b]$ and if w_i is the supremum of $F(b') - F(a')$ for all (a', b') with $a_i < a' < b' < b_i$, then w_i satisfies the convergence condition satisfied by $|T(a_i, b_i)|$ in III. There are functions $f(x)$ which are integrable in the generalized Denjoy sense which are not integrable in the specialized sense, i.e. functions $f(x)$ for which the original conditions (III) hold, but not the modified conditions.

6.4. Descriptive definitions of generalized integrals. Descriptive definitions of integrals are as old as the theory of integration itself. The first was that of Newton: If $f(x)$ is finite at each point of $[a, b]$ and there is a continuous function $F(x)$ such that $F'(x) = f(x)$, then $F(x) - F(a)$ is the integral of $f(x)$ over the interval $[a, x]$. There are also descriptive definitions of the generalized integrals of Section 6.3. These definitions, and the properties of the resulting integrals, may be found in the two books by Saks [58, 59]. These definitions are also suggested by a property of continuous functions $F(x)$ which have finite derivatives.

THEOREM 6.13. *If $F(x)$ is continuous and is such that*

$F'(x)$ is finite at each point of $[a, b]$ except possibly a denumerable set then there is a finite or denumerably infinite set of sets $A_1, A_2, \ldots$ which cover $[a, b]$ and on each of which $F(x)$ is absolutely continuous.

Let $\delta_1 > \delta_2 > \ldots$ be a sequence of positive numbers with $\delta_n \to 0$. Let E_{nk} be the points of $[a, b]$ which are such that

$$\frac{|F(x + h) - F(x)|}{|h|} < n$$

when $|h| < \delta_k$. Every point of $[a, b]$ except the denumerable exceptional set is contained in E_{nk} for some n and k, both sufficiently great. If $(x_i x'_i)$ is any set of non-overlapping intervals with x_i, x'_i points of E_{nk} for which $x'_i - x_i < \delta_k$,

$$\sum|F(x'_i) - F(x_i)| < \sum(x'_i - x_i)n.$$

Hence $\sum |F(x_i) - F(x_i)|$ is small if $\sum(x' - x_i)$ is sufficiently small, from which we conclude that $F(x)$ is AC on E_{nk}. Since $F(x)$ is continuous, if a single point is added to a set E_{nk}, $F(x)$ remains AC on the enlarged set. Hence if one point of the exceptional denumerable set is added to each of the denumerable set of sets E_{nk}, the interval $[a, b]$ is covered by a denumerable set of sets on each of which $F(x)$ is AC. This property of F is described by saying that $F(x)$ is generalized absolutely continuous (ACG).

If the function $F(x)$ is defined on the interval $[a, b]$ and this interval can be covered by a denumerable sequence of sets on each of which $F(x)$ is AC, then $F(x)$ is generalized absolutely continuous, ACG, on $[a, b]$.

As a matter of fact functions $F(x)$ which satisfy the conditions of Theorem 6.13 can be shown to satisfy a property which is more restrictive then that of being ACG.

Let $F(x)$ be defined on $[a, b]$ and let A be a set on $[a, b]$. Let (a_i, b_i) be a set of non-overlapping intervals with end-points in A, and let $w_i = sup|F(b') - F(a')|$ for $a_i \leq a' < b' \leq b_i$. If $\sum w_i$ is arbitrarily small when $\sum(b_i - a_i)$ is sufficiently small then $F(x)$ is absolutely continuous in the restricted sense, AC_*, on A. If $[a, b]$ can be covered by a denumerable sequence of sets on each *of which $F(x)$ is AC_* then $F(x)$ is generalized absolutely continuous in the restricted sense, ACG_*, on $[a, b]$.*

Functions $F(x)$ which satisfy the conditions of Theorem 6.13 can be shown by similar methods to be ACG_* on $[a, b]$, and this has led to the following:

DEFINITION 6.4. *Let $f(x)$ be finite almost everywhere on $[a, b]$ and be measurable. If there exists a continuous function $F(x)$ which is ACG_* on $[a, b]$ and which is such that $F'(x) = f(x)$ almost everywhere on $[a, b]$ then $F(x) - F(a)$ is the Denjoy integral of $f(x)$ on the interval $[a, x]$.*

It can be shown that the function $F(x)$ of Definition 6.4 is the special Denjoy integral described in Section 6.3. A further study of functions which are ACG suggests a definition of an integral which is equivalent to the general Denjoy integral.

If the function F is continuous on $[a, b]$ and is AC on a set A it is AC on $\bar{A}$, the closure of A. For if for some $\lambda > 0$, $\sum |F(x'_i) - F(x_i)| > \lambda$ for some set of non-overlapping intervals (x_i, x'_i) with x_i and x'_i points of $\bar{A}$ and $\sum(x'_i - x_i)$ arbitrarily small, it is possible to use the continuity of F to obtain a similar set of intervals satisfying the same relation with x_i, x'_i points of A and $\sum(x'_i - x_i)$ arbitrarily small. This contradicts the hypothesis that $F(x)$ is AC on the set A.

It now follows that if the continuous function F is ACG on $[a, b]$ there is a sequence of closed sets $A_1, A_2, \ldots$ covering $[a, b]$ with F AC on each A_n. By Theorem 6.3 F is BV on A_n, and by Theorem 5.17, ${}_{A_n}DF$ exists and is finite for almost all points of A_n. The set A_n is closed and consequently measurable. It then follows from Theorem 5.6 that at almost all points of A_n the density of $\tilde{A}_n$ is zero. Then since the sets A_n cover $[a, b]$ and ${}_{A_n}DF$ exists and is finite for almost all points of A_n, it can be stated that for almost all points of $[a, b]$

$$\lim_{\xi \to x} \frac{F(\xi) - F(x)}{\xi - x}$$

exists and is finite, except for a set ξ of density zero at x. We are thus led to the following definition and theorem:

DEFINITION 6.5. *If the function* $F(x)$ *defined on* $[a, b]$ *is such that at a point* x

$$\lim_{\xi \to x} \frac{F(\xi) - F(x)}{\xi - x}$$

exists except for a set ξ *of density zero at* x *then this limit is the approximate derivative of* $F(x)$ *at the point* x.

The foregoing considerations now give us

THEOREM 6.14. *If the continuous function* $F(x)$ *is* ACG *on* $[a, b]$ *then* $F(x)$ *has an approximate derivative almost everywhere on* $[a, b]$.

This theorem suggests a second descriptive definition for a generalized integral.

DEFINITION 6.6. *Let the function* $f(x)$ *be finite almost everywhere on* $[a, b]$ *and be measurable. If there exists a continuous function* $F(x)$ *which is* ACG *on* $[a, b]$ *and which has almost everywhere an approximate derivative equal to* $f(x)$ *then the function* $F(x)$ *is the generalized integral of* $f(x)$ *on the interval* $[a, x]$.

It can be shown that the integral of this definition is equivalent to the general Denjoy integral.

The full story of these generalized integrals is long and interesting. The space is not available to go into it here. We have given in detail only the processes which arise naturally from a study of derivatives and their inversion. The complete story of the constructive definitions suggested by Theorems 6.9—6.12 may be found in [28, 41]. There is a different approach to the problem of generalized integrals which was originated by O. Perron. For an introduction to this the reader is referred to [44, 58, 59].

Problems

6.1. If $F(x)$ and $G(x)$ are two functions which are AC on a set A show that $F(x) + G(x)$, $F(x)G(x)$ are AC on A. If there is a number $d > 0$ with $|G(x)| > d$ on A show that $F(x)/G(x)$ is AC on A.

6.2. If the function $F(x)$ is AC on the half open interval

$[a, b)$ and continuous at b show that $F(x)$ is AC on the closed interval $[a, b]$.

6.3. If the function $f(x)$ is integrable on the interval $[a, b]$ and (x_{i-1}, x_i) is a subdivision of $[a, b]$ then

$$\sum_{i=1}^{n} \left| \int_{x_{i-1}}^{x_i} f(x)dx \right| \to \int_a^b |f(x)|dx$$

as $\max(x_i - x_{i-1})$ tends to zero.

6.4. If $F(x)$ is AC on an interval $[a, b]$ then the total variation (Problem 1.5) of $F(x)$ on $[a, b]$ is

$$\int_a^b |F'(x)|dx.$$

([62], p. 393.)

6.5. If $F(x)$ and $G(x)$ are two functions which are AC on an interval $[a, b]$ and $F'(x) = G'(x)$ almost everywhere on $[a, b]$ then $F(x) - G(x)$ is constant on $[a, b]$.

6.6. If $F(x)$ is continuous on the interval $[a, b]$ and if $[a, b]$ can be covered by a denumerable sequence of sets $A_1, A_2, \ldots$ on each of which $F(x)$ is constant then $F(x)$ is constant on $[a, b]$.

6.7. Let $F(x)$ be continuous on the interval $[a, b]$ and let $F(x)$ be AC on each set of a denumerable sequence of sets $A_1, A_2, \ldots$ which covers $[a, b]$. Show that if E is a closed set on $[a, b]$ with $|E| = 0$ then for $\epsilon > 0$ and $\delta > 0$ there is a finite set of non-overlapping intervals $(a_1, b_1), \ldots, (a_n, b_n)$ which contain all of E either as interior points or as end points and for which

$$\sum_{i=1}^{n} \{F(b_i) - F(a_i)\} < \epsilon \text{ and } \sum_{i=1}^{n} (b_i - a_i) < \delta.$$

6.8. Let $F(x)$ be non-decreasing and continuous on $[a, b]$. If E_x is a set on $[a, b]$ let E_y be the set on the y-axis defined by $y = F(x)$, $x \in E_x$. Show that a necessary and sufficient condition that $F(x)$ be AC is that $|E_x| = 0$ implies that $|E_y| = 0$.

6.9. If $F(x)$ is defined on the closed interval $[a, b]$ and is such that $F'(x)$ is finite at each point of $[a, b]$ show that $[a, b]$ can be covered by a denumerable set of sets $A_1, A_2, \ldots$ on each of which $F(x)$ is AC.

6.10. If $F(x)$ is defined on the closed interval $[a, b]$ and if $DF \geq 0$ on a set A contained on $[a, b]$, show that for $\epsilon > 0$ there exists $\delta > 0$ such that

$$\sum \{F(x'_i) - F(x_i)\} > -\epsilon$$

whenever (x_i, x'_i) is a set of non-overlapping intervals with x_i, x'_i points of A and $\sum(x_i - x_{i-1}) < \delta$.

6.11. If $DF(x) \geq 0$ at each point of a closed interval $[a, b]$ then $F(x)$ is non-decreasing on $[a, b]$.

6.12. Let E be a closed set on the interval $[a, b]$, (α_i, β_i) the intervals of the set $\tilde{E}$. Let $F(x)$ be AC on E and on each closed interval $[\alpha_i, \beta_i)$. If $T[\alpha_i, \beta_i]$ is the total variation (Problem 5.1) of $F(x)$ on the closed interval $[\alpha_i, \beta_i]$ and $\sum T[\alpha_i, \beta_i]$ converges show that $F(x)$ is AC on the interval $[a, b]$.

6.13. Construct a function satisfying the conditions of Problem 6.12, except that $\sum T[\alpha_i, \beta_i]$ does not converge, which is not AC on $[a, b]$.

6.14. Let E be a closed set on $[a, b]$, (α_i, β_i) the intervals of the set $\tilde{E}$. Let the function $F(x)$ be absolutely continuous on E, and for x on an interval (α_i, β_i) let $y = F(x)$ be the ordinate of the point (x, y) on the linear segment joining the points $[\alpha_i, F(\alpha_i)]$, $[\beta_i, F(\beta_i)]$. Show that $F(x)$ is AC on $[a, b]$.

6.15. On the interval $1/(n + 1) < x \leq 1/n$ let $f(x) = \pm(n + 1)\sqrt{n}$ accordingly as n is odd or even, $n = 1, 2, \ldots$ and let $f(0) = 0$. If

$$F(x) = \int_x^1 f(x)dx$$

show that $F(x)$ tends to a limit as x tends to $0+$. If $g(x)$ is continuous and BV on $[0, 1]$ and $g(0) = 0$ show that

$$\int_x^1 f(x)g(x)dx \to \text{a limit}$$

as x tends to $0+$. Construct on $[0, 1]$ a function $u(x)$ continuous at $x = 0$ with $u(0) = 0$, and for which

$$\int_x^1 f(x)u(x)dx$$

does not tend to a limit as x tends to 0.

CHAPTER VII

DERIVED NUMBERS AND DERIVATIVES

Introduction: This chapter continues the study of derivatives started in Chapter V. It includes a detailed discussion of the approximate derived numbers of arbitrary functions defined on arbitrary sets.

7.1. Derivates or derived numbers. If $f(x)$ is a function defined on a set A, the ratio

$$\frac{f(x+h)-f(x)}{h}, \quad x \in A, \; x+h \in A,$$

may not tend to a limit as $h \to 0$. But if x is a limit point of A on the right and x, $x+h$ are points of A, then

$$\limsup_{h \to 0+} \frac{f(x+h)-f(x)}{h}, \quad \liminf_{h \to 0+} \frac{f(x+h)-f(x)}{h}$$

both exist. These limits are denoted by ${}_AD^+f$, ${}_AD_+f$ respectively, and are called the upper right and lower right derivates of $f(x)$ over A. There are corresponding definitions for the upper and lower left derivates, ${}_AD^-f$, ${}_AD_-f$. Concerning these derivates we now prove

THEOREM 7.1. *Let the function $f(x)$ be defined and be measurable on the measurable set A. Then at all points $x \in A$, except possibly a denumerable set, the four derivates of $f(x)$ over A exist, and are measurable on A.*

If f is defined on a set A and $x \in A$ is a limit point of A on both sides, then all four derived numbers exist at x. A point $x \in A$ which is not a limit point of A on one side at least is an end point of an open interval of the set complementary to the closure of A. Since this set of intervals is denumerable it follows that the points of A which are not limit points of A on both sides form at most a denumerable set. This establishes the first part of the theorem.

The second part of the theorem will be established for ${}_AD^+f$ the proofs for the other three derivates being similar. We note that it is not possible to use the method of Theorem 5.15 where the corresponding result for derivatives was proved. Even when the set A is the interval (a, b) it could not be said that the function φ_n of that theorem tends to ${}_AD^+f$.

For a real number a let E^a, E_a be respectively the sets $E({}_AD^+f < a)$, $E({}_AD^+f \geq a)$. If ${}_AD^+f$ is not measurable then for some value of a the set E^a is not measurable. Hence, since A is measurable and $E^a + E_a = A$, it follows from Theorem 2.20 that E^a and E_a are not metrically separated. Let $c_1 < c_2 < \ldots$ be a sequence of real numbers with $c_n \to a$. Let E_{jk} be the points of E^a for which

$$(5.16) \qquad \frac{f(\xi + h) - f(\xi)}{h} < c_j, \ \xi \in E^a,$$

when $0 < h < 1/k$, ξ and $\xi + h$ points of A. If $j_2 \geq j_1$, $k_2 \geq k_1$ then $E_{j_2k_2} \supset E_{j_1k_1}$. Also if $x \in E^a$ then $x \in E_{jk}$ for some sufficiently great j and k. Hence it follows from Theorem 2.20 that for j and k sufficiently great E_{jk} and E_a are not metrically separated. Then by Theorem 5.7, there is a set $E \subset E_a$ with $|E|^\circ > 0$ at which the density of E_{jk} is greater than zero. By Theorem 5.9 f is approximately continuous at almost all points of A. Then since $|E|^\circ > 0$ there are points of E at which f is approximately continuous. Let x be such a point, let c be a real number with $c_j < c < a$, and let h' be a value of h, $0 < h' < 1/2k$ for which

$$(5.17) \qquad \frac{f(x + h') - f(x)}{h'} > c,$$

$x + h' \in A$. Such a number h' exists for the reason that $x \in E_a$. Let ξ be a point of E_{jk}, and take h satisfying (5.16) with $\xi + h = x + h'$. Then from (5.16) and (5.17) we get

$$f(x + h') - f(x) > h'c,$$
$$f(\xi + h) - f(\xi) < hc_j,$$

$\xi + h = x + h'$, $c_j < c$. These give

$$f(\xi) - f(x) > h'\left(c - \frac{h}{h'} c_j\right).$$

As $\xi \to x$, $h/h' \to 1$. Hence

$$\liminf_{\xi \to x} [f(\xi) - f(x)] \geq h'(c - c_j),$$

and the set $\xi \subset E_{jk}$ has density greater than zero at x. Consequently x cannot be a point of approximate continuity of f. This contradiction allows us to conclude that ${}_AD^+f$ is measurable on A.

If the set A is the interval (a, b) then the derivates exist at every point of A. If at any point x all four derived numbers have the same value their common value is the derivative of $f(x)$, $Df(x)$ or $f'(x)$. The next question with which we shall be concerned is the existence of the derivative of a function $f(x)$ defined on an interval (a, b).

If the derivative exists and is finite at a point x of (a, b), then $f(x)$ is continuous at this point. For, if $[f(x + h) - f(x)]/h$ tends to a finite limit as $h \to 0$, it follows that $f(x + h) - f(x)$ tends to zero. The converse of this is not true. If $f(x) = |x|$ then $f(x)$ is continuous at the origin, but the derivative of $f(x)$ does not exist at the origin. For

$$\lim_{h \to 0+} \frac{f(x + h) - f(x)}{h} = 1 \neq \lim_{h \to 0-} \frac{f(x + h) - f(x)}{h} = -1.$$

It is easy to construct continuous functions which fail to have a derivative at a finite number of points, or even at the points of a denumerably infinite set. As to whether or not a function continuous on an interval (a, b) could fail to have a derivative at every point of the interval remained for long an open question. That such a function can be constructed was demonstrated by the German mathematician Weierstrass. This was published by du Bois-Reymond in 1875 with Weierstrass's own proof. There is, moreover, evidence that Bolzano constructed such a function as early as 1834.

The function defined by Weierstrass was

$$f(x) = \sum_{n=0}^{\infty} b^n \cos(a^n \pi x),$$

$0 < b < 1$, a an odd positive integer. If the product ab is sufficiently great the ratio $[f(x+h) - f(x)]/h$ fails to tend to a limit, finite or infinite, for any value of x.

The function

$$f(x) = \sum_{n=1}^{\infty} a^{-n} \sin a^n x$$

which is due to Cellerier, and which was published in 1890 fails to have a finite derivative at every value of x if a is a sufficiently great even integer. This function, however, is not considered to be non-differentiable in the same strict sense as that of Weierstrass, for it can be shown that there is an everywhere dense set at which $[f(x+h) - f(x)]/h \to \infty$, and another everywhere dense set at which $[f(x+h) - f(x)]/h \to -\infty$. References to these studies of continuous functions which do not have a derivative at any point may be found in [29, pp. 401-421].

7.2. The Weierstrass non-differentiable function. Titchmarsh [62, p. 351] gives a simple proof of the fact that the function defined by Weierstrass does not have a finite derivative for any value of x if $ab > 1 + 3\pi/2$. By slightly modifying this proof we shall show that if $ab > 1 + 3\pi/2$, then for every value of x, $[f(x+h) - f(x)]/h$ fails to tend to a limit finite or infinite, and that there are everywhere dense sets at the points of which the limit is $+\infty$ on one side and $-\infty$ on the other side. The function under consideration is

$$f(x) = \sum_{n=0}^{\infty} b^n \cos a^n \pi x,$$

a an odd integer, $0 < b < 1$. Write

$$f(x+h) - f(x) = \sum_{n=0}^{m-1} b^n \cos [a^n\pi(x+h)] - \cos (a^n \pi x)$$
$$+ \sum_{n=m}^{\infty} b^n[\cos a^n\pi(x+h) - \cos (a^n\pi x).$$

Using the law of the mean,

$$|\cos a^n\pi(x+h) - \cos (a^n\pi x)| = |a^n\pi|h| \sin [a^n\pi(x+\theta h)]|$$
$$\leq a^n\pi|h|.$$

Hence, writing $f(x + h) - f(x) = S_m + R_m$, it follows that

$$|S_m| \leq |h|\pi \frac{a^m b^m - 1}{ab - 1} < \pi|h| \frac{a^m b^m}{ab - 1}.$$

To obtain a lower limit for R_m we write

$$a^m x = r_m + \xi_m,$$

where r_m is an integer and $-1/2 \leq \xi_m < 1/2$. Then, if $h = (1 - \xi_m)/a^m$,

$$a^n\pi(x + h) = a^{n-m}\pi(r_m + 1),\ a^n\pi x = a^{n-m}\pi(r_m + \xi_m),$$

and

$$\begin{aligned}\cos a^n\pi(x + h) &- \cos a^n\pi x \\ &= (-1)^{r_m+1} + (-1)^{r_m+1} \cos(\pi a^{n-m}\xi_m) \\ &= (-1)^{r_m+1}[1 + \cos(a^{n-m}\pi\xi_m)].\end{aligned}$$

From this it follows that

$$R_m = \sum_{n=m}^{\infty} (-1)^{r_m+1} b^n[1 + \cos(a^{n-m}\pi\xi_m)].$$

There is a sequence of values of m with $m \to \infty$ such that every r_m is odd or such that every r_m is even. In the first case R_m is the sum of a positive term series and consequently not less than the first term of the series, which is b^m. Hence noticing that $0 < h < 3/2a^m$ we see that

$$\frac{R_m}{h} > \frac{b^m}{h} > \frac{2}{3}a^m b^m,$$

and

$$\frac{f(x + h) - f(x)}{h} \geq \frac{R_m - |S_m|}{h} > a^m b^m\left(\frac{2}{3} - \frac{\pi}{ab - 1}\right).$$

If $ab > 1 + \frac{3}{2}\pi$ it follows that $D^+f = \infty$. If $h = (-1 - \xi_m)/a^m$ then

$$R_m = (-1)^{r_m-1} \sum_{n=m}^{\infty} b^n[1 + \cos a^{n-m}\pi\xi_m].$$

If r_m is odd then

$$\frac{R_m}{h} < \frac{b^m}{h} < -\frac{2}{3}a^m b^m,$$

and it follows that $D^-f = -\infty$. If r_m is a sequence of even integers it follows in a similar manner that $D^+f = -\infty$, $D^-f = \infty$. Hence for every x the ratio $[f(x+h) - f(x)]/h$ fails to tend to a limit, finite or infinite.

It will next be shown that there is an everywhere dense set at which $f(x)$ has a right-hand derivative equal to ∞ and a left-hand derivative equal to $-\infty$. Let x be an odd integer. Then $a^m x$ is an odd integer, and

$$\cos a^n\pi(x+h) - \cos a^n\pi x = 1 - \cos a^n\pi h,$$

$$f(x+h) - f(x) = \sum_{n=0}^{\infty} b^n(1 - \cos a^n\pi h) = 2\sum_{n=0}^{\infty} b^n \sin^2 \tfrac{1}{2}a^n\pi h.$$

But for $0 < a^n\pi h < \pi$, $0 < h < \pi/a^n$

$$\sin \frac{1}{2}\, a^n\pi h > \frac{1}{\pi}\,(a^n\pi h).$$

Hence for $1/a^{m+1} \leq h < 1/a^m$,

$$\begin{aligned}
\frac{f(x+h) - f(x)}{h} &> 2a^m \sum_{n=0}^{m} b^n (a^{n-m-1})^2, \\
&> 2a^m \sum_{n=0}^{m} b^n\, a^{2n}\, a^{-2m}\, a^{-2}, \\
&> \frac{2}{a^{m+2}} \sum_{n=0}^{m} b^n\, a^{2n}, \\
&> \frac{2}{a^{m+2}}\, \frac{b^m\, a^{2m} - 1}{a^2 b - 1}, \\
&> \frac{2}{a^2}\, \frac{a^m b^m - 1}{a^2 b - 1}.
\end{aligned}$$

As m increases indefinitely, $h \to 0$. If $ab > 1$, $a^m b^m \to \infty$. Consequently $[f(x+h) - f(x)]/h \to \infty$ and the right derivative of $f(x)$ is ∞. Thus for x an odd integer the right-hand derivative is ∞. For a fixed value of m

$$\begin{aligned}
f(x) &= \sum_{n=0}^{m-1} b^n \cos a^n\pi x + \sum_{n=m}^{\infty} b^n \cos a^n\pi x, \\
&= \varphi_m(x) + \varphi(x).
\end{aligned}$$

Each of the finite number of terms in $\varphi_m(x)$ is a constant times the cosine of a constant times x from which it follows that $\varphi_m(x)$ has a finite derivative. For x an odd integer the right derivative of $f(x)$ is $+\infty$, and consequently the right derivative of $\varphi(x)$ is $+\infty$. Now for x an odd integer let $x' = x - 2r/a^m$, r a positive or negative integer, m a positive integer. For such values of r and m

$$f(x') = \varphi_m(x') - \varphi(x').$$

As in the case of $\varphi(x)$ the derivative of $\varphi_m(x')$ is finite. Also

$$\varphi(x') = \sum_{n=m}^{\infty} b^n \cos a^n\pi\left(x - \frac{2r}{a^m}\right) = \sum_{n=m}^{\infty} b^n \cos a^n\pi x = \varphi(x).$$

Consequently the right derivative of $\varphi(x')$ at x' is equal to the right derivative of $\varphi(x)$ at x, which is $+\infty$. It then follows that the right derivative of $f(x')$ is $+\infty$, and it is easily verified that the set x' is everywhere dense. If the number h satisfies

$$-\frac{1}{a^m} < h < -\frac{1}{a^{m-1}},$$

it is easily verified that

$$\frac{f(x+h) - f(x)}{h} < -\frac{2}{a^{m+2}}\,\frac{a^m b^m - 1}{a^2 b - 1},$$

from which it follows that for x an odd integer the left-hand derivative is $-\infty$, and the same is true for the everywhere dense set x'.

By starting with x an even integer it can be shown in a similar way that there is an everywhere dense set at which the derivative on the right is $-\infty$ and the derivative on the left is $+\infty$. It is easily verified that in both cases the set x is denumerable.

It thus appears that the function of Weierstrass has cusps at each of two everywhere dense sets, with the cusps pointing in opposite directions at the points of the respective sets. The question as to whether or not there exist non-differentiable functions without cusps was for long open, in spite of the fact that after the work of Weierstrass the whole problem of non-differentiable functions received the attention of many eminent mathematicians. The construction of a function for which at every point $D_+f < D^+f$, $D_-f < D^-f$ had to wait more than half a century for the genius of A. S. Besicovitch [5].

Later Pepper [49] revised the work of Besicovitch, giving a different exposition. We shall now give Pepper's interpretation of this function, but obtain its properties by methods which are different. These methods are in part geometrical. A. P. Morse [45] has constructed a function which has at no point a unilateral derivative by a method which is wholly arithmetical.

7.3. A function which has no unilateral derivative. The first step in establishing the existence of such a function is the construction of a non-dense closed set on an interval $[0, a]$. Let α_{01} be an open interval with centre at the centre of $[0, a]$ and with $|\alpha_{01}| = a/4$. Let u_{11}, u_{12} be the two closed intervals on $[0, a]$ complementary to α_{01}. Let α_{11}, α_{12} be two open intervals with centres at the centres of u_{11}, u_{12} respectively, and with $|\alpha_{1i}| = a/4^2$, $i = 1, 2$. Continuing this process there is obtained the set of open intervals $\alpha = \sum_k \sum_i \alpha_{ki}$, $i = 1, 2, \ldots, 2^k$, $k = 0, 1, \ldots$, for which

$$|\alpha| = \frac{a}{4} + \frac{2a}{4^2} + \frac{2^2a}{4^3} + \ldots .$$

Consequently the non-dense closed set E complementary to α has $|E| = a/2$. There are some further properties of this set E which we shall use, and these we now obtain.

(i) At the point $x = 0$ the right-hand density of E is unity and at the point $x = a$ the left-hand density of E is unity.

Suppose there is a sequence of values $c_1 > c_2 > \ldots$ of x with $c_n \rightarrow 0$ and such that

$$\frac{|E(0,c_n)|}{c_n} < \lambda < 1. \tag{7.1}$$

Consider the first value of k which is such that $u_{k1} \ni c_n$ and $\alpha_{k1} \ni c_n$ or lies to the left of c_n. If $\alpha_{k1} \ni c_n$ then from (7.1) we get

$$\frac{|Eu_{k+1,1}|}{|u_{k+1}| + |\alpha_{k1}|} \leq \frac{|Eu_{k+1,1}|}{c_n} < \lambda. \tag{7.2}$$

It follows from the construction of E that $|Eu_{ki}| = |Eu_{kj}|$,

$i \neq j$. Hence, since $|a_{ki}| = |a_{kj}|$, $i \neq j$, it follows from (7.2) that

$$|E| = \sum_i |Eu_{k+1,\,i}| \leq \lambda \sum |u_{k+1,\,i}| + \lambda \sum_i |a_{ki}|.$$

As $c_n \to 0$, $k \to \infty$. But as $k \to \infty$ $\sum_i u_{k+1,\,i} \to |E|$, $\sum_i |a_{ki}| \to 0$, and since $\lambda < 1$ this, with the preceding relation, leads to a contradiction.

Now suppose a_{k1} falls to the left of c_n. Then c_n is to the right of the centre of u_{k1}. Let x_k be the right-hand end-point of u_{k1}. Then $Eu_{k1} = E(0, c_n) + E(c_n, x_k)$. Hence, from (7.1),

$$|Eu_{k1}| < \lambda c_n + (x_k - c_n) < \lambda' |u_{k1}|,$$

where $\lambda' = (1 + \lambda)/2 < 1$. We then have

$$|E| = \sum_i |Eu_{ki}| < \lambda' \sum_i |u_{ki}|,$$

which, as in the previous case, leads to a contradiction.

We can now conclude that $|E(0, c_n)|/c_n \to 1$ as $c_n \to 0$. Thus the right-hand density of E is unity at 0, and it can be shown in a similar way that at $x = a$ the left-hand density of E is unity.

(ii) If x_0 is a limit point of E on the right (left) then $x_0 \in u_{ki}$ for every k and some value i_k of i. If $u_{ki_k} = [x_k, x'_k]$ then $x_k \leq x_0 < x'_k (x_k < x_0 \leq x'_k)$,

$$\limsup_{x'_k \to x_0} \frac{|E(x_0, x'_k)|}{x'_k - x_0} = 1 \left(\limsup_{x_k \to x_0} \frac{|E(x_k, x_0)|}{x_0 - x_k} = 1 \right).$$

There will be an infinite set of values of k for which a_{ki_k} is to the right of x_0. This means that x_0 is to the left of the centre of u_{ki_k}. Suppose that for such values of k

$$\frac{|E(x_0, x'_k)|}{x'_k - x_0} < \lambda < 1.$$

Then

$$\begin{aligned} |Eu_{ki_k}| &< |E(x_k, x_0)| + |E(x_0, x'_k)|, \\ &\leq x_0 - x_k + \lambda(x'_k - x_0), \\ &< \lambda'(x'_k - x_k) = \lambda' |u_{ki_k}|, \end{aligned}$$

where $\lambda' = (1 + \lambda)/2 < 1$. This relation can be used as in (i) to lead to a contradiction. A similar proof holds for the second relation in (ii).

(iii) There is a number $\mu > 0$ such that

$$\frac{|E(x, a)|}{a - x} \geq \mu > 0$$

for $0 \leq x < a$.

Let $m(x) = |E(x, a)|/(a - x)$, $x \neq a$, $m(a) = 1$. The function $m(x)$ is continuous for x on $0 \leq x < a$, and by (i) $m(x) \to 1$ as $x \to a$. Hence $m(x)$ is continuous on the closed interval $[0, a]$. Then, since $m(0) = 1/2$, $m(a) = 1$, and $m(x) \neq 0$ for $0 \leq x \leq a$, it follows that $m(x)$ is bounded from zero. This means that there is a number $\mu > 0$ for which $m(x) \geq \mu$, $0 \leq x \leq a$. Thus (iii) is established.

For b a positive real number, define $\varphi(x)$ on the interval $0 \leq x \leq a$ by the relation

$$\varphi(x) = \frac{2b}{a}|E(0, x)|.$$

If follows at once that $\varphi(a) = b$. Furthermore, it is possible to prove

(iv) If x_0 is a limit point of points of E on the right (left) then at $x_0, D^+\varphi \geq 2b/a$, $(D^-\varphi \geq 2b/a)$.

If $h > 0$ then

$$\frac{\varphi(x_0 + h) - \varphi(x_0)}{h} = \frac{2b}{a}\frac{|E(x, x + h)|}{h}.$$

If h is so taken that $x_0 + h$ is the right-hand end-point of $u_{ki} \ni x_0$, then (iv) follows from (ii). A similar proof holds with left replacing right.

On $0 \leq x \leq a$ let $\varphi_0(x) = \varphi(x)$, and on the range $a < x \leq 2a$ let $\varphi_0(x) = \varphi(2a - x)$. Let E_0 be the set E on $[0, a]$, and E'_0 be the reflection of E in the point a. Let α'_{ki} be the reflection of α_{ki} in the point a. The function $\varphi_0(x)$ is now defined on the interval $[0, 2a]$, and on the intervals α_{ki}, α'_{ki} respectively the graph of $\varphi_0(x)$ consists of two line segments l_{ki}, l'_{ki} parallel to and the same distance from the x-axis. The graph of $\varphi_0(x)$ on $[0, 2a]$ has been called by Pepper a step-triangle. We shall denote it by Δ_0.

On l_{01}, l'_{01} construct respectively the step-triangles Δ_{01},

Δ'_{01} congruent to each other, with vertices below the base, constructed in a manner similar to that used in constructing the step-triangle on $[0, 2a]$, and with the altitude of each step-triangle equal to $b/2$. Carry out a similar construction on each of the segments $l_{11}, l_{12}, l'_{11}, l'_{12}$, with the altitude of each step-triangle equal to $b/2^2$. Let this process of construction be continued for all the segments l_{ki}, l'_{ki} where for each k the altitude of the corresponding step-triangle is $b/2^{k+1}$. If a' is the half-base and b' the altitude of the congruent step-triangles $\Delta_{ki}, \Delta'_{ki}$ defined on l_{ki}, l'_{ki}, then

$$a' = \frac{1}{2}\frac{a}{4^{k+1}}, \; b' = \frac{b}{2^{k+1}}, \quad \frac{2b'}{a'} = 2^{k+3}\frac{b}{a} > \frac{2b}{a}.$$

Let $\varphi_1(x) = \varphi_0(x)$ on E_0 and on E'_0. For x a point on α_{ki} or α'_{ki} let the ordinate of $\varphi_1(x)$ be the ordinate of the point in the side of the step-triangle Δ_{ki} or Δ'_{ki} of which x is the projection.

Let Δ_k be a step-triangle of the set $\Delta_{ki}, \Delta'_{ki}$, and let E_k, E'_k be the projection on the x-axis of the points in the base of Δ_k which correspond to the points E_0, E'_0 respectively in the base of Δ_0. For the points of these sets the following holds:

(v) If x_0 is a limit point on the right (left) of E_k then at x_0, $D_+\varphi_1 \leq -2b'/a' < -2b/a$ $(D_-\varphi_1 \leq -2b'/a' < -2b/a)$. If x_0 is a limit point on the right (left) of E'_k then at x_0, $D^+\varphi_1 \geq 2b'/a' > 2b/a$ $(D^-\varphi_1 \geq 2b'/a' > 2b/a)$, where in each case b' is the altitude, a' the half-base of the step-triangle.

The proof of (v) is similar to that of (iv).

Let us now examine the derived numbers of $\varphi_1(x)$ at the points of E_0. Let x_0 be a limit point on the right of E_0. The point x_0 lies between two intervals α_{pi} and α_{qj}, where the first of these intervals is to the left of x_0. The step-triangle on the line segment l_{qj} has its vertex on the line containing the segment l_{pi}. If γ is the mid-point of α_{qj} then $\varphi_1(\gamma)$ is the length of the ordinate of the segment l_{pi}. Furthermore, $\varphi_1(x_0) = \varphi_0(x_0) \geq$ ordinate of l_{pi}. Hence

$$\frac{\varphi_1(\gamma) - \varphi_1(x_0)}{\gamma - x_0} \leq 0,$$

and it follows that at x_0, $D_+\varphi_1 \leq 0$. Again, since $x \in E_0$, $\varphi_1(x) = \varphi_0(x)$, it follows that at x_0, $D^+\varphi_1 \geq D^+\varphi_0 \geq 2b/a$. We have thus shown

(vi) If x_0 is a limit point of E_0 on the right, then at x_0 $D^+\varphi_1 - D_+\varphi_1 > 0$.

Let x_0 be a limit point of E_0 on the left. Then x_0 is on an infinite set of the intervals u_{ki} with a_{ki} to the left of x_0. From this it follows that for such a set of intervals x_0 is to the right of the centre of each interval of this infinite set u_{ki}. Let $a_{k-1,\,j}$ be the interval of the set a which is immediately to the left of u_{ki}. Let γ be the mid-point, x_1 the right end-point of $a_{k-1,\,j}$. Then

$$\frac{\varphi_1(\gamma) - \varphi_1(x_0)}{\gamma - x_0} = \frac{\varphi_1(x_0) - \varphi_1(x_1)}{x_0 - \gamma} + \frac{\varphi_1(x_1) - \varphi_1(\gamma)}{x_0 - \gamma}.$$

The points x_0 and x_1 belong to E_0. Hence $\varphi_1(x_0) = \varphi_0(x_0)$, $\varphi_1(x_1) = \varphi_0(x_1)$, and

$$\varphi_1(x_0) - \varphi_1(x_1) = \varphi_0(x_0) - \varphi_0(x_1) = \frac{2b}{a}\left|E(x_1, x_0)\right|.$$

Again, $\varphi_1(x_1) - \varphi_1(\gamma)$ is the altitude of the triangle on $l_{k-1,\,j}$, and is, therefore, equal to $b/2^k$. It now follows that

$$\frac{\varphi_1(\gamma) - \varphi_1(x_0)}{\gamma - x_0} = \frac{2b}{a}\,\frac{\left|E(x_1, x_0)\right|}{x_0 - \gamma} + \frac{b}{2^k}\,\frac{1}{x_0 - \gamma}.$$

Also, $x_0 - \gamma = (x_0 - x_1) + (x_1 - \gamma)$, and

$$\frac{\left|u_{ki}\right|}{2} < x_0 - x_1 \leq \left|u_{ki}\right|,\ x_1 - \gamma = \frac{1}{2}\,\frac{a}{4^k}.$$

We next evaluate $\left|u_{ki}\right|$. The complement of the set $u_{k1}, \ldots, u_{k2^k}$ on the interval $[0, a]$ is the set $a_{01}, a_{11}, a_{12}, \ldots, a_{k-1,\,1}, \ldots, a_{k-1,\,2^{k-1}}$, and the measure of this set is

$$\frac{a}{4} + \frac{2a}{4^2} + \ldots + \frac{2^{k-1}a}{4^k} = \frac{a}{2}\,\frac{2^k - 1}{2^k}.$$

Hence

$$\sum\left|u_{ki}\right| = a - a\frac{2^k - 1}{2^{k+1}} = a\frac{2^k + 1}{2^{k+1}}.$$

Since there are 2^k intervals in the set $u_{k1}, \ldots, u_{k2^k}$, it follows that

$$|u_{ki}| = a\frac{2^k+1}{2^{2k+1}}.$$

We then get

$$\frac{x_1-\gamma}{x_0-x_1} < \frac{\frac{a}{2}}{\frac{a}{2}} \cdot \frac{\frac{1}{2^{2k}}}{\frac{2^k+1}{2^{2k+1}}} = \frac{2}{2^{k+1}},$$

which tends to zero as $k \to \infty$. We also have

$$\frac{\varphi_1(\gamma)-\varphi_1(x_0)}{\gamma-x_0} > \frac{2b}{a}\frac{|E(x_1, x_0)|}{(x_0-x_1)+(x_1-\gamma)} + \frac{b}{2^k}\frac{1}{(x_1-x_0)+(x_0-\gamma)},$$

$$> \frac{2b}{a}\frac{\frac{|E(x_1, x_0)|}{x_0-x_1}}{1+\frac{x_1-\gamma}{x_0-x_1}} + \frac{b}{2^k}\frac{1}{|u_{ki}|+\frac{a}{2}\frac{1}{4^k}}.$$

Using the value obtained for $|u_{ki}|$, the second term of this reduces to

$$\frac{2b}{a} \cdot \frac{2^k}{2^k+2},$$

which tends to $2b/a$ as $k \to \infty$. Using this, (ii), and the fact that $(x_1-\gamma)/(x_0-x_1) \to 0$, it follows that

$$\limsup_{\gamma \to x_0} \frac{\varphi_1(\gamma)-\varphi_1(x_0)}{\gamma-x_0} \geq \frac{4b}{a},$$

and therefore at x_0 $D^-\varphi_1 \geq 4b/a$. Again

$$\frac{\varphi_1(x_1)-\varphi_1(x_0)}{x_1-x_0} = \frac{\varphi_0(x_0)-\varphi_0(x_1)}{x_0-x_1} = \frac{2b}{a}\frac{|E_0(x_1, x_0)|}{x_0-x_1},$$

which, by (ii), tends to $2b/a$ as $x_1 \to x_0$. Thus, $D_-\varphi_1 \leq 2b/a$. These results combine to give

(vii) If x_0 is a limit point of E_0 on the left then $D^-\varphi_1 - D_-\varphi_1 > 0$ at x_0.

Using similar arguments it is possible to prove

(viii) If x_0 is a limit point of E'_0 on the right (left), then $D^+\varphi_1 - D_+\varphi_1 > 0 (D^-\varphi_1 - D_-\varphi_1 > 0)$ at x_0.

A consideration of the construction of $\varphi_1(x)$ together with the results already obtained for $\varphi_0(x)$ and $\varphi_1(x)$ easily give

(ix) If (x_l, x_r) is an interval of the set a_{ki}, a'_{ki} then at x_l the right derivative of φ_1 is $-2b'/a'$ and at x_r the left derivative of φ_1 is $2b'/a'$, where a' is the half base, b' the altitude of the step-triangle Δ_{lr} the projection of whose base is the interval (x_l, x_r).

On the line segments in the sides of each of the step-triangles Δ_{lr} construct step-triangles with vertices above the base, using the same method of construction as that used in constructing the set Δ_{lr}. Let E_1, E'_1 be the sets in the intervals (x_l, x_r) which correspond to the sets E_0, E'_0 in $[0, 2a]$. The sets E_1, E'_1 then have the end-points of the intervals (x_l, x_r) in common with E_0, E'_0.

On E_0, E'_0 and the remaining points of E_1, E'_1 let $\varphi_2(x) = \varphi_1(x)$. On the projections of the set of step-triangles last defined let the ordinate of $\varphi_2(x)$ be the ordinate of the corresponding point in the side of the step-triangle.

It follows from (vii) and (viii) that $D_+\varphi_1 \leq 0$ at $x = 0$ and $D_-\varphi_1 \leq 0$ at $x = 2a$. This also follows easily from the fact that the vertices of the step-triangles Δ_{k1}, Δ'_{k1} are in the base of Δ_0, and similar reasoning can now be used to show that $D^+\varphi_2 \geq 0$ at x_l and $D_-\varphi_2 \leq 0$ at x_r. This can now be combined with (vi), (vii), (viii), (ix) and the fact that $\varphi_2(x) = \varphi_1(x)$ on E_0, E'_0, E_1, E'_1, to give

(x) At all points of E_0, E'_0 the relations $D^+\varphi_2 - D_+\varphi_2 > 0$, $D^-\varphi_2 - D_-\varphi_2 > 0$ hold.

This procedure can be continued to give a sequence of continuous functions defined on $[0, 2a]$ for which

(xi) $\varphi_n(x) = \varphi_{n-1}(x)$ on $E_0, E'_0, E_1, E'_1, \ldots, E_{n-1}, E'_{n-1}$, and $D^+\varphi_n - D_+\varphi_n > 0$, $D^-\varphi_n - D_-\varphi_n > 0$ at all points of the sets $E_0, E'_0, E_1, E'_1, \ldots, E_{n-2}, E'_{n-2}$.

Furthermore for $p > n$,

$$|\varphi_n(x) - \varphi_{n+p}(x)| < \frac{b}{2^n} + \frac{b}{2^{n+1}} + \ldots + \frac{b}{2^{n+p}} < \frac{b}{2^{n-1}}.$$

Then, making use of Theorem 1.6, Definition 1.26, and Theorem 1.11, we conclude that $\varphi_n(x)$ tends to a continuous function $\varphi(x)$, and it follows from (xi) that $D^+\varphi - D_+\varphi > 0$, $D^-\varphi - D_-\varphi > 0$ at all points of E_0, E'_0, E_1, $E'_1, \ldots$. It remains to show that the latter relations hold at the remaining points of $[0, 2a]$.

Let x be a point which is on an interval α_k of the form α_{ki} or α'_{ki} at every stage of the construction of $\varphi(x)$. Suppose first that x is to the left of the centre of α_k for an infinite sequence of these intervals. Let γ be the mid-point, x_1 the right end-point of α_k. The point $[x, \varphi(x)]$ is interior to the step-triangle Δ_k. Let $\varphi_k(x)$ be the function in the sequence defining $\varphi(x)$ which has ordinates defined by means of the step-triangle Δ_k, and suppose for definiteness that the vertex of Δ_k is above the base. Then $\varphi(x) \leq \varphi_k(x)$, $\varphi(\gamma) = \varphi_k(\gamma)$, and making use of (iii) we get

$$\frac{\varphi(\gamma) - \varphi(x)}{\gamma - x} \geq \frac{\varphi_k(\gamma) - \varphi_k(x)}{\gamma - x} \geq \mu\frac{2b'}{a'} > \mu\frac{2b}{a},$$

where a' is the half base, b' the altitude of Δ_k. Also

$$\frac{\varphi(x_1) - \varphi(x)}{x_1 - x} \leq 0.$$

We can now conclude that if x is on the left half of an infinite sequence of intervals of the form α_{ki} or α'_{ki} then $D^+\varphi - D_+\varphi > 0$, and it can be shown in a similar way that if x is on the right half of an infinite sequence of such intervals then $D^-\varphi - D_-\varphi > 0$.

We next consider the case in which the point x is on the right half of all but a finite set of the intervals of the form (x_l, x_r). Two step-triangles Δ_1, Δ_2 entering into the construction of $\varphi(x)$ are consecutive if Δ_2 has its base on a line segment in the side of Δ_1. There are two cases to consider, that for which there is an infinite sequence of pairs Δ_1, Δ_2 containing the point $[x, \varphi(x)]$ for which the projection on the x-axis of

Δ_2 is not for some k a last interval on the right of the set a'_{ki} in the base of Δ_1, and that for which there are only a finite set of such pairs. Taking the first case, suppose for definiteness that the vertex of Δ_1 is above its base. The point $[x, \varphi(x)]$ is interior to Δ_1 and Δ_2. Let a_1, a_2 be respectively the projection on the x-axis of Δ_1, Δ_2, and let x_1, x_2 be the right end-points of these respective intervals. Then the vertex of Δ_2 is below its base. Let $\varphi_1(x)$ be the function in the sequence defining $\varphi(x)$ which has ordinates defined by means of Δ_1. Let x' be such that $\varphi(x) = \varphi_1(x')$. Then, since $\varphi(x_1) = \varphi_1(x_1)$, we have

$$\frac{\varphi(x_1) - \varphi(x)}{x_1 - x} = \frac{\varphi_1(x_1) - \varphi_1(x')}{(x_1 - x') + (x' - x)}.$$

Dividing numerator and denominator by $(x_1 - x')$, making use of (iii) and the fact that $(x' - x)/(x_1 - x') < 1$, it follows that

$$\frac{\varphi(x_1) - \varphi(x)}{x_1 - x} < -\frac{\mu}{2}\frac{b'}{a'} < -\frac{\mu}{2}\frac{b}{a}.$$

Since $[x, \varphi(x)]$ is interior to Δ_2, and since $[x_2, \varphi(x_2)]$ is the right end-point of the base of Δ_2, it follows that

$$\frac{\varphi(x_2) - \varphi(x)}{x_2 - x} \geq 0,$$

and we can conclude that $D^+\varphi - D_+\varphi > 0$.

For the second case, if the subscript k in the set a'_{ki} is sufficiently great, for every consecutive pair Δ_1, Δ_2, the interval a_2 is for some k the last interval on the right of the set a'_{ki} in the interval a_1. Also there is a step-triangle Δ_3 on a line segment in the side of Δ_2, with vertex above the base, and with a_3 the last interval on the right of some set a'_{ki} in the projection of the base of Δ_2, and such that $[x, \varphi(x)]$ is interior to Δ_3. It follows from these considerations that $\varphi(x) - \varphi_1(x) > [\varphi_1(x_2) - \varphi_1(x_1)]/2$. Hence, since $\varphi_1(x_2) = \varphi(x_2)$ and $\varphi_1(x_1) = \varphi(x_1)$,

$$\frac{\varphi(x_1) - \varphi(x)}{x_1 - x} < \frac{[\varphi(x_1) - \varphi(x_2)]/2}{(x_1 - x_2) + (x_2 - x)}.$$

It is easily verified that $(x_2 - x)/(x_1 - x_2) < 1$. Then, dividing the numerator and denominator of the right member of the second last inequality by $x_1 - x_2$ and using (iii), it is seen that

$$\frac{\varphi(x_1) - \varphi(x)}{x_1 - x} < - \frac{\mu}{4} \frac{b}{a}.$$

Furthermore, it follows as in the previous case that

$$\frac{\varphi(x_2) - \varphi(x)}{x_2 - x} \geq 0.$$

Consequently we can conclude that $D^+\varphi - D_+\varphi > 0$.

A similar study leads to the conclusion that when x is on the left half of an infinite set of the intervals a_{ki}, or a'_{ki}, then $D^-\varphi - D_-\varphi > 0$, and this completes the demonstration that the function $\varphi(x)$ has no unilateral derivative.

7.4. The derived numbers of arbitrary functions defined on arbitrary sets. So far our attention has been mainly directed to the derivatives of functions $f(x)$ which were specialized in one way or another. In Chapter V we saw that if $f(x)$ is BV it has a finite derivative almost everywhere; if $f(x)$ is measurable then its derived numbers, and consequently its derivative, if it exists, are measurable. In the first part of this chapter it was shown that there exist functions $f(x)$ continuous on an interval (a, b) which failed to have a derivative at each point of the interval. It was also pointed out at the beginning of this chapter that if the function $f(x)$ is defined on a set A, the derivates exist at all of A except possibly a denumerable set. This about covers the information so far obtained and, with the exception of the existence of the derived numbers, it is concerned with specialized functions. There are many other questions of interest, even for specialized functions. For example, it was shown that at a certain denumerable everywhere dense set the Weierstrass function had a right derivative equal to ∞ and a left derivative equal to $-\infty$. Could this happen at a more than denumerable set? If for any function ${}_AD^+f$ is finite, can ${}_AD_-f$ be infinite? What can be said of the set at which ${}_AD^+f = -\infty$? These and other questions will be answered by considering functions $f(x)$ defined on sets A. We prove

THEOREM 7.2. *If $f(x)$ is defined and finite on the set A then the set $B \subset A$ at the points of which one or both of the relations ${}_AD_-f > {}_AD^+f$, ${}_AD_+f > {}_AD^-f$ hold is at most denumerable. The set $E \subset A$ at which the right-hand and left-hand derivatives over A exist and are different is denumerable.*

It is sufficient to consider the first relation, ${}_AD_-f > {}_AD^+f$. Let h, k be two rational numbers, $h < k$. For n a positive integer let E_{hkn} be the points of E for which

$$\text{(a)}\ \frac{f(\xi) - f(x)}{\xi - x} < h, \quad \text{(b)}\ \frac{f(\xi') - f(x)}{\xi' - x} > k,$$

$\xi - x$, $x - \xi' < 1/n$. There is then no point of E_{hkn} other than x on the interval $(x - 1/n, x + 1/n)$. For suppose $x_1 < x$ is such a point. Replacing ξ by x and x by x_1 in (a), and replacing ξ' by x_1 in (b) there is obtained

$$\frac{f(x) - f(x_1)}{x - x_1} < h, \quad \frac{f(x_1) - f(x)}{x_1 - x} > k.$$

Since $h < k$ these two relations are inconsistent. If x_1 is taken greater than x similar relations result. It then follows that the points of E_{hkn} are isolated, and consequently denumerable. Furthermore, every point for which ${}_AD_-f > {}_AD^+f$ is in some E_{hkn}. But the set of triples (h, k, n) is denumerable by Note 0.1. We conclude, therefore, that the set $E({}_AD_-f > {}_AD^+f$ is denumerable, which is the first part of the theorem.

To prove the second part of the theorem let f'_-, f'_+, be respectively the left and right derivatives at the point x, and let $E = E(f'_- < f'_+)$. If $r_1, r_2, \ldots$ is the set of rational numbers there is a smallest integer k for which

$$f'_- < r_k < f'_+,$$

a smallest integer m for which

$$\frac{f(\xi) - f(x)}{\xi - x} < r_m,\ r_m < \xi < x,\ \xi \in A,$$

and a smallest integer n for which

$$\frac{f(\xi) - f(x)}{\xi - x} > r_k, x < \xi < r_n, \xi \in A.$$

For every number x there is a unique triad. For if x_1, x_2, $x_1 < x_2$, have the same triad, $\xi = x_1$, $x = x_2$ in the first relation gives

$$f(x_1) - f(x_2) > (x_1 - x_2)r_k,$$

while $\xi = x_2$, $x = x_1$ in the second relation gives

$$f(x_2) - f(x_1) > (x_2 - x_1)r_k,$$

and these relations are obviously inconsistent. We conclude, therefore, that to each $x \in E$ there corresponds a unique triad of rational numbers. By Note 0.1 the triads of rational numbers are denumerable, and it follows that the set E is denumerable, which is the second part of the theorem.

NOTE 7.1. The first question raised in the introduction to this section can now be answered. Is there more than a denumerable set at the points of which the Weierstrass function has $f'_- = -\infty$, $f'_+ = \infty$? It follows from the theorem just proved that this set is at most denumerable.

THEOREM 7.3. *Let the function $f(x)$ be finite at each point of the set A. At the points of a set $A' \subset A$ let ${}_AD^+f < \infty$. Then at all of A', with the possible exception of a null set, ${}_AD^+f$, ${}_AD_-f$ are finite and equal.*

Let $M_1 < M_2 < \ldots$ be a sequence of positive numbers with $M_n \to \infty$. Let $E = E(|f| < M_n)$. Then $E_n \supset E_{n-1}$ and, since f is finite at each point of A, $E_1 + E_2 + \ldots$ is the set A. It then follows from Theorem 2.18 that $|E_n|^\circ \to |A|^\circ$. Again let E_{nk} be the points of A' for which

$$\frac{f(x + h) - f(x)}{h} < M_n, 0 < h < 1/k, \ x + h \in A.$$

Then $E_{nk} \supset E_{n-1,\ k-1}$ and $\sum E_{nk} = A'$. Consequently it follows from Theorem 2.18 that $|E_{nk}|^\circ \to |A'|^\circ$ as n, $k \to \infty$. These considerations permit us to assert that if $\epsilon > 0$ is given, and then $M > 0$ and $\delta > 0$ are fixed with M sufficiently great and δ sufficiently close to zero, the set $A_1 \subset A'$ for which

$$(7.3) \qquad |f(x)| < M, \frac{f(x+h) - f(x)}{h} < M, 0 < h < \delta,$$

is such that

$$(7.4) \qquad |A_1|^\circ > |A'|^\circ - \epsilon.$$

Let (c, d) be an interval containing points of A_1 with $d - c < \delta$, c and d points of A_1. For $c \le x \le d$ let $x_0 = c < x_1 < x_2 \ldots < x_n = x$ be a subdivision of $[c, x]$, with x_i points of A_1. Let $P(x)$ be the supremum of the positive terms in the sum $\sum[f(x_i) - f(x_{i-1})]$ for all possible such subdivisions of the interval $[c, x]$. From (7.3) it follows that $0 \le P(x) \le \delta M$. Let $N(x)$ be the lower bound of the sums of the negative terms of $\sum[f(x_i) - f(x_{i-1})]$. Then since

$$f(x) - f(c) = P(x) + N(x),$$

with $|f(x)| < M$ and $P(x) < \delta M$ on $A_1[c, d]$ it follows that $N(x)$ is bounded on $A_1[c, d]$ and consequently $f(x)$ is of bounded variation on the part of A_1 on $[c, d]$. It then follows from Theorem 5.14 that ${}_{A_1}Df$ exists and is finite at almost all of A_1. We now show that at all of A_1, except for at most a null set,

$${}_AD^+f = {}_{A_1}Df = {}_AD_-f.$$

Let A_2 be the points of density of A_1 at which ${}_{A_1}Df$ exists and is finite. By Theorem 5.2 and what we have just proved, A_2 contains all of A_1 except a null set.

Suppose for $x \in A_2$, ${}_AD^+f > {}_{A_1}Df + \eta$, $\eta > 0$. Then for a sequence $\xi_1, \xi_2, \ldots, \xi_n > x$, and $\xi_n \to x$,

$$(7.5) \qquad \frac{f(\xi_n) - f(x)}{\xi_n - x} > {}_{A_1}Df + \eta.$$

At x the density of A_1 is unity. Hence for n fixed in (7.5) and ξ_n sufficiently close to x

$$(7.6) \qquad \frac{f(\xi) - f(x)}{\xi - x} < {}_{A_1}Df + \eta', 0 < \eta' < \eta,$$

$\xi \in A_1$, $\xi < \xi_n$, $\xi_n - \xi = t(\xi_n - x)$. The point ξ is any point of A_1 on (x, ξ_n), and the density of A_1 at x is unity. Hence if ξ_n is first chosen sufficiently close to x, ξ can then be found sufficiently close to ξ_n that t is arbitrarily small. Relations (7.5) and (7.6) now give

$$f(\xi_n) - f(x) > (\xi_n - x)\ {}_{A_1}Df + \eta(\xi_n - x),$$
$$f(\xi) - f(x) < (\xi - x)\ {}_{A_1}Df + \eta'(\xi - x).$$

Subtracting the second from the first gives,

$$\begin{aligned} f(\xi_n) - f(\xi) & \\ &> (\xi_n - x - \xi + x)\ {}_{A_1}Df + \eta(\xi_n - x) - \eta'(\xi - x) \\ &= (\xi_n - \xi)\ {}_{A_1}Df + (\xi_n - x)\left[\eta - \frac{\xi - x}{\xi_n - x}\eta'\right], \end{aligned}$$

$$\frac{f(\xi_n) - f(\xi)}{\xi_n - \xi} > {}_{A_1}Df + \frac{\xi_n - x}{\xi_n - \xi}\left[\eta - \frac{\xi - x}{\xi_n - x}\eta'\right], \tag{7.7}$$

for ξ any point of A_1 on (x, ξ_n). Since $x < \xi < \xi_n$ it follows that $(\xi - x)/(\xi_n - x) < 1$. Also, from (7.5), $(\xi_n - x)/(\xi_n - \xi) = 1/t$. The point ξ can be any point of A_1 on the (x, ξ_n) and, as explained above, if ξ_n is first chosen sufficiently close to x, $\xi \in A_1$ can be found sufficiently close to ξ_n to make $1/t$ arbitrarily great. Hence $\xi \in A$ can be found so that (7.7) contradicts the second part of (7.3). We conclude, therefore, that at points of A_2, ${}_AD^+f$ is not greater than ${}_{A_1}Df$. Obviously ${}_AD^+f$ cannot be less than ${}_{A_1}Df$. Hence at points of A_2, ${}_AD^+f = {}_{A_1}Df$, and in a similar way it can be shown that at points of A_2, ${}_AD_-f = {}_{A_1}Df$. The set A_2 contains all of A_1 except a null set and $A_2 \subset A$. It therefore follows that at all of A_1 except a null set

$${}_AD^+f = {}_AD_-f. \tag{7.8}$$

In relation (7.4) ϵ is arbitrary. Hence there is a set $A'' \subset A'$ with $|A''|^\circ = |A'|^\circ$ for which (7.8) holds. Nevertheless relations $A'' \subset A'$, $|A''|^\circ = |A'|^\circ$ do not insure that A'' is all of A except a null set. Let A''' be the part of A' for which (7.8) does not hold. The points of A''' satisfy the conditions of the theorem, and if $|A'''|^\circ > 0$ it contains a part with metric greater than zero at which (7.8) does hold. This contradicts the definition of A''', and the proof of the theorem is complete.

THEOREM 7.4. *Let the function $f(x)$ be finite at each point of a set A. Then at almost all of A, ${}_AD^+f > -\infty$.*

If at the points of $A' \subset A$ with $|A'|^\circ > 0$ the relation ${}_AD^+f = -\infty$ holds, then for this set A' the conditions of

Theorem 7.3 hold, and consequently there is a part A'' of A' with $|A''|^\circ = |A'|^\circ$ at which ${}_AD^+f$ is finite which contradicts the supposition that at all of A', ${}_AD^+f = -\infty$. Hence the theorem.

If in Theorem 7.3 the condition ${}_AD_-f > -\infty$ at the points of A' replaces ${}_AD^+f < \infty$ the same conclusion is reached in a similar way. Likewise the supposition ${}_AD^-f < \infty$ leads to ${}_AD^-f$, ${}_AD_+f$ finite and equal, and ${}_AD_+f > -\infty$ leads to ${}_AD_+f$, ${}_AD^-f$ finite and equal, both relations holding at almost all points of A'. We thus have

THEOREM 7.5. *Let the function $f(x)$ be defined and finite at the points of a set A. Then for at most a null part of A*

$${}_AD^+f = -\infty,\ {}_AD_+f = \infty;\ {}_AD^-f = -\infty,\ {}_AD_-f = \infty.$$

Furthermore, except for at most a null set, the points of A are in one of the four sets:

A_1: *${}_ADf$ exists and is finite.*

A_2: *${}_AD^+f$, ${}_AD_-f$ are finite and equal;*
${}_AD_+f = -\infty$, ${}_AD^-f = \infty$

A_3: *${}_AD_+f$, ${}_AD^-f$ are finite and equal;*
${}_AD^+f = \infty$, ${}_AD_-f = -\infty$

A_4: ${}_AD^+f = {}_AD^-f = \infty$, ${}_AD_+f = {}_AD_-f = -\infty$.

EXAMPLE 7.1. Let A be the non-measurable set of Section 2.7. From (v) of that example it follows that there are three different rational transformations A_1, A_2, A_3 of A, which are mutually exclusive and all on $(-1, 2)$. The method of Theorem 2.25 can be used to show that

$$|A_1|^\circ = |A_2|^\circ = |A_3|^\circ = |A|^\circ.$$

Now for a given $\epsilon > 0$ let $\alpha^i = \alpha_{i1} + \ldots + \alpha_{in_i}$ be such that

$$|A_1|^\circ - \epsilon < |A_1\alpha^i|^\circ < |A_1|^\circ + \epsilon, \quad i = 1, 2, 3.$$

The finite set of non-overlapping intervals in $\alpha^2 - \alpha^2\alpha^1$ can be subdivided into smaller intervals and some or all of these smaller intervals be carried by rational translations onto $\alpha^1 - \alpha^1\alpha^2$ in such a way that the translated intervals do not overlap, and such that if A'_2 is the translated part of A_2 then

$$|\alpha^1(A_2 + A'_2)|^\circ > |A_2|^\circ - 2\epsilon.$$

That this can be accomplished by rational translations follows from the fact that the rational numbers are everywhere dense. This property of the rational numbers, together with Section 2.7 (v), permits the translations to be carried out in such a way that $A_1A_2 = 0$. This process can be repeated with α^3 and A_3 replacing α^2 and A_2, and since there are only a finite number of intervals and operations involved in all the operations, it follows from Section 2.7 (v), that those involving A_3 can be carried out in such a way that A'_3 has no point in common with A_1 or with $A_2 + A'_2$. Since $|A_i|^\circ = |A|^\circ$, $i = 1, 2, 3$, we now have, $|A|^\circ - \epsilon < |\alpha^1 A_1|^\circ < |A|^\circ + \epsilon$, and

$$|A|^\circ - 2\epsilon < |\alpha'(A_i + A'_i)|^\circ < |\alpha'| < |A|^\circ + \epsilon, \quad i = 2, 3.$$

Since ϵ is arbitrary, and since the sets A_1, $A_2 + A'_2$, $A_3 + A'_3$ are mutually exclusive the theorems on the metric density of sets permit us to conclude that there exist three mutually exclusive sets E_1, E_2, E_3 with $|E_1|^\circ = |E_2|^\circ = |E_3|^\circ = \lambda > 0$, and such that at each point of any one of these sets the density of all three sets is unity. Let $E = E_1 + E_2 + E_3$ and let

$$f(x) = -1 \text{ on } E_1, f(x) = 0 \text{ on } E_2, f(x) = 1 \text{ on } E_3.$$

It is easily verified that the derived numbers of f are distributed as follows:

$$E_1\colon\ {}_ED_+f = {}_ED^-f = 0;\ {}_ED^+f = \infty,\ {}_ED_-f = -\infty.$$
$$E_2\colon\ {}_ED^+f = {}_ED^-f = \infty;\ {}_ED_+f = {}_ED_-f = -\infty.$$
$$E_3\colon\ {}_ED^+f = {}_ED_-f = 0;\ {}_ED^+f = -\infty,\ {}_ED^-f = \infty.$$

If now we take a single interval ω with $0 < |E\omega|^\circ < |E|^\circ$, let $f(x) = 0$ on $E\omega$, $f(x)$ defined as above on $E - E\omega$ we have a function for which all four sets of Theorem 7.5 exist other than null sets.

7.5. Approximate derived numbers over arbitrary sets. The definition of an approximate derivative for a function $f(x)$ defined on an interval (a, b) was given in Definition 6.5. We now enlarge that definition to include right and left approximate derivatives and upper and lower approximate derived numbers. Similar definitions and some of the following results may be found in [5, 11, 12].

DEFINITION 7.1. *Let $f(x)$ be defined on the set A. If for $x \in A$ the ratio*

$$\frac{f(\xi) - f(x)}{\xi - x}, \ \xi > x, \ \xi \in A$$

tends to a limit except for a set $\xi \subset A$ of zero density on the right at x then this limit is the approximate derivative over A on the right of $f(x)$ at the point x. The approximate derivative over A on the left is defined in a similar way. If the two are equal their common value is the approximate derivative of $f(x)$ over A at the point x, ${}_A\mathbf{D}f(x)$.

We note that if x is a point of density of A for which the right (left) approximate derivative exists and E_0 is the exceptional set, then if $E = A - E_0$ the point ξ may take on all values of E and E has unit density on the right (left) at x.

Consider the function $f(x)$ of Example 7.1. For this example the function $f(x)$ is defined on $A = E_1 + E_2 + E_3$, and at each point of A the density of all three sets is unity. Let x be a point of E_2. Then the ratio

$$\frac{f(\xi) - f(x)}{\xi - x}, \ \xi > x,$$

tends to $-\infty$, 0, ∞ according as ξ is on E_1, E_2 or E_3. If $\xi \in E_2$ the limit is zero, but the right density of the exceptional set $E_0 = E_1 + E_3$ is unity. Consequently zero does not qualify as an approximate derivative on the right. Neither do the numbers $-\infty$, ∞ for the same reason. Nevertheless in all three cases the limit is approached for ξ on a set of unit density on the right at x. These considerations lead us to state

DEFINITION 7.2. *Let $f(x)$ be defined on the set A. If for $x \in A$ the ratio*

$$\frac{f(\xi) - f(x)}{\xi - x}, \ \xi > x, \ \xi \in A,$$

tends to a limit for ξ on a set E with unit density on the right at x

then this limit is an approximate derived number on the right at x. There is a corresponding definition for an approximate derived number on the left. If the two are the same their common value is an approximate derived number of $f(x)$ at the point x, ${}_E\Lambda f(x)$, $E \subset A$.

For the function $f(x)$ of Example 7.1, if $x \in E_2$ there is an approximate derived number equal to zero. In this case the set E over which ξ may vary is the set E_2. If E consists of the points of E_1 to the left of x and the points of E_3 to the right of x then for $\xi \in E$ $[f(\xi) - f(x)]/(\xi - x) \to \infty$ as $\xi \to x$. The set E has density unity at x, and consequently f has an approximate derived number ${}_E\Lambda f = \infty$ at x. If $E = E_3$ the limit is ∞ on the right and $-\infty$ on the left.

It is now clear that the ratio $[f(\xi) - f(x)]/(\xi - x)$ can behave in many ways for ξ on sets of unit density at x. It serves no useful purpose to try to formulate definitions to cover all cases. We consider another example.

EXAMPLE 7.2. Let E_0 be an everywhere dense null set and let $A = (E_1 + E_2 + E_3) - E_0$ where E_1, E_2, E_3 are the sets of Example 7.1. Since E_0 is a null set it remains true that at every point of A the density of each of the sets E_1, E_2, E_3 is unity. For $x_0 \in AE_2$ let $f(x) = -(x - x_0)$ on E_1, 0 on E_2, $f(x) = (x - x_0)$ on E_3, $f(x) = 2(x - x_0)$ on E_0. It is evident that $f(x)$ has three finite approximate derived numbers $-1, 0, 1$ at x_0. Let $E \subset A$ be any set with $EE_0 = 0$. Then if $x_0 \in E_2$

$$\limsup_{\xi \to x_0} \frac{f(\xi) - f(x_0)}{\xi - x_0} \leq 1, \quad \xi \in E.$$

It can, therefore, be said that this limit exists, $\xi \in A$, except for a set ξ of zero density at x_0 The exceptional set is E_0. Furthermore for a set ξ of unit density at x_0,

$$\lim_{\xi \to x_0} \frac{f(\xi) - f(x_0)}{\xi - x_0} = 1$$

at x. This set of unit density is the set E_3.

It was a study of an example similar to this which gave rise to the following definition [35].

Let $f(x)$ be defined on the set A. If there exists a real number a such that

$$\limsup_{\xi \to x} \frac{f(\xi) - f(x)}{\xi - x} \leq a, \ \xi > x, \ \xi \in A,$$

except for a set ξ of right density zero at x, and if

$$\lim_{\xi \to x} \frac{f(\xi) - f(x)}{\xi - x} = a, \quad \xi > x,$$

for a set $\xi \subset A$ of unity density on the right at x, then this number a is the upper approximate derived number on the right of $f(x)$ at the point x, ${}_A\mathbf{D}^+f$.

It was remarked by S. Saks [60] that this definition was not clear to him. While there are reasons why it is an undesirable definition, it is difficult to see what there is about it that is not clear. One objection to it is that it does not cover the case for which the second limit holds, not for a set of unit density at x, but for a set of density λ where $0 < \lambda < 1$. A more concise and inclusive definition is

DEFINITION 7.3. *Let $f(x)$ be defined on the set A. The upper right approximate derived number of $f(x)$ at the point x over the set A, ${}_A\mathbf{D}^+f$, is the supremum of real numbers a for which*

$$\frac{f(\xi) - f(x)}{\xi - x} \geq a, \ \xi > x, \quad \xi \in A,$$

for a set ξ of right density greater than zero at x. There are corresponding definitions for the other approximate derived numbers ${}_A\mathbf{D}_+f$, ${}_A\mathbf{D}^-f$, ${}_A\mathbf{D}_-f$.

In our study of approximate derived numbers we shall use the following definition and theorems.

DEFINITION 7.4. *The function $f(x)$ defined on the set A is metrically separable relatively to A if for every real number a the sets $E^a = E(f < a)$, $E^a = E(f \geq a)$ are metrically separated according to Definition 2.5.*

THEOREM 7.6. *If the function $f(x)$ defined on the set A is metrically separable relatively to A then at almost all points of A the function $f(x)$ is approximately continuous over A according to Definition 5.4.*

Let $(a_{n,\,i-1}, a_{ni})$ be a sequence of subdivisions of the range $(-\infty, \infty)$ where $a_{ni} - a_{n,\,i-1} \to 0$ as $n \to \infty$, and let $e_{ni} = E(a_{n,\,i-1} \leq f < a_{ni})$. Since f is metrically separable relatively to A the sets e_{ni}, e_{nj}, $i \neq j$ are metrically separated. Hence if for n and i fixed there are excluded from e_{ni} the points which are not points of density of e_{ni}, and the points at which the density of e_{nj} is not zero for all j except $j = i$, there is excluded at most a null set. This follows from Theorems 5.2 and 5.3. If e'_{ni} is the set that remains then $\sum_i e'_{ni}$ contains almost all of A. Let A' be the part of A that remains when this exclusion process has been carried out for all values of n. Then, since at most a null set was excluded for each value of n it follows, since the sum of a denumerable set of null sets is a null set, that A' contains almost all of A. Now let $\epsilon > 0$ be given. Fix n so that $a_{ni} - a_{n,\,i-1} < \epsilon$. Let x be a point of A'. Then for some i the point x is in the set e'_{ni} and consequently $|f(\xi) - f(x)| \leq a_{ni} - a_{n,\,i-1} < \epsilon$ for $\xi \in e'_{ni}$. But at x the density of e'_{ni} is unity and the density of e_{nj}, $i \neq j$ is zero. Hence $f(x)$ is approximately continuous over A at all points $x \in A'$ according to Definition 5.4.

THEOREM 7.7. *Let the function $f(x)$ be defined on the set A. If ${}_AD^+f < \infty$ at the points of a set $A' \subset A$ then the function $f(x)$ is metrically separable relatively to the set A'.*

For a real, let E^a, E_a be the points of A' for which $f < a$, $f \geq a$ respectively. Suppose E^a and E_a are not metrically separated Let $d_1 < d_2 \ldots$ be a sequence of positive numbers with $d_n \to a$ and let E_n be the part of A for which $f < a - d_n$. Then $E_n \supset E_{n-1}$, and it follows from Theorem 2.18 that $|E_n|^\circ \to |E^a|^\circ$. Consequently for n sufficiently great E_n and E_a are not metrically separated. There are then points x in E_n at which the density of E_a is unity, and for such a point $f(x) < a - d_n$. Consequently if $\xi \in E_a$, $f(\xi) - f(x) > d_n$. Hence if a' is arbitrarily great,

$$\frac{f(\xi) - f(x)}{\xi - x} > a', \quad \xi \in E_a,$$

for a set ξ of unit density at x. It follows from this and

Definition 7.3 that at this point $x \in A'$, ${}_AD^+f = \infty$, which is a contradiction. We conclude, therefore, that f is metrically separable relative to A'.

THEOREM 7.8. *Let $f(x)$ be defined on the set A and at the points of a set $A' \subset A$ let a finite approximate derived number ${}_E\Lambda f$, $E \subset A'$, exist. If ${}_A\mathbf{D}^+f < \infty$ at the points of A' then*

$$ {}_A\mathbf{D}^+f = {}_E\Lambda f = {}_A\mathbf{D}_-f $$

at all points of the set A'. If in addition $f(x)$ is metrically separable relative to A then at all points $x \in A$, ${}_A\mathbf{D}^+f = {}_A\mathbf{D}_+f$.

Let $\eta > 0$ be given. If ${}_A\mathbf{D}^+f > {}_E\Lambda f + \eta$ at a point $x \in A'$ then the set ξ for which

$$ \frac{f(\xi) - f(x)}{\xi - x} > {}_E\Lambda f + \eta,\ \xi > x,\ \xi \in A \tag{7.9} $$

is such that $|\xi(x, x + h)|^\circ > \lambda h$ for some number λ with $0 < \lambda < 1$, $0 < h < \delta$, provided δ is sufficiently small. Furthermore, since ${}_E\Lambda f$ exists at the point x, for $0 < \eta' < \eta$,

$$ \frac{f(\xi') - f(x)}{\xi' - x} < {}_E\Lambda f + \eta',\ \xi' > x,\ \xi' \in A', \tag{7.10} $$

and $|\xi'(x, x + h)|^\circ > (1 - \lambda)h$, $0 < h < \delta' < \delta$, provided δ' is sufficiently small. Then for $0 < h < \delta'$ the sets ξ and ξ' are not metrically separated on the interval $(x, x + h)$. Consequently there is a point ξ'_1, of the set ξ' at which the right-hand density of ξ is unity. Using ξ'_1 in (7.10) and subtracting (7.9) with $\xi > \xi'_1$ we get

$$ f(\xi) - f(\xi'_1) > (\xi - \xi'_1)\,{}_E\Lambda f + \eta(\xi - x) - \eta'(\xi'_1 - x). $$

$$ \frac{f(\xi) - f(\xi'_1)}{\xi - \xi'_1} > {}_E\Lambda f + \frac{\xi - x}{\xi - \xi'_1}\left[\eta - \eta'\frac{\xi'_1 - x}{\xi - x}\right]. $$

As $\xi \to \xi'_1$ the ratio $(\xi'_1 - x)/(\xi - x) \to 1$, and since for $\xi > \xi'_1$, $\xi - x > \xi'_1 - x > 0$, the ratio $(\xi - x)/(\xi - \xi'_1) \to \infty$. Then, since $\eta' < \eta$ and since at ξ'_1 the density on the right of the set ξ is unity, it follows that ${}_A\mathbf{D}^+f = \infty$ at the point $\xi'_1 \in A'$. This is a contradiction and, since ϵ is arbitrary, we conclude that at all points of A' the relation ${}_A\mathbf{D}^+f \leq {}_E\Lambda f$ holds. But it is obvious that ${}_A\mathbf{D}^+f \geq {}_E\Lambda f$ at all points of A', and consequently it follows that at all points of this set ${}_A\mathbf{D}^+f = {}_E\Lambda f$.

To show that ${}_A\mathbf{D}_-f = {}_E\Lambda f$ at points of A' let $\eta > 0$ be given, and suppose that for $x \in A'$. If $\delta > 0$ is sufficiently small there is a number λ for which

$$\frac{f(\xi) - f(x)}{\xi - x} < {}_E\Lambda f - \eta, \quad \xi < x, \ \xi \in A, \tag{7.11}$$

for a set ξ with $|\xi(x - h, x)|^\circ > \lambda h$, $0 < h < \delta$, $0 < \lambda < 1$. Since $x \in A'$, if $\delta' < \delta$ is sufficiently small and $\eta' < \eta$, then

$$\frac{f(\xi') - f(x)}{\xi' - x} > {}_E\Lambda f - \eta', \ \xi' < x, \ \xi' \in A', \tag{7.12}$$

and $|\xi'(x - h, x)|^\circ > (1 - \lambda)h$, $0 < h < \delta'$. It then follows that for $0 < h < \delta'$ the sets ξ and ξ' are not metrically separated on the interval $(x - h, x)$. There is then a point $\xi'_1 \in A'$ which satisfies (7.12) and at which the right density of the set ξ satisfying (7.11) is unity. Noting that both $\xi - x$ and $\xi'_1 - x$ are negative, the foregoing relations give

$$f(\xi) - f(x) > (\xi - x)\, {}_E\Lambda f - (\xi - x)\eta,$$
$$f(\xi'_1) - f(x) < (\xi'_1 - x)\, {}_E\Lambda f - (\xi'_1 - x)\eta'.$$

Keeping $\xi > \xi'_1$ and subtracting the second of these from the first we get

$$f(\xi) - f(\xi'_1) > (\xi - \xi'_1)\, {}_E\Lambda f - (\xi - x)\eta - (\xi'_1 - x)\eta',$$
$$\frac{f(\xi) - f(\xi'_1)}{\xi - \xi'_1} > {}_E\Lambda f + \frac{x - \xi}{\xi - \xi'_1}\left[\eta - \eta'\frac{x - \xi'_1}{x - \xi}\right].$$

As in the previous case, since the right density of ξ at the point $\xi'_1 \in A'$ is unity this leads to ${}_A\mathbf{D}^+f = \infty$ at ξ'_1, which is a contradiction. Hence, since η is arbitrary, ${}_A\mathbf{D}_-f \geq {}_E\Lambda f$ and since it is obvious that the relation $>$ cannot hold we conclude that ${}_A\mathbf{D}_-f = {}_E\Lambda f$ at all points of the set A'. The proof of the first part of the theorem is now complete.

For the second part of the theorem the function $f(x)$ is metrically separable relatively to the set A. We begin by supposing that at a point $x \in A'$ the relation ${}_A\mathbf{D}_+f < {}_E\Lambda f - \eta$ holds where $\eta > 0$ is arbitrary. We then have, as in the previous cases, for $0 < \eta' < \eta$,

(7.13) $f(\xi) - f(x) < (\xi - x)\,{}_E\Lambda f - \eta(\xi - x),\ \xi > x,\ \xi \in A,$

(7.14) $f(\xi') - f(x) > (\xi' - x)\,{}_E\Lambda f - \eta'(\xi' - x),\ \xi' > x,\ \xi' \in A',$

(7.15) $|\xi(x, x + h)|^\circ > \lambda h,\quad |\xi'(x, x + h)|^\circ > (1 - \lambda)h,$

where $0 < \lambda < 1$, $0 < h < \delta$, provided δ is sufficiently small. It follows from (7.15) that the set e over which ξ varies in (7.13) is not metrically separated on the interva' $(x, x + h)$ from the set e' over which ξ' varies in (7.14). Consequently there is a point $c \in e \subset A$ with $x < c < x + h$ at which the right density of the set $e \subset A$ is unity, and which is a point of density of e'. If a point d is fixed with $c < d < x + h$, and $d - c$ sufficiently small it then follows, since $c - x > 0$ and $\eta' < \eta$, that for ξ' on $e'(c, d)$ the lower bound M of the right side of (7.14) is greater than the upper bound m of the right side of (7.13) when ξ is on $e(c, d)$. We then have

$$f(\xi') > f(x) + M,\ f(\xi) < f(x) + m,$$

$M > m$, ξ' on $e'(c, d)$, ξ on $e(c, d)$ and, since at c the density of both e and e' is unity, the sets $e'(c, d)$ and $e(c, d)$ are not metrically separated. It follows from these considerations, since $e' \subset A$, $e \subset A$, that f is not metrically separated relative to A. This is a contradiction and since η is arbitrary we conclude that ${}_A\mathbf{D}^+ f \geq {}_E\Lambda f$. It is obvious that the relation $>$ cannot hold, and we conclude that at points $x \in A'$ the relation ${}_A\mathbf{D}_+ f = {}_E\Lambda f = {}_A\mathbf{D}^+ f$ holds. This completes the proof of the theorem.

At first glance it is surprising that we have been able to obtain Theorem 7.8 for *all* points of the set A'. There is however a tacit assumption on the set A' which makes this possible. When it is assumed that at each point of A' a finite approximate derived number *over* A' exists it is implied that every point of A' is a point of density of this set. This means that at every point $x \in A'$ the density of A' on both the right and left is unity at x. Again it is natural to ask if it is not sufficient to assume that at every point of A' there is a finite approximate derived number over A? The answer is no, for then it could not be asserted that the points ξ' of (7.11) and (7.13) were points of A', and this is essential to the proofs, for the point ξ'_1 which comes from this set ξ' must belong to A'. With these considerations in mind we can state,

THEOREM 7.9. *Let $f(x)$ be defined on the set A. If there is a set $A' \subset A$ at the points of which there are two finite approximate derived numbers over A', then ${}_A\mathrm{D}^+f = \infty$ at every point of the set A'.*

For otherwise the method of Theorem 7.8 could be used to show that ${}_A\mathrm{D}^+f$ is equal to each of the two different approximate derived numbers over A'.

In the two preceding theorems it is assumed that a finite approximate derived number over the set A' exists. It will next be shown that if ${}_A\mathrm{D}^+f < \infty$ at the points of A' then a finite approximate derived number over the set A' does indeed exist at almost all points of A'. This we state as

THEOREM 7.10. *Let $f(x)$ be defined on the set A. At each point of $A' \subset A$ let ${}_A\mathrm{D}^+f < \infty$. Then at almost all points of A' there exists a finite approximate derived number, ${}_E\Lambda f$, $E \subset A'$.*

If ${}_A\mathrm{D}^+f < M$ at a point x, then if $0 < \lambda < 1$

$$\frac{f(\xi) - f(x)}{\xi - x} < M, \ \xi > x, \ \ \xi \in A$$

except for a set ξ with $|\xi(x, x + h)|^\circ < \lambda h$ provided $h > 0$ is sufficiently small. Let positive numbers M, δ, $\lambda < 1/4$, and ϵ be given. Let A_1 be the part of A' for which

$$\frac{f(\xi) - f(x)}{\xi - x} < M, \ \xi > x, \ \ \xi \in A, \tag{7.16}$$

except for a set ξ with $|\xi(x, x + h)|^\circ < \lambda h$ when $0 < h < \delta$. If M is sufficiently great and δ sufficiently small it follows from Theorem 2.18, as in the proof of Theorem 7.3, that

$$|A_1|^\circ > |A'|^\circ - \epsilon.$$

By Theorems 7.7 and 7.6 the function f is approximately continuous over A' at almost all points of A'. Using this and Theorem 5.2, the existence of a set $A_2 \subset A_1$ can be asserted with

$$|A_2|^\circ > |A_1|^\circ - \epsilon > |A'|^\circ - 2\epsilon,$$

and for which

(a) $x \in A_2$, f is approximately continuous at x over A'.

(b) $x \in A_2$ is a point of density of A_1.

(c) There exists $\delta' < \delta$ such that if $x \in A_2$ and $0 < h < \delta'$ then $|A_1(x - h, x)|^\circ > (1 - \lambda)h$, $\lambda < 1/4$ as in (7.16).

Now set $f_1(x) = f(x) - Mx$. It follows from (7.15) that

$$(7.17) \qquad \frac{f_1(\xi) - f_1(x)}{\xi - x} < 0, \quad \xi > x,\ \xi \in A,\ x \in A_1$$

except for a set ξ with $|\xi(x, x + h)|^\circ < \lambda h$ if $0 < h < \delta$. Let (c, d) be an interval containing points of A_2 with $d - c < \delta' < \delta$. For x on (c, d) let $\varphi(x)$ be the infimum of $f_1(\xi)$ for $\xi \in A_2(c, x)$. Obviously for x a point of A_2, $\varphi(x) \leq f_1(x)$. We shall show that for $x \in A_2$, $\varphi(x)$ cannot be less than $f_1(x)$. For suppose that $\varphi(x) = f_1(x) - \eta$, $\eta > 0$, $x \in A_2$. There is then $\xi_0 \in A_2(c, x]$ with

$$(7.18) \qquad f_1(\xi_0) < f_1(x) - \eta/2.$$

Since $\xi_0 \in A_2 \subset A_1$ relation (7.17) is satisfied with ξ_0 replacing x which gives

$$(7.19) \qquad \frac{f_1(\xi) - f_1(\xi_0)}{\xi - \xi_0} < 0, \quad \xi > \xi_0,\ \xi \in A$$

except for a set ξ with $|\xi(\xi_0, x)|^\circ < \lambda(x - \xi_0)$, for the reason that $|x - \xi_0| < \delta$. Since $x - \xi_0 < \delta'$ it follows from (c) that $|A_1(\xi_0, x)|^\circ > (1 - \lambda)(x - \xi_0)$. Hence there is a set $\xi \subset A_1$ with $|\xi(\xi_0, x)|^\circ > (1 - 2\lambda)(x - \xi_0)$ for which (7.19) holds, hence for which

$$(7.20) \qquad f_1(\xi) < f_1(\xi_0) < f_1(x) - \eta/2, \quad \xi \in A_1,$$

$|\xi(\xi_0, x)|^\circ > (1 - 2\lambda)(x - \xi_0) > (x - \xi_0)/2$. It is then possible to choose a point $\xi_1 \subset A_1$ satisfying (7.20) with $x - \xi_1 < (x - \xi_0)/2$. This point ξ_1 can replace x in (7.17) to give

$$(7.21) \qquad \frac{f(\xi) - f(\xi_1)}{\xi - \xi_1} < 0, \quad \xi > \xi_1,\ \xi \in A,$$

except for a set ξ with $|\xi(\xi_1, x)|^\circ < \lambda(x - \xi_1)$. Again it follows from (c) and (7.21) that there is a set $\xi \subset A_1$ with $|\xi(\xi_1, x)|^\circ > (x - \xi_1)/2 > (x - \xi_0)/4$ for which

$$(7.22) \qquad f_1(\xi) < f_1(\xi_1) < f_1(x) - \eta/2,$$

$\xi \in A_1$, $|\xi(\xi_1, x)|^\circ > (x - \xi_1)/2 > (x - \xi_0)/4$. There is then a point $\xi_2 \in A_1$ satisfying (7.22) with $x - \xi_2 < (x - \xi_1)/2 < (x - \xi_0)/2^2$. This point ξ_2 can now replace x in (7.17) to give

$$\frac{f_1(\xi) - f_1(\xi_2)}{\xi - \xi_2} < 0, \quad \xi > \xi_2, \ \xi \in A, \tag{7.23}$$

except for a set ξ with $|\xi(\xi_2, x)|^\circ < \lambda(x - \xi_2)$, and it again follows from (c) and (7.23) that there is a set $\xi \subset A_1$ with

$$f_1(\xi) < f_1(\xi_2) < f_1(x) - \eta/2, \ \xi \in A_1, \tag{7.24}$$

$|\xi(\xi_2, x)|^\circ > (x - \xi_2)/2 > (x - \xi_0)/2^3$. This reasoning can be continued to give a sequence $\xi_0, \xi_1, \ldots$ with $x - \xi_n < (x - \xi_0)/2^{n+1}$, and with

$$f(\xi) < f(\xi_n) < f_1(x) - \eta/2, \quad \xi \in A_1,$$

$|\xi(\xi_n, x)|^\circ > (x - \xi_n)/2$. Then since $A_1 \subset A$ this contradicts (a) which says that x is a point of approximate continuity of f, and consequently of f_1, over A. We can now conclude that $\varphi(x) = f_1(x)$, $x \in A_2(c, d)$.

The function φ is non-increasing on A_2, and the same is therefore true of f_1. It then follows from Theorem 5.14 that ${}_{A_2}Df_1$ exists at almost all points of A_2 and is finite. Then, since f_1 differs from f by a linear function, the same is true of f and, since almost all points of A_2 are points of density of A_2, it follows that at almost all points of A_2 an approximate derived number ${}_E\Lambda f = {}_{A_2}Df$, $E \subset A'$, exists and is finite.

We have $|A_2|^\circ > |A'|^\circ - 2\epsilon$ and since ϵ is arbitrary it follows that there is a set $A'' \subset A'$ with $|A''|^\circ = |A'|^\circ$ at which f has a finite approximate derived number ${}_E\Lambda f$, $E \subset A'$. The fact that $|A''|^\circ = |A'|^\circ$ does not insure that A'' contains almost all of A'. However, if there is a set $A''' \subset A'$ with $|A'''|^\circ > 0$ at which no finite approximate derived number exists, the set A''' satisfies the conditions of the theorem we are proving. Hence there is a part of A''' with metric equal to that of A''' at which a finite approximate derived number does exist. But this is inconsistent with the definition of the set A'''. We conclude, therefore, that the set at which a finite approximate derived number ${}_E\Lambda f$, $E \subset A'$, exists contains almost all of A'. This completes the proof of the theorem.

If in Theorem 7.8 the assumption ${}_AD^+f < \infty$ is replaced by the assumption ${}_AD_-f > -\infty$ it may be shown in a way similar to that used in the proof of Theorem 7.8 that ${}_A\mathbf{D}_-f = {}_A\mathbf{D}^+f$ and if f is metrically separable relative to A then ${}_AD_-f = {}_AD^-f$, these results holding at all points of the set A'. The assumption that ${}_AD^-f < \infty$, or ${}_AD_+f > -\infty$ leads to the corresponding results. These considerations give

THEOREM 7.11. *Let the function $f(x)$ be defined on A and be metrically separable relatively to A. If at the points of a set $A' \subset A$ there exists a finite approximate derived number ${}_E\Lambda f$, $E \in A'$, and if at the points of the set A' one of the upper or lower approximate derived numbers is finite, then the function $f(x)$ has a finite approximate derivative over A, ${}_A\mathbf{D}f$, at all points of the set A'.*

From Theorems 7.8, 7.9, 7.10 and 7.11 there follows

THEOREM 7.12. *Let the function $f(x)$ be defined on the set A, and at the points of a set $A' \subset A$ let ${}_A\mathbf{D}^+f < \infty$. Then ${}_A\mathbf{D}^+f = {}_A\mathbf{D}_-f$ at almost all points of the set A', and at almost all points of the set A', a finite approximate derivative over A', ${}_{A'}\mathbf{D}f$ exists. There are corresponding results if one of the other three extreme derived numbers is assumed to be finite.*

There also follow from Theorems 7.8—7.11

THEOREM 7.13. *Let $f(x)$ be defined on the set A. Then, except for at most a null set, the points of A fall into one or the other of the sets:*

E_1: *A finite approximate derivative ${}_A\mathbf{D}f$ exists.*

E_2: ${}_A\mathbf{D}^+f$, ${}_A\mathbf{D}_-f$ *are finite and equal,* ${}_A\mathbf{D}^-f = \infty$, ${}_A\mathbf{D}_+f = -\infty$.

E_3: ${}_A\mathbf{D}_+f$, ${}_A\mathbf{D}^-f$ *are finite and equal,* ${}_A\mathbf{D}^+f = \infty$, ${}_A\mathbf{D}_-f = -\infty$.

E_4: ${}_A\mathbf{D}^+f = {}_A\mathbf{D}^-f = \infty$, ${}_A\mathbf{D}_+f = {}_A\mathbf{D}_-f = -\infty$.

The function $f(x)$ is metrically separable relatively to the sets E_i, $i = 1, 2, 3$. At all points of the set E_i, $i = 2, 3$, except at most a null set, ${}_{A_i}\mathbf{D}f$ exists, is finite, and is equal to the common value of the finite extreme approximate derived numbers over A.

THEOREM 7.14. *Let $f(x)$ be defined on the set A and be*

metrically separable relative to A. Then all points of A, except possibly a null set, fall into one or the other of the sets:

E_1: *A finite approximate derivative $_A\mathbf{D}f$ exists.*

E_2: $_A\mathbf{D}^+f = {_A\mathbf{D}^-f} = \infty$; $_A\mathbf{D}_+f = {_A\mathbf{D}_-f} = -\infty$.

7.6. Approximate derived numbers of measurable functions, and relations between arbitrary functions and measurable functions.

THEOREM 7.15. *Let the function $f(x)$ be measurable on the measurable set A. Then all points of A, with the possible exception of a null set, fall into one or other of the sets*

E_1: A finite approximate derivative $_A\mathbf{D}f$ exists.

E_2: $_A\mathbf{D}^+f = {_A\mathbf{D}^-f} = \infty$; $_A\mathbf{D}_+f = {_A\mathbf{D}_-f} = -\infty$.

If the function f is measurable on A it is metrically separable relative to A and the theorem follows from Theorem 7.14.

Theorem 7.15 was proved by Burkill and Haslam-Jones [11] by considering only measurable functions. Theorem 7.14 then follows from Burkill's theorem by means of the following

THEOREM 7.16. *Let the function $f(x)$ be defined on the set A and be metrically separable relative to A. There is then a measurable function $\varphi(x)$ which is equal to $f(x)$ at the points of A.*

Let the set e_{ni} be defined as in Theorem 7.6. By Theorem 2.17 there is a measurable set $E_{ni} \supset e_{ni}$ with $|E_{ni}| = |e_{ni}|^\circ$. Since e_{ni}, e_{nj} are metrically separated for $i \neq j$, it follows from Theorem 2.19 that the same is true for the sets E_{ni}, E_{nj}, $i \neq j$. Then $\sum_i E_{ni} \supset A$ and by Theorems 2.7 and 2.14

$$\left|\sum_i E_{ni}\right| = \sum_i |E_{ni}| = \sum_i |e_{ni}|^\circ = |A|^\circ.$$

Let $E_n = \sum_i E_{ni}$, and let $E = E_1E_2 \ldots$. Then E is measurable by Theorem 2.16, and since $E_n \supset A$ for every n, $E \supset A$. Let $\varphi_n(x) = a_{ni}$ on EE_{ni}. Then φ_n is measurable on E by Theorem 3.9. Also for $x \in E$

$$|\varphi_n - \varphi_{n+p}| < a_{ni} - a_{n,\,i-1}, \quad p = 1, 2, \ldots$$

and it follows from Theorem 1.6 that φ_n converges on E to a function $\varphi(x)$. Furthermore, for $x \in A \subset E$, $|\varphi - f| < a_{ni} -$

$a_{n, i-1}$ for every n. Hence for $x \in A$, $\varphi = f$. That φ is measurable follows from the measurability of φ_n and Theorem 3.7.

THEOREM 7.17. *Let $f(x)$ be defined on the set A and be metrically separable relative to A. Then the extreme approximate derived numbers of $f(x)$ over A are metrically separable relative to A.*

This theorem will be proved for the upper right approximate derived number, ${}_A\mathbf{D}^+f$. The proof for the other three derived numbers may be obtained in a similar way. Let $E^a = E({}_A\mathbf{D}^+f < a)$, $E_a = E({}_A\mathbf{D}^+f \geq a)$, and suppose that for some real number a the sets E^a and E_a are not metrically separated. Let $\epsilon > 0$ be given such that if $E_1 \subset E^a$, $E_2 \subset E_a$ with

$$(7.25) \qquad |E_1|^\circ > |E^a|^\circ - 2\epsilon,\ |E_2|^\circ > |E_a|^\circ - 2\epsilon,$$

then E_1 and E_2 are not metrically separated. Let E_n be the set for which ${}_A\mathbf{D}^+f < a - 1/n$. Then, by using Theorem 2.18, it can be shown that for n sufficiently great $|E_n|^\circ > |E^a|^\circ - \epsilon$. With n so fixed let $E_{\lambda\delta n}$ be the points $x \in E_a$ for which

$$(7.26) \qquad \frac{f(\xi) - f(x)}{\xi - x} > a - \frac{1}{2n}$$

for a set ξ with

$$(7.27) \qquad |\xi(x, x + h)|^\circ > \lambda h,\ 0 < h < \delta.$$

If λ is first chosen sufficiently small, and then δ chosen sufficiently small, the set $E_{\lambda n\delta}$ is such that

$$|E_{\lambda\delta n}|^\circ > |E_a|^\circ - \epsilon.$$

Now for $\lambda' < \lambda/4$ and $\delta' < \delta$ let $E_{\lambda'\delta' n}$ be the points x' of E_n which are such that

$$(7.28) \qquad \frac{f(\xi') - f(x')}{\xi' - x'} < a - \frac{1}{n}$$

except for a set ξ' with

$$(7.29) \qquad |\xi'(x', x' + h')|^\circ < \lambda' h',\ 0 < h' < \delta'.$$

If $\lambda' < \lambda/4$ is first fixed, and then $\delta' < \delta$ chosen sufficiently small

$$|E_{\lambda'\delta'n}|^\circ > |E_n|^\circ - \epsilon > |E^a|^\circ - 2\epsilon.$$

It follows from (7.25) that $E_{\lambda\delta n}$ and $E_{\lambda'\delta'n}$ are not metrically separated. Let x be a point of $E_{\lambda\delta n}$ which is a point of density of $E_{\lambda'\delta'n}$ and a point at which $f(x)$ is approximately continuous over A. Then from (7.26) and (7.27) it follows that

$$f(\xi) - f(x) > (\xi - x)\left(a - \frac{1}{2n}\right) \tag{7.30}$$

for a set ξ with $|\xi(x, x + h)|^\circ > \lambda h$, $0 < h < \delta$. Let x' be a point of $E_{\lambda'\delta'n}$ with h' fixed, and with

$$x < x',\ x' + h' < x + h,\ 0 < h' < \delta',\ 0 < h < \delta.$$

Then from (7.28) and (7.29) it follows that

$$f(\xi') - f(x') < (\xi' - x')\left(a - \frac{1}{n}\right) \tag{7.31}$$

except for a set ξ' with $|\xi'(x', x' + h')|^\circ < \lambda' h'$. Again referring to (7.27) and (7.29) we see that if h' is fixed (7.30) holds for a set $\xi \subset A$ with $|\xi(x, x + h')|^\circ > \lambda h'$, and that (7.31) holds for all $\xi' \in A(x', x' + h')$ *except* a set ξ' with $|\xi'(x', x' + h')|^\circ < \lambda' h'$ where $\lambda' < \lambda/2$. It then follows that to every $x' > x$ and sufficiently close to x there corresponds a point ξ'' for which both (7.30) and (7.31) are satisfied and which is such that $\xi'' - x > \lambda/2h'$. Using ξ'' in (7.30) and (7.31) and combining the two results there is obtained,

$$\begin{aligned} f(x') - f(x) &> (x' - x)a + \frac{1}{n}(\xi'' - x') - \frac{1}{2n}(\xi'' - x), \\ &> (x' - x)a + \frac{1}{n}\left(\xi'' - x' - \frac{\xi'' - x}{2}\right). \end{aligned}$$

Since n, h', and λ are positive constants and the density of x' is unity at x, this contradicts the fact that x is a point of approximate continuity of $f(x)$ over A. The theorem now follows.

THEOREM 7.18. *Let $f(x)$ be measurable on the measurable set A. Then the extreme approximate derived numbers of $f(x)$ over A are measurable on A.*

If f is measurable on A it is metrically separable relative to A. By Theorem 7.17 the extreme approximate derived numbers of f over A are metrically separable relative to A. The theorem now follows from Theorem 2.20.

DEFINITION 7.5. *Let $f(x)$ be defined on the set A. The metrical upper boundary of $f(x)$ is the function $u(x)$ which is the infimum of numbers a for which $f(\xi) > a$ for at most a set ξ of zero density at x. The function $u(x)$ is then defined for all values of x. If x is a point of zero density of the set A then $u(x) = -\infty$.*

THEOREM 7.19. *The function $u(x)$ is measurable, and for all $x \in A$, except possibly a null set, $u(x) \geq f(x)$.*

Let $E^a = E(u < a)$, $E_a = E(u \geq a)$, and let $A_n = E(u < a - 1/n)$. It follows from the definition of $u(x)$ that at a point $x \in E_n$ the density of the set E_a is zero. Hence at every point of the set $E^a = A_1 + A_2 + \ldots$ the density of E_a is zero. It then follows from Theorem 5.5 that the sets E^a and E_a are metrically separated. The measurability of these sets then follows from Theorem 2.20. To prove the second part of the theorem let $A_n \subset A$ be the set for which $f(x) > u(x) + 1/n$, and suppose for some n, $|A_n|^\circ > 0$. Let $x \in A_n$ be a point of density of A_n and a point of approximate continuity of $u(x)$. Then $u(\xi) > u(x) - 1/2n$ except for a set ξ of density zero at x. Then for $\xi \in A_n, f(\xi) > u(\xi) + 1/n > u(x) + 1/2n$ for a set $\xi \in A_n$ of density unity at x. This contradicts the definition of $u(x)$. Hence $|A_n|^\circ = 0$ for every n. It then follows that the set $A = A_1 + A_2 + \ldots$ for which $f(x) > u(x)$ is a null set.

DEFINITION 7.6. *Let $f(x)$ be defined on the set A. The metrical lower boundary of $f(x)$ is the function $l(x)$ which is the supremum of numbers a for which $f(\xi) < a$ for at most a set ξ of density zero at x. The function $l(x)$ is defined for all x. If the density of A is zero at a point x then $l(x) = \infty$.*

THEOREM 7.20. *The function $l(x)$ is measurable, and for almost all points of A, $l(x) \leq f(x)$.*

The proof is similar to that of the corresponding theorem for $u(x)$.

These functions $u(x)$ and $l(x)$ were first defined by H. Blumberg [10]. He made use of them in conjunction with the known properties of measurable functions to obtain, among other things, the results of Theorem 7.5 of this chapter for arbitrary functions. The known results for measurable functions which he used are those of Theorems 7.3—7.5 of this chapter, stated for measurable functions, and are as difficult to obtain for measurable functions as they are for arbitrary functions. S. E. Chow [17] has shown that the functions $u(x)$, $l(x)$ can be used in conjunction with Theorem 7.15 for measurable functions to obtain some of the results of Theorem 7.13 of this chapter for the approximate derivatives of arbitrary functions. It is, however, unlikely that the metric separability of f over E_i, $i = 1, 2, 3$, the existence of ${}_{E_i}Df$, $i = 2, 3$, or the results of Theorem 7.7 can be obtained in this way.

CHAPTER VIII

THE STIELTJES INTEGRAL

Introduction: This chapter gives the definition and principal properties of the Riemann-Stieltjes integral [28, 66]; it also gives the function-theory background for the ideas of measure and distribution which were introduced by L. Schwartz [61].

8.1 The Riemann-Stieltjes integral.

DEFINITION 8.1. *Let the function $f(x)$ be bounded on the interval $[a, b]$, and let $g(x)$ be a bounded function on this interval. Let (x_{i-1}, x_i) be a subdivision of $[a, b]$ and let ξ_i be any point on $[x_{i-1}, x_i]$. Form the sum*

$$S_n = \sum_{i=1}^{n} f(\xi_i)\{g(x_i) - g(x_{i-1})\}.$$

If the sum S_n tends to a limit as n increases and $max(x_i - x_{i-1})$ tends to zero then this limit is the Riemann-Stieltjes integral of $f(x)$ with respect to $g(x)$ on $[a, b]$

$$RS(f, a, b, g) = \int_a^b f(x)dg(x).$$

Let M_i, m_i be respectively sup $f(x)$, inf $f(x)$, $x_{i-1} \leq x \leq x_i$, $S = \sum M_i\{g(x_i) - g(x_{i-1})\}$, $s = \sum m_i\{g(x_i) - g(x_{i-1})\}$.

THEOREM 8.1. *A necessary and sufficient condition that $RS(f, a, b\ g)$ exist is that $S - s \to 0$ as $max(x_i - x_{i-1}) \to 0$.*

THEOREM 8.2. *If $f(x)$ is continuous on $[a, b]$ and $g(x)$ is BV on this interval then $RS(f, a, b, g)$ exists.*

The proofs of these theorems are similar to the proofs of the corresponding theorems for the ordinary Riemann integral (Problem 5.13).

NOTE 8.1. A single point of discontinuity of $f(x)$ can lead to the non-existence of $RS(f, a, b, g)$. Let $f(x) = 0$, $0 \leq x < 1/2$; $f(x) = 1$, $1/2 \leq x \leq 1$. Let $g(x) = f(x)$. If (x_{i-1}, x_i) is any subdivision of [0, 1] and $x = 1/2$ is not an end-point of any subinterval then the sum S_n can be made unity or zero by suitably choosing ξ on the interval which contains $x = 1/2$.

THEOREM 8.3 (THE FORMULA FOR INTEGRATION BY PARTS FOR THE RIEMANN-STIELTJES INTEGRAL). *If $f(x)$ is BV on $[a, b]$ and $g(x)$ is continuous on this interval then $RS(f, a, b, g)$ exists and*

$$\int_a^b f(x)dg(x) = \Big[f(x)g(x)\Big]_a^b - \int_a^b g(x)df(x).$$

Forming the sum whose limit is the integral on the left,

$$S_n = \sum_{i=1}^{n} f(\xi_i)\{g(x_i) - g(x_{i-1})\},$$

the terms can be rearranged to give

$$-\sum_{i=0}^{n-1} g(x_i)\{f(\xi_{i+1}) - f(\xi_i)\} + f(\xi_n)g(x_n) - f(\xi_0)g(x_0).$$

Using Theorem 8.2 it is easily seen that the limit of this sum is

$$f(b)g(b) - f(a)g(a) - \int_a^b gdf,$$

which is the theorem.

8.2. Properties of the Riemann-Stieltjes integral.

(8.1) $$\int_a^b dg(x) = g(b) - g(a).$$

(8.2) If $g(x) = c$ then $\int_a^b f(x)dg(x) = 0$.

(8.3) If $a < c < b$ then $$\int_a^b f(x)dg(x) = \int_a^c f(x)dg(x) + \int_c^b f(x)dg(x).$$

Let $V_{ab}{}^g = \sup \sum |g(x_i) - g(x_{i-1})|$ for all possible subdivisions (x_{i-1}, x_i) of $[a, b]$. Then

(8.4) $$\left|\int_a^b f(x)dg(x)\right| \leq \sup_{a \leq x \leq b} |f(x)|\, V_{ab}{}^g.$$

Let $g(x)$ be non-decreasing on $[a, b]$, and let m, M be respectively $\inf f(x)$, $\sup f(x)$, $a \leq x \leq b$. Then

$$(8.5)\quad m\{g(b) - g(a)\} \le \int_a^b f(x)dg(x) \le M\{g(b) - g(a)\}.$$

If $f(x)$ is continuous and $g(x)$ is non-decreasing on the interval $[a, b]$, then there is a value ξ of x between a and b for which

$$(8.6)\qquad \int_a^b f(x)dg(x) = f(\xi)\{g(b) - g(a)\}.$$

If the functions $f_1(x)$ and $f_2(x)$ are integrable with respect to $g(x)$ and if c_1, c_2 are any two constants, real or complex, then

$$(8.7)\qquad \int_a^b \{c_1f_1(x) + c_2f_2(x)\}dg(x) = c_1\int_a^b f_1(x)dg(x) + c_2\int_a^b f_2(x)dg(x).$$

Properties (8.1)—(8.7) follow immediately from Definition 8.1.

THEOREM 8.4. *If $f(x)$ is non-decreasing and $g(x)$ is continuous on the interval $[a, b]$ then for some ξ, $a \le \xi \le b$,*

$$\int_a^b f(x)dg(x) = f(a)\int_a^\xi dg(x) + f(b)\int_\xi^b dg(x).$$

By Theorem 8.3 and Properties (8.6) and (8.1)

$$\begin{aligned}\int_a^b fdg &= f(b)g(b) - f(a)g(a) - \int_a^b gdf \\ &= f(b)g(b) - f(a)g(a) - g(\xi)\int_a^b df \\ &= f(a)\{g(\xi) - g(a)\} + f(b)\{g(b) - g(\xi)\} \\ &= f(a)\int_a^\xi dg + f(b)\int_\xi^b dg,\end{aligned}$$

which is the theorem.

THEOREM 8.5. *On the interval $[a, b]$ let $f(x)$ be bounded and measurable and let $g(x)$ be AC. Let $RS(f, a, b, g)$ exist. Then*

$$\int_a^b f(x)dg(x) = \int_a^b f(x)g'(x)dx,$$

where the integral on the right is a Lebesgue integral.

Since g' is summable and f is bounded and measurable, it follows that the product fg' is summable. Furthermore, since g' exists and is finite almost everywhere there is a set E with $|E| = b - a$ such that if $x \in E$ then for $\epsilon > 0$ and $h > 0$ and sufficiently small

$$\left| \frac{1}{h} \int_x^{x+h} fg'dx - f(x) \frac{g(x+h) - g(x)}{h} \right| < \epsilon.$$

This relation associates with the points of the set E a Vitali family of intervals, and a finite non-overlapping set of these intervals can be selected with

$$\left| \int_{x_k}^{x'_k} fg'dx - f(x_k)\{g(x'_k) - g(x_k)\} \right| < \epsilon\,(x'_k - x_k),$$

and with $\sum(x'_k - x_k)$ arbitrarily near to $|E| = b - a$. If these inequalities are added over the intervals (x_k, x'_k) the sum of the integrals on the left is close to the integral of fg' over $[a, b]$. It follows from the existence of $RS(f, a, b, g)$, the boundedness of f, and the absolute continuity of g that the second sum on the left is arbitrarily near to $RS(f, a, b, g)$, provided $x'_k - x_k$ is sufficiently small and $\sum(x'_k - x_k)$ is sufficiently close to $b - a$. The sum on the right side is less than $\epsilon(b - a)$ where ϵ is arbitrary. Hence the theorem.

THEOREM 8.6. *Let $\varphi(x)$ be summable and $f(x)$ non-decreasing on the interval $[a, b]$. Then $f(x)\,\varphi(x)$ is summable and for some ξ, $a \leq \xi \leq b$,*

$$\int_a^b f(x)\varphi(x)dx = f(a) \int_a^\xi \varphi(x)dx + f(b) \int_\xi^b \varphi(x)dx.$$

Let

$$g(x) = \int_a^x \varphi(x)dx.$$

Then g is AC and $g' = \varphi$ for almost all x. By Theorem 8.5

$$\int_a^b fdg = \int_a^b f\varphi dx.$$

By Theorem 8.4

$$\int_a^b fdg = f(a) \int_a^\xi dg + f(b) \int_\xi^b dg.$$

Combining these results and again using Theorem 8.5,

$$\int_a^b f\varphi dx = f(a)\int_a^\xi \varphi dx + f(b)\int_\xi^b \varphi dx,$$

which is the required theorem.

THEOREM 8.7. *If* $g(x)$ *is continuous and* $f(x)$ *is non-negative on the interval* $[a, b]$, *then, accordingly as* $f(x)$ *is non-decreasing or non-increasing,*

$$\int_a^b f(x)dg(x) = f(b)\int_\xi^b dg(x), \quad \int_a^b f(x)dg(x) = f(a)\int_a^\xi dg(x),$$

where in each case ξ *is some number between* a *and* b.

We prove the first relation. The proof of the second is similar. By Theorem 8.4

$$\int_a^b fdg = f(b)g(b) - f(a)g(a) - g(\xi)\{f(b) - f(a)\}.$$

Since f is non-decreasing and g is continuous it then follows that

$$f(b)g(b) - f(a)g(a) - \max g(x)\{f(b) - f(a)\} \leq \int_a^b fdg$$
$$\leq f(b)g(b) - f(a)g(a) - \min g(x)\{f(b) - f(a)\},$$

which gives

$$f(b)\{g(b) - \max g(x)\} - f(a)\{g(a) - \max g(x)\} \leq \int_a^b fdg$$
$$\leq f(b)\{g(b) - \min g(x)\} - f(a)\{g(a) - \min g(x)\}.$$

Since $g(a) - \max g(x) \leq 0 \leq g(a) - \min g(x)$ it follows that

$$f(b)\{g(b) - \max g(x)\} \leq \int_a^b fdg \leq f(b)\{g(b) - \min g(x)\}.$$

Since $g(x)$ is continuous there is then some point ξ between a and b for which

$$\int_a^b fdg = f(b)\{g(b) - g(\xi)\} = f(b)\int_\xi^b dg,$$

which is the theorem.

THEOREM 8.8. *Let* $\varphi(x)$ *be summable on* $[a, b]$ *and let* $f(x)$ *be non-negative. Then accordingly as* $f(x)$ *is non-decreasing or non-increasing*

$$\int_a^b f(x)\varphi(x)dx = f(b)\int_\xi^b \varphi(x)dx, \quad \int_a^b f(x)\varphi(x)dx = f(a)\int_a^\xi \varphi(x)dx,$$

where in each case ξ *is a point between* a *and* b.

This theorem is proved by setting

$$g(x) = \int_a^x \varphi(x)dx$$

in Theorem 8.3 and using Theorem 8.5.

NOTE 8.2. Theorems 8.6 and 8.8 are known as second mean value theorems They can be proved without the use of the Stieltjes integral theory. See problems 3.13, 4.10, and [28, p. 618].

THEOREM 8.9. *On the interval* $[a, b]$ *let* $f(x)$ *be continuous and* $g(x)$ *be* BV. *If*

$$F(x) = \int_a^x f(x)dg(x)$$

then $F'(x) = f(x)g'(x)$ *almost everywhere on* $[a, b]$.

It follows from (8.3) that

$$\begin{aligned}\frac{F(x+h) - F(x)}{h} &= \frac{1}{h}\int_x^{x+h} f(t)dg(t) \\ &= f(x)\frac{1}{h}\int_x^{x+h} dg(t) + \frac{1}{h}\int_x^{x+h} \xi(t)dg(t),\end{aligned}$$

where $\xi(t) = f(t) - f(x)$. It follows from (8.1) that the first term on the right is equal to $f(x)\{g(x+h) - g(x)\}/h$, and since $f(x)$ is BV on $[a, b]$ this tends to $f(x)g'(x)$ for almost all x on $[a, b]$. In order to evaluate the second term on the right we use (8.4) and write

$$\left|\frac{1}{h}\int_x^{x+h} \xi(t)dg(t)\right| \leq \sup |\xi(t)| \frac{V_{a,\,x+h}{}^g - V_{ax}{}^g}{h}.$$

Since $V_{ax}{}^g$ is a non-decreasing function the ratio on the right tends to a finite limit for almost all x, and since $f(t)$ is continuous sup $|\xi(t)|$ tends to zero as $h \to 0$. It then follows that for almost all x the left side of the foregoing inequality tends to zero. We can now conclude that for almost all x the relation $F'(x) = f(x)g'(x)$ holds.

THEOREM 8.10. *On the interval* $[a, b]$ *let* $f(x)$ *be summable* *and let $g(x)$ be BV. Then the product $f(x)g(x)$ is summable and*

$$\int_a^b f(x)g(x)dx = \Big[F(x)g(x) \Big]_a^b - \int_a^b F(x)dg(x),$$

where $F(x) = L(f, a, x)$ and where the integral on the right is a Stieltjes integral.

By Theorem 5.13 $g = g_1 - g_2$ where g_1 and g_2 are non-decreasing. Then, since F is continuous it follows that the integrals of F with respect to g, g_1 and g_2 all exist, and the first is equal to the second minus the third. Hence it is sufficient to prove the theorem for g non-decreasing. Thus, with g non-decreasing, we set

$$H(x) = F(x)g(x) - \int_a^x F(x)dg(x),$$

and prove that H is AC and that $H' = fg$ for almost all x. With this established it follows from Theorem 6.5 that fg is summable and that

$$\int_a^b fgdx = H(b) - H(a).$$

To show that H is AC let (α, β) be a subinterval of $[a, b]$. Then by (8.3)

$$H(\beta) - H(\alpha) = F(\beta)g(\beta) - F(\alpha)g(\alpha) - \int_\alpha^\beta Fdg.$$

With g non-decreasing (8.6) gives

$$H(\beta) - H(\alpha) = F(\beta)g(\beta) - F(\alpha)g(\alpha) - F(\xi)\{g(\beta) - g(\alpha)\},$$

where $\alpha \leq \xi \leq \beta$. This in turn gives

$$H(\beta) - H(\alpha) = g(\beta)\{F(\beta) - F(\xi)\} + g(\alpha)\{F(\xi) - F(\alpha)\}.$$

Since g is bounded and F is AC it now follows that H is AC.

It follows from the definition of F that $F' = f$ almost everywhere, and since g is non-decreasing g' exists almost everywhere. It then follows from Theorem 8.9 that

$$H' = Fg' + F'g - Fg' = F'g = fg$$

for almost all x on $[a, b]$, and the proof of the theorem is complete.

When the function g is absolutely continuous Theorems 8.5 and 8.10 give

$$\int_a^b fg\,dx = \Big[Fg \Big]_a^b - \int_a^b Fg'\,dx,$$

which is the formula of the elementary calculus for integration by parts.

8.3. Interval functions and measure functions. Let I be an interval, open, closed, or half open, or a single point. Let $\mu(I)$ be a real number associated with the sets I on the interval $[a, b]$.

DEFINITION 8.2. *Let I be an interval and $I_1, I_2, \ldots$ a finite or denumerable sequence covering I, $I = I_1 + I_2 + \ldots$, $I_j I_k = 0$, $j \neq k$. If for every interval I and every such covering of I,*

$$\mu(I) = \sum \mu(I_i)$$

then $\mu(I)$ is a completely additive interval function. If there exists a number $M > 0$ such that for every set $I_1, I_2, \ldots$ with $I_j I_k = 0, j \neq k$

$$\sum |\mu(I_i)| < M,$$

then $\mu(I)$ is of bounded variation on $[a, b]$. If $\mu(I)$ is completely additive and of bounded variation then $\mu(I)$ is a measure function.

Let $\mu(I)$ be a measure function on $[a, b]$, and let $f(x)$ be bounded on this interval. Let $[a, b] = I_1 + I_2 + \ldots$ where $I_j I_k = 0, j \neq k$, and let ξ_i be any point on I_i. If $\sum f(\xi_i)\mu(I_i)$ tends to a limit as max $|I_i|$ tends to zero this limit is the Stieltjes integral of $f(x)$ with respect to $\mu(I)$.

If $\mu(I)$ is a measure function on $[a, b]$ and $f(x)$ is continuous on this interval it can be shown as in the case of the Riemann-Stieltjes integral that the integral of $f(x)$ with respect to $\mu(I)$ exists. If $I = [a, b]$ is the sum of two mutually exclusive intervals, $I = I_1 + I_2$, $I_1 I_2 = 0$, then

$$\int_a^b f\,d\mu = \int_{I_1} f\,d\mu + \int_{I_2} f\,d\mu.$$

However, it is not necessarily true, even when $f(x)$ is continuous, that if $a < c < b$ then

$$\int_a^b f\,d\mu = \int_a^c f\,d\mu + \int_c^b f\,d\mu.$$

This relation does hold if $\mu(c) = 0$. Let $g(x)$ be BV on $[a, b]$. A measure function $\mu(I)$ may be associated with $g(x)$ in the following way: Let $g(a - 0) = g(a)$, $g(b + 0) = g(b)$. Then if I is a single point x, $\mu(I) = g(x + 0) - g(x - 0)$. If $\alpha, \beta, \alpha < \beta$, defines an interval on $[a, b]$,

$$I = [\alpha, \beta],\ \mu(I) = g(\beta + 0) - g(\alpha - 0),$$
$$I = (\alpha, \beta],\ \mu(I) = g(\beta + 0) - g(\alpha + 0),$$
$$I = [\alpha, \beta),\ \mu(I) = g(\beta - 0) - g(\alpha - 0),$$
$$I = (\alpha, \beta),\ \mu(I) = g(\beta - 0) - g(\alpha + 0).$$

The fact that $g(x)$ is BV on $[a, b]$ assures that $\mu(I)$ is also BV on this interval, and it is easy to verify that $\mu(I)$ is completely additive. Hence $\mu(I)$ is a measure function on the interval $[a, b]$. Furthermore, if $f(x)$ is continuous on $[a, b]$ the integrals of $f(x)$ over this interval with respect to $g(x)$ and with respect to $\mu(I)$ both exist, and it is easy to show that the two are equal.

8.4. Linear functionals.

DEFINITION 8.2. *Let (B) be the class of functions of x which are bounded on $-\infty < x < \infty$. The class (B) is known as the space of bounded functions. Let $\mathfrak{L}(f)$ be a real number associated with $f \in (B)$. $\mathfrak{L}(f)$ is a functional defined on the space of bounded functions (B). If $\mathfrak{L}(f)$ is such that for any two functions f_1 and f_2 in (B) and any two constants c_1, c_2*

$$\mathfrak{L}(c_1f_1 + c_2f_2) = c_1\,\mathfrak{L}(f) + c_2\,\mathfrak{L}(f_2)$$

then $\mathfrak{L}(f)$ is a linear functional defined on (B).

$\mathfrak{L}(f) = f(0)$ is an example of a linear functional. In Definition 8.2 the functions f, the functional $\mathfrak{L}(f)$, and the constants c_1, c_2 may be complex, and the inclusion of complex values would call for no essential changes in the discussion. We shall, however, have in mind only real values. For a more comprehensive study of functionals see [3].

DEFINITION 8.3. *For $f \in (B)$ let $\|f\| = sup\ |f(x)|$, $-\infty < x < \infty$. The number $\|f_1 - f_2\|$ thus associated with two functions f_1, f_2 in (B) is a distance function or metric of the space (B). Also $\|f - 0\| = \|f\|$ is called the norm of the function f. If* *there is a sequence of functions* f_n *with* $f_n \in (B)$ *and a function* $f \in (B)$ *for which* $\|f_n - f\| \to 0$ *as* $n = \infty$, *then* f *is the limit of the sequence* f_n. *If a sequence of functions* f_n *with* $f_n \in (B)$ *is such that* $\|f_n - f_m\| \to 0$ *as* n, $m \to \infty$ *then the sequence is a Cauchy sequence.*

THEOREM 8.10. *Every Cauchy sequence in* (B) *has a limit* f *with* f *in* (B).

Let x be fixed. Then

$$|f_n(x) - f_m(x)| \leq \|f_n - f_m\|.$$

Hence for each $x, f_n(x)$ is a Cauchy sequence in the ordinary sense, and consequently for each $x, f_n(x)$ tends to a limit $\varphi(x)$. It remains to show that φ is a function in (B). The sequence $f_n(x)$ tends to $\varphi(x)$ uniformly. For suppose there is $d > 0$ such that for an infinite number of values of n there exists x_n with $|f_n(x_n) - \varphi(x_n)| > d$. Fix N such that $\|f_n - f_m\| < d/2$, $m, n > N$. Fix $n > N$ and x_n so that $|f_n(x_n) - \varphi(x_n)| > d$. Now take $m > n$ so that $|f_m(x_n) - \varphi(x_n)| < d/2$. The last two inequalities combine to give

$$\|f_n - f_m\| \geq |f_n(x_n) - f_m(x_n)| > d/2,\ m, n > N$$

which is a contradiction. We conclude, therefore, that $f_n(x) \to \varphi(x)$ uniformly.

To show that $\varphi \in (B)$ let $D > 0$ be given. Fix N so that $|f_n(x) - \varphi(x)| < D$, $n > N$. Since $f_n \in (B)$ for n fixed, $n > N$ there exists $M > 0$ such that $|f_n(x)| < M$, $-\infty < x < \infty$. It then follows that $|\varphi(x)| < M + D$, $-\infty < x < \infty$. Consequently $\varphi(x)$ is a function in (B).

NOTE 8.3. Because the limit of every Cauchy sequence in (B) is a function in (B) the space (B) is said to be *complete*. There are subspaces of (B) which are not complete. Let (B_0) be the class of functions f which are bounded and equal to zero outside some finite interval $[a, b]_f$, the interval varying with the function. It is easy to show that the function $\varphi(x) = 1/(1 + x^2)$ is the limit of a sequence of functions in (B_0), and it is obvious that φ is not in (B_0). Let (B_1) be the class of functions f which are bounded and such that $|f(x)| \to 0$ as $|x| \to \infty$. Obviously $(B_1) \supset (B_0)$ and it is easy to show that with the distance function as in Definition 8.3 the space (B_1) is complete.

DEFINITION 8.4. *Let $u = [a, b]$ be a fixed finite closed interval. Let (B_u) be the sub-class of functions f_u of (B) which are zero outside of u. Let $\mathfrak{L}(f)$ be a linear functional defined on (B). If f_{un} is a sequence of functions in (B_u) and if $\mathfrak{L}(f)$ defined on (B) is such that $\mathfrak{L}(f_{un}) \to \mathfrak{L}(f_u)$ whenever the sequence $f_{un} \to f_u$ in the sense of Definition* 8.3 *then $\mathfrak{L}(f)$ is continuous on* (B). (See Remark 8.4).

Since $\mathfrak{L}(f)$ is linear on (B), $\mathfrak{L}(f_u - f_{un}) = \mathfrak{L}(f_u) - \mathfrak{L}(f_{un})$. If the functional $\mathfrak{L}(f)$ is continuous according to Definition 8.4 then the right side of this equation tends to zero as $f_{un} \to f_u$ according to Definition 8.3. Consequently the left side tends to zero. On the other hand, if the left side tends to zero whenever $||f_u - f_{un}|| \to 0$ so does the right side, and $\mathfrak{L}(f)$ is continuous under Definition 8.4. We have thus proved

THEOREM 8.11. *The necessary and sufficient condition that the linear functional $\mathfrak{L}(f)$ defined on (B) be continuous under Definition* 8.4 *is that for every finite closed interval u, $\mathfrak{L}(f_{un}) \to 0$ whenever $f_{un} \to 0$ in the sense of Definition* 8.3.

It follows from Definition 8.4 and Theorem 8.11 that if $\mathfrak{L}(f)$ is continuous on (B) and $f(x) = 0$ identically then $\mathfrak{L}(f) = 0$.

THEOREM 8.12. *Let the linear functional $\mathfrak{L}(f)$ be continuous on (B). Let $u = [a, b]$ be any fixed finite closed interval. There exists a number $M_u > 0$ such that*

$$|\mathfrak{L}(f_u)| \leq M_u||f_u||$$

for every function f_u in (B_u).

Suppose the contrary to be true. There then exists a sequence of positive numbers M_n with $M_n \to \infty$ as $n \to \infty$ and a sequence of functions $f_{un} \in (B_u)$ for which

$$|\mathfrak{L}(f_{un})| > M_n||f_{un}||.$$

We note that this relation, in conjunction with the remark following Theorem 8.11, implies $||f_{un}|| \neq 0$. For if $||f_{un}|| = 0$ then f_{un} is identically zero and $|\mathfrak{L}(f_{un})| = 0$. Now set

$$y_n = \frac{1}{M_n} \frac{f_{un}}{||f_{un}||}.$$

Then y_n is in (B_u) and $||y_n|| \to 0$ as $n \to \infty$. Hence it follows from Theorem 8.11 that $\mathfrak{L}(y_n) \to 0$. But

$$|\mathfrak{L}(y_n)| = \frac{1}{M_n} \frac{|\mathfrak{L}(f_{un})|}{||f_{un}||} > 1.$$

This contradicts the hypothesis that $\mathfrak{L}(f)$ is continuous on (B), and the theorem follows.

THEOREM 8.13. *Let $\mathfrak{L}(f)$ be a linear continuous functional defined on (B). There exists a function $g(x)$ defined on $-\infty < x < \infty$, which is of bounded variation on every finite closed interval $[a, b]$, and which is such that if $\psi(x) \in (B)$ is continuous on $[a, b]$ and zero outside of $[a, b]$ then*

$$\mathfrak{L}(\psi) = \int_a^b \psi(x)dg(x).$$

For $x < 0$ let

$$\begin{aligned} \xi_x(t) &= -1,\ x \leq t < 0 \\ &= 0 \text{ elsewhere.} \end{aligned}$$

For $x \geq 0$ let

$$\begin{aligned} \xi_x(t) &= 1,\ 0 \leq t < x \\ &= 0 \text{ elsewhere.} \end{aligned}$$

For every x on $-\infty < x < \infty$ the function $\xi_x(t)$ is in (B). Let $g(x) = \mathfrak{L}[\xi_x(t)]$. Then $g(x)$ is defined for every x on $-\infty < x < \infty$. We now show that if $[a, b]$ is a finite interval then $g(x)$ is BV on this interval.

Let $a = x_0 < x_1 < \ldots < x_n = b$ be a subdivision of $[a, b]$. Let

$$V_n = \sum|g(x_i) - g(x_{i-1})| = \sum\epsilon_i\{g(x_i) - g(x_{i-1})\}$$

where ϵ_i is 1 or -1 accordingly as $g(x_i) - g(x_{i-1})$ is positive or zero, or negative. Substituting for $g(x)$ and using the fact that $\mathfrak{L}(f)$ is linear,

$$\begin{aligned} V_n &= \sum\epsilon_i\{\mathfrak{L}[\xi_{x_i}(t)] - \mathfrak{L}[\xi_{x_{i-1}}(t)]\} \\ &= \mathfrak{L}[\sum\epsilon_i\{\xi_{x_i}(t) - \xi_{x_{i-1}}(t)\}]. \end{aligned}$$

It is easily verified that the function $\sum\epsilon_i\{\xi_{x_i}(t) - \xi_{x_{i-1}}(t)\}$ is zero outside of $[a, b]$, zero at b, and 1 on $x_{i-1} \leq t < x_i$, $i = 1, 2, \ldots, n$. Hence $\|\sum \epsilon_i \{\xi_{x_i}(t) - \xi_{x_{i-1}}(t)\}\| = 1$, and, using Theorem 8.12, we get

$$V_n \leq M_u, \quad u = [a, b].$$

Since M_u depends on the interval $[a, b]$ and not on n it follows that $g(x)$ is BV on $[a, b]$.

Now let ψ be the functions of class (B) which are continuous on $[a, b]$ and zero outside of this interval. Let $a = x_0 < x_1 < \ldots < x_n = b$ be a subdivision of $[a, b]$. Define a function $z_n(t)$ on $-\infty < x < \infty$ as follows:

$$z_n(b) = \psi(b)$$

$$z_n(t) = \sum_{i=1}^{n} \psi(x_i)\{\xi_{x_i}(t) - \xi_{x_{i-1}}(t)\}, \quad t \neq b.$$

It is easily verified that $\xi_{x_i}(t) - \xi_{x_{i-1}}(t) = 1$, $x_{i-1} \leq t < x_i$, and vanishes outside of $[a, b]$. Consequently, since $\psi(x)$ is continuous on $[a, b]$, $z_n(t) \to \psi(t)$ uniformly and, therefore, $z_n(t) \to \psi(t)$ in the sense of Definition 8.3. Then, since $\psi(t)$ and $z_n(t)$ are zero outside of $[a, b]$, and since $\mathfrak{L}(f)$ is continuous under Definition 8.4, it follows that $\mathfrak{L}[z_n(t)] \to \mathfrak{L}[\psi(t)]$. Furthermore, since $\mathfrak{L}(f)$ is linear,

$$\begin{aligned} \mathfrak{L}[z_n(t)] &= \mathfrak{L}[\sum \psi(x_i)\{\xi_{x_i}(t) - \xi_{x_{i-1}}(t)\} \\ &= \sum \psi(x_i)\{\mathfrak{L}[\xi_{x_i}(t)] - \mathfrak{L}[\xi_{x_{i-1}}(t)]\} \\ &= \sum \psi(x_i)\{g(x_i) - g(x_{i-1})\}. \end{aligned}$$

Then, as $n \to \infty$ and $\max(x_i - x_{i-1}) \to 0$, the left side of this relation tends to $\mathfrak{L}[\psi(t)] = \mathfrak{L}(\psi)$. Furthermore, since $\psi(x)$ is continuous and $g(x)$ is BV on $[a, b]$, the right side tends to the Riemann-Stieltjes integral of ψ with respect to g,

$$\mathfrak{L}(\psi) = \int_a^b \psi(x)dg(x).$$

This completes the proof of the theorem.

Even though the function ψ is continuous on $[a, b]$ and zero outside this interval it does not follow that

$$\int_a^b \psi dg = \int_{-\infty}^{\infty} \psi dg.$$

For example, this is not the case if $\psi(a) \neq 0$ and $g(a - 0) \neq g(a)$. In order that the foregoing relation hold, a further restriction on the class of functions ψ is necessary.

Let $\varphi(x)$ be the subclass (C) of functions of (B) which are continuous and which vanish outside some finite interval $[a, b]_\varphi$, the interval varying with the function. Then for each function φ in (C) there is an interval $[a, b]_\varphi$ with $\varphi(a) = \varphi(b) = 0$ and for which

$$\mathfrak{L}(\varphi) = \int_a^b \varphi dg = \int_{-\infty}^{\infty} \varphi dg.$$

Let $\mu(I)$ be the measure function of §8.3 which is associated with $g(x)$. Then $\mu(I)$ is defined for every finite interval I on $-\infty < x < \infty$ and

$$\mathfrak{L}(\varphi) = \int_{-\infty}^{\infty} \varphi dg = \int_{-\infty}^{\infty} \varphi d\mu.$$

If $u = [a, b]$ is a fixed finite interval and φ_u the functions of class (C) which are zero outside of u, then

$$\mathfrak{L}(\varphi_{un}) = \int_{-\infty}^{\infty} \varphi_{un} d\mu$$

tends to zero as $\varphi_{un} \to 0$ under Definition 8.3, for in this case $||\varphi_{un}|| \to 0$ and consequently $\varphi_{un}(x) \to 0$ uniformly on $u = [a, b]$. Hence, by Theorem 8.11 $\mathfrak{L}(\varphi)$ is continuous on (C) under Definition 8.4.

NOTE 8.4. For $\mathfrak{L}(f)$ defined on (B) a natural definition of continuity is that $\mathfrak{L}(f_n) \to \mathfrak{L}(f)$ when $f_n \to f$ under Definition 8.3, f_n and f contained in (B). But under this definition $\mathfrak{L}(\varphi)$ would not be continuous for φ in (C), for it is easy to construct a sequence of functions φ_n in (C) with $||\varphi_n|| \to 0$ and with

$$\int_{-\infty}^{\infty} \varphi_n d\mu$$

not tending to zero. It was to insure the continuity of $\mathfrak{L}(\varphi)$ on (C) that Definition 8.3 was adopted.

Now let $\mu(I)$ be any function of sets I which is a measure function on every finite interval $[a, b]$. For φ in (C) define $\mathfrak{L}(\varphi)$ by

$$\mathfrak{L}(\varphi) = \int_{-\infty}^{\infty} \varphi d\mu.$$

Then $\mathfrak{L}(\varphi)$ is a linear functional defined on (C) which is continuous on (C) in the sense of Definition 8.4. However, this relation does not define a functional for all the functions $f \in (B)$, or even for all the functions of (B) which are zero outside of some finite interval, for there are such functions for which

$$\int_{-\infty}^{\infty} f d\mu$$

does not exist.

We have now reached the stage at which we can say that if $\mathfrak{L}(f)$ is a linear continuous functional defined on (B), then there is an interval function $\mu(I)$ associated with $\mathfrak{L}(f)$ which is a measure function on every finite interval, and which is such that for $\varphi \in (C)$

$$\mathfrak{L}(\varphi) = \int_{-\infty}^{\infty} \varphi d\mu.$$

If $\mu(I)$ is any interval function whatever which is a measure function on every finite interval, then

$$\mathfrak{L}(\varphi) = \int_{-\infty}^{\infty} \varphi d\mu$$

is a linear continuous functional on (C).

It seemed to be these considerations which led Schwartz to call the functional $\mathfrak{L}(\varphi)$ a measure denoted by

$$\mu(\varphi) = \int_{-\infty}^{\infty} \varphi d\mu.$$

Let $f(x)$ be summable on every finite interval and let a be a fixed value of x. Let

$$g(x) = \int_{a}^{x} f(x) dx.$$

Then $g(x)$ is absolutely continuous, and if $\mu(I)$ is the interval function associated with $g(x)$ then $\mu(I)$ is a measure function on every finite interval and the measure

$$\mu(\varphi) = \int_{-\infty}^{\infty} \varphi d\mu = \int_{-\infty}^{\infty} \varphi dg = \int_{-\infty}^{\infty} f \varphi dx$$

is said to be absolutely continuous. Thus the class of locally summable functions $f(x)$ defines a linear functional on (C)

$$f(\varphi) = \int_{-\infty}^{\infty} f\varphi dx$$

which is continuous on (C) under Definition 8.4, and which is a measure in the sense of Schwartz.

If a functional $T(\varphi)$ is defined by the relation

$$T(\varphi) = \varphi'(0),$$

then $T(\varphi)$ exists for all functions φ in (C) which have a derivative. Furthermore, it is easily verified that $T(\varphi)$ is linear over the class of functions for which it is defined. However, over this class of functions $T(\varphi)$ is not continuous in the sense of Definition 8.4. For if φ_{un} is a sequence of functions for which φ_{un} tends to zero in the sense of Definition 8.3 and for which φ'_{un} exists, it does not follow that $T(\varphi_{un}) = \varphi'_{un}(0)$ tends to zero.

Denote by (D) the class of functions $\chi \in (C)$ which are indefinitely differentiable. Given any function $\chi \in (D)$ it is also in (C) and consequently there is a finite interval $[a, b]_\chi$ such that χ and all its derivatives vanish outside of this interval. We shall say that a sequence of functions χ_n tends to zero in the sense of (D) if χ_n and all derivatives χ'_n tend to zero in the sense of Definition 8.3. Let $u = [a, b]$ be a fixed finite interval. Let χ_u be the functions in (D) which are such that χ_u and all its derivatives vanish outside of u. A linear functional defined on (D) is continuous in the sense of (D) if for every fixed finite interval u, $T(\chi_{un}) \to 0$ when the sequence $\chi_{un} \to 0$ in the sense of (D). The class of functionals which are continuous on (D) in this sense is what Schwartz calls *distributions*. Thus, for $\chi \in (D)$, $T(\chi) = \chi'(0)$ is a distribution.

We have now accomplished our purpose of giving the theoretical setting for the ideas of measure and distribution introduced by Schwartz [61]. We leave the reader to look elsewhere for the technical development of these ideas. There is an excellent introduction to this work by Schwartz in collaboration with I. Halperin [61].

BIBLIOGRAPHY

[1] Adams, C. R., and Clarkson, A. J., "Properties of Functions $f(x, y)$ of Bounded Variation," *Transactions of the American Mathematical Society*, vol. 36 (1934), pp. 711-730.

[2] ——— "On the Space *B V*," *Transactions of the American Mathematical Society*, vol. 42 (1937), pp. 194-205.

[3] Banach, S., *Théorie des opérations linéares* (Warsaw, 1932).

[4] Besicovitch, A. S., "On the fundamental Geometrical Properties of Linearly Measurable Plane Sets," *Mathematische Annalen*, vol. 115 (1938), pp. 296-329.

[5] ——— "Discussion der stetigen Funktionen im Zusammenhang mit der Frage über ihre Differentiierbarkeit," *Bulletin de l'Academie des Sciences de Russie*, vol. 19(1925), pp. 527-540.

[6] Birkhoff, G. D., "Proof of a Recurrence Theorem for Strongly Transitive Systems," *Proceedings of the National Academy, U.S.A.*, vol. 17 (1931), pp. 650-655.

[7] ——— "Proof of the Ergodic Theorem," *Proceedings of the National Academy, U.S.A.*, vol. 17 (1931), pp. 656-660.

[8] Birkhoff, G. D., and Koopman, B. O., "Recent Contributions to the Ergodic Theorem, " *Proceedings of the National Academy of Sciences, U.S.A.*, vol. 18 (1932), pp. 279-282.

[9] Birkhoff, Garrett, "The Mean Ergodic Theorem," *Duke Mathematical Journal*, vol. 5 (1939), pp. 19-20.

[10] Blumberg, H., "The Measurable Boundaries of an Arbitrary Function," *Acta Mathematica*, vol. 65 (1935).

[11] Burkill, J. C., and Haslam-Jones, U. S., "Derivatives and Approximate Derivatives of Measurable Functions," *Proceedings of the London Mathematical Society*, vol. 32 (1930), pp. 345-355.

[12] ——— "Relative Measurability and the Derivatives of Non-Measurable Functions," *Quarterly Journal of Mathematics*, vol. 4 (1933), pp. 234-239.

[13] Busemann, H., and Feller, W., "Fur Differentiation der Lebesgue Integral," *Fundamenta Mathematicae*, vol. 22 (1936), pp. 226-256.

[14] Cantor, George, *Contributions to the Founding of the Theory of Transfinite numbers* (Translated by Philip E. Jourdain, Chicago and London, 1924).

[15] Carathéodory, C. E., *Vorlesungen über reelle Funktionen* (Leipzig and Berlin, 1927).

[16] ——— "Uber das lineare Mass von Punktinengen—eine Verallgemeinerung des Längenbegriffs," *Nachr. Ges. Wiss. Göttingen* (1914), pp. 404-426.

[17] Chow, S. E., "On Approximate Derivatives," *Bulletin of the American Society*, vol. 34 (1948), pp. 793-802.

[18] Clarkson, J. A., and Adams, C. R., "On Definitions of Bounded Variation for Functions of Two Variables," *Transactions of the American Mathematical Society*, vol. 35 (1933), pp. 824-854,

[19] Courant, R., and Robbins, H., *What is Mathematics?* (New York, 1941).

[20] Dedekind, Richard, *Essay on the Theory of Numbers* (Translated by W. W. Berman, Chicago, 1909).

[21] Fan, S. C., "Integration with Respect to an Upper Measure Function," *American Journal of Mathematics*, vol. 63 (1941), pp. 319-337.

[22] Goursat, É., and Hedrick, E. R., *Mathematical Analysis*, vol. I (Cambridge, 1904).

[23] Graves, L. M., *The Theory of Functions of Real Variables* (New York and London, 1946).

[24] Hahn, H. E., *Theorie der reellen Funktionen* (Berlin, 1921).

[25] Hahn, H., and Rosenthal, A., *Set Functions* (Albuquerque, 1948).

[26] Hardy, G. H., and Wright, E. M., *Theory of Numbers* (Oxford, 1938).

[27] Hildebrandt, T. H., "On Integrals related to and extension of the Lebesgue Integral," *Bulletin of the American Mathematical Society*, vol. XXIV (1917), p. 113.

[28] Hobson, E. W., *Theory of Functions of a Real Variable*, second edition, vol. I (Cambridge, 1921).

[29] ——— *Theory of Functions of a Real Variable*, second edition, vol. II (Cambridge, 1926).

[30] Hopf, E., *Ergodentheorie* (Leipzig, 1927).

[31] Huntington, E. V., *The Continuum* (Cambridge, 1917).

[32] Hurewicz, W., "Ergodic Theorem without Invariant Measure," *Annals of Mathematics*, vol. 45 (1944), pp. 192-206.

[33] Jeffery, R. L., "Relative Summability," *Annals of Mathematics*, vol. 33 (1932) pp. 443-459.

[34] ——— "Non-absolutely Convergent Integrals With Respect to Functions of Bounded Variation," *Transactions of the American Mathematical Society*, vol. 34 (1932), pp. 645-675.

[35] ——— "Derivatives of Arbitrary Functions over Arbitrary Sets," *Annals of Mathematics*, vol. 36 (1935), pp. 438-447.

[36] ——— "Integrations in Abstract Space," *Duke Mathematical Journal*, vol. 6 (1940), pp. 706-718.

[37] Kestleman, H., *Modern Theories of Integration* (Oxford, 1927).

[38] Koopman, B. O., "Hamiltonian Systems and Transformations in Hilbert Space," *Proceedings of the National Academy of Sciences, U.S.A.*, vol 17 (1931), pp. 315-18.

[39] Koopman, B. O., and Neumann, J. V., "Dynamical Systems of Continuous Spectra," *Proceedings of the National Academy of Sciences, U.S.A.*, vol. 18 (1932), pp. 255-263.

[40] Landau, E., *Grundlagen der Analysis* (Leipzig, 1930).

[41] Lebesgue, H., *Leçons sur l'integration et la fonction primitive* (Paris, 1928).

[42] Macphail, M. S., "Integration of Functions in a Banach Space," *National Mathematics Magazine*, vol. 20 (1945), pp. 67-78.

[43] ——— "Functions of Bounded Variation in Two Variables," *Duke Mathematical Journal*, vol. 8 (1941), pp. 215-222.

[44] McShane, E. J., *Integration* (Princeton, 1944).

[45] Morse, A. P., "A Continuous Function with no Unilateral Derivatives," *Transactions of the American Mathematical Society*, vol. 44 (1938), pp. 406-507.

[46] Morse, A. P., and Randolph, J. F., "Gillespie Measure," *Duke Mathematical Journal*, vol. 6 (1940), pp 408-419.

[47] ——— "The Rectifiable Subsets of the Plane," *Transactions of the American Mathematical Society*, vol. 55 (1944), pp. 236-305.

[48] von Neumann, J., "Proof of the Quasiergodic Hypothesis," *Proceedings of the National Academy, U.S.A.*, vol. 18 (1932), pp. 70-82.

[49] Pepper, E. D., "On Continuous Functions without a Derivative," *Fundamenta Mathematicae*, vol. 12 (1928), pp. 244-253.

[50] Pierpont, J., *Theory of Functions of a Real Variable*, vol. II (New York, 1912).

[51] Radó, T., *Length and Area* (American Mathematical Society Colloquium Publications, vol. XXX, New York, 1948).

[52] Randolph, J. F., "Carathéodory Linear Measure and a Generalization of the Gauss-Green Lemma," *Transactions of the American Mathematical Society*, vol. 38 (1935), pp. 531-548.

[53] ——— "Metric Separability and Outer Integrals," *Bulletin of the American Mathematical Society*, vol. 46 (1940), pp. 934-939.

[54] Riesz, F., "Sur l'integrale de Lebesgue," *Acta Mathematica*, vol. 42 (1920), pp. 191-205.

[55] Robinson, G. de B., *The Foundations of Geometry* (Toronto, 1940).

[56] Russell, Bertrand, *The Principles of Mathematics* (Cambridge, 1903).

[57] ——— *Introduction to Mathematical Philosophy* (London, 1924).

[58] Saks, S., *Théorie de l'Integrale* (Warsaw, 1932).

[59] ——— *Theory of the Integral* (Warsaw, 1937).

[60] ——— *Zentralblatt für Mathematik*, vol. II (1935), p. 431.

[61] Schwartz, L., *Théorie des distributions*, t. I (Paris, 1950); t. II (Paris, 1951); *Theory of Distributions* (with I. Halperin (Toronto, 1951)).

[62] Titchmarsh, E. C., *Theory of Functions*, second edition (Oxford, 1939.)

[63] Van Vleck, E. B., "On Non-Measurable Sets of Points, with an Example," *Transactions of the American Mathematical Society*, vol. 9 (1908), pp. 237-244.

[64] Weiner, N., "Homogeneous Chaos," *American Journal of Mathematics*, vol. 60 (1939), p. 897.

[65] ——— "The Ergodic Theorems," *Duke Mathematical Journal*, vol. 5 (1939), pp. 1-18.

[66] Widder, D. V., *The Laplace Transform* (Princeton, 1941).

[67] Young, W. H., "On Upper and Lower Integration," *Proceedings of the London Mathematical Society*, vol. II (1905), p. 52.

[68] ——— "On the General Theory of Integration," *Philosophical Transactions*, vol. CCIV (1905), p. 221.

[69] Zermelo, E., *Math. Annalen*, vol. LIX (1904), p. 514.

[70] Zygmund, A., "On the Summability of Multiple Fourier Series," *American Journal of Mathematics*, vol. LXIX (1947), pp. 836-850.

INDEX OF SUBJECTS

ABEL, lemma of, 42; test of (for convergence of series), 42; theorem of, 43

Absolute continuity, of functions, 140, 141; of set functions, 131; generalized, 160; in the restricted sense, 160; generalized in the restricted sense, 160, 161; of indefinite LEBESGUE integral, 141

Absolutely convergent integrals, 85

Additivity, of functions of sets, 131; complete, 131, 211

Algebraic numbers, 17, 18; denumerability of, 17, 18

Almost everywhere, 52

Approximate continuity, 118

Approximate derived numbers, 187-198; distribution of values of, 198; of measurable functions, 199

Arbitrary functions, 181-203; derived numbers of, 165, 181-187; approximate derived numbers of, 187-199; measurable bounds of, 202, 203

Arc length, 130

Axiom, of choice, 64, 97 (*see* principle of selection, ZERMELO axiom); of DEDEKIND, (Axiom 0.1) 13, 20, 24, 27; of nested intervals (Axiom 1.1), 25

BAIRE's theorem, 60

BOLZANO-WEIERSTRASS theorem, 26, 27

Bounded convergence theorem, 93

Bounded variation, *see* functions of bounded variation

Bounds, of functions, 31, 32, 202; of sequences, 20-23; of sets, 26-28

Cantor ternary set, 16, 64; nondenumerability of, 17; nondensity of, 16

CARATHÉODORY measure of linear sets, 64 (Problem 2.5); linear of plane sets, 130

CAUCHY, criterion for convergence, 24; sequences, 24, 213; test for convergence of series, 43

Complement, of a set, 46

Completely additive, 131, 211

Condensation points, 29

Continuity, of functions, 33, 34; absolute, 131, 140, 141; approximate, 118; generalized absolute, 160; generalized absolute in the restricted sense, 160, 161; of the LEBESGUE integral, 141; of the limit of a sequence of continuous functions, 39; necessary and sufficient conditions for the continuity of the limit of a sequence of, 38, 39; of a function of two variables, 39, 40; uniform, 25

Continuous functions with no unilateral derivatives, 172

Convergence, 36-40, 42 (*see* uniform convergence)

DEDEKIND section (Axiom 0.1), 13, 20, 24, 27

DENJOY integrals, 158, 161, 162; special, 159; general, 159-162

Denumerability, of sets, 14; of discontinuities of functions of

bounded variation, 118; of the set at which the right-hand and left-hand derivatives exist and are different, 182; of sets of open intervals, 47, 48; of rational numbers, 14; of rational number pairs and triples, 15
Dense sets, 13
Density, 110f.; metric density of sets 110, 114-118
Derivates, 165
Derivatives, approximate, 187-198; of arbitrary functions over arbitrary sets, 181f.; distribution of values of, 186, 187, 198, 199; distributions of values of derivatives of measurable functions, 199; of functions of bounded variation, 122f.; of functions of sets, 125, 126; inversion of, 140f.; inversion of non-summable, 146-158; measurability of, 124, 200, 201 (Theorem 7.18); upper and lower over sets, 122, 165f.
Derived numbers (*see* derivatives) 165f.; of arbitrary functions, 181f.; approximate, 187f.
DIRICHLET's test for convergence of series, 43
Discontinuities, of RIEMANN integrable functions, 71, 72; of functions of bounded variation, 119
Distributions of L. SCHWARTZ, 219
Division, operation of, 4, 5; by zero, 7, 12

Ergodic theorem, 81, 91, 100
EGOROFF's theorem, 65
Exterior measure, 45 (Introduction to Chapter II)

Fan integral, 74
FATOU's theorem, 97
Functions, 30; absolutely continuous, 140f. (*see* absolute continuity); approximately continuous, 118; of bounded variation (*see* functions of bounded variation); continuous, 33; continuous non-differentiable, 167, 168; continuous with no unilateral derivative, 172-181; infimum of, 31, 33; of intervals, 211-218; as the integral of a derivative, 143f.; of class L^2, 107 (Problems, 4.6, 4.7, 4.8); limits of, 32, 33; measurable, 76f. (*see* measurable functions); measure function, 211f.; monotone 119, 129 (*see* monotone functions); non-differentiable of BESICOVITCH, 172-181; non-measurable, 95 (Example 4.3), 186 (Example 7.1); relations between arbitrary and measurable, 199-203; WEIERSTRASS non-differentiable, 166-172; of sets (*see* set functions) ; of two variables 39-41, 95-97
Functions of bounded variation of one variable, 110, 118, 130, 211, 215, 216; derivatives of, 122-125; as the difference of two non-decreasing functions, 121, 122; discontinuities of, 118, 119; denumerability of discontinuities of, 118, 119; existence of right-hand and left-hand limits of, 121; with discontinuities everywhere dense,119-121, 138 (Problem 5.7); measurability of, 121; summability of derivatives of, 127-129; total variation of, 137 (Problems 5.1, 5.2); absolutely continuous, 141 (Theorem 6.3); functions of sets, 125 (*see* set functions); of two or more variables, 130, 131
Functions defined by integrals, 140f.

Functionals, 212; linear, 212; continuous, 214, 215; measure function of L. SCHWARTZ, 218

Generalized integrals (*see* integral), 158 (§ 6.3); descriptive definitions of, 159 (§ 6.4); of DENJOY, 158, 159, 161, 162; of KHINTCHINE, 159; of PERRON, 162; of W. H. YOUNG, 162

Generalized absolute continuity (*see* absolute continuity)

Greatest lower bound, of sets, 20; of functions, 31

Half open interval, 13

HEINE-BOREL theorem, 28

HILDEBRANDT integral, 74

Infimum, of functions, 31, 35; of sets, 20

Inner measure, 45

Integers, geometrical representation of, 17; negative, 5; positive, 3; sets of, 5

Integrals, absolutely convergent, 85; containing a parameter, 95f.; DENJOY special, 158, 159, 161, 162; DENJOY general, 159, 162; descriptive, 159-162; functions defined by, 140; generalized, 158f.; of LEBESGUE, 66f. (*see* LEBESGUE integral); non-absolutely convergent, 90; of PIERPONT, 74; of PERRON, 162; of RIEMANN, 66, 69-73; RIEMANN-STIELTJES, 204 (*see* RIEMANN-STIELTJES integral); of W. H. YOUNG, 74

Integrability of sequences, 92 (§ 4.4), 97 (§ 4.7)

Interior measure, 45 (Introduction to Chapter II)

Interval functions, 211, 212, 217, 218

Inversion of derivatives, 140; of summable, 142-145; of bounded, 145, 146; of non-summable, 147-158

Irrational numbers, 9, 15-18; non-denumerability of, 15

Least upper bound, of functions, 31; of sets, 20, 27

LEBESGUE integral, of bounded functions, 66, 67f.; of unbounded functions, 73f.; absolute summability of, 85; alternative definitions of, 73 (Definition 3.5), 75 (Definition 3.7); extension to unbounded sets, 88f. (§ 4.3); general discussion of, 74; properties of, 81f.; integration by parts for, 210, 211; relation to RIEMANN integrals, 86; second mean value theorems for, 207 (Theorem 8.6), 208 (Theorem 8.8), 209 (Note 8.2)

Limits, of sequences, 20f.; of sets, 26; upper and lower of sequences, 20-23; upper and lower of functions, 31, 32; limit function of sequences of functions, 36-44

Linear measure of two dimensional sets, 130

Lower derivatives, 122 (*see* derivative)

LUSIN'S theorem, 77

Mean convergence theorem, 98, 107 (Problem 4.8)

Mean-value theorem, LEBESGUE and STIELTJES integrals, 108 (Problem 4.10), 207-209; for RIEMANN integrals, 79 (Problem 3.10)

Measurability, of bounds of arbitrary functions, 202, 203; of closed sets, 55; of functions, 211f.;

of limits of sequences of functions, 76 (Theorem 3.7); of open sets, 54; of products and unions of sequences of sets, 56f.; of functions of bounded variation, 121; of sets 56-59
Measurable functions, 66f.; continuous on a closed set, 77; limit of a sequence of functions, 76 (Theorem 3.7); measurable bounds of arbitrary functions, 202, 203; as the limit of a sequence of continuous functions, 94 (Theorem 4.15)
Measure, CARATHÉODORY linear of two dimensional sets, 130; of closed sets, 55; inner, 45; LEBESGUE outer, 45; of non-uniform convergence, 43; of open sets, 54; of products and unions of sets, 56 (Theorem 2.12); of products and unions of sequences of sets, 56-59; of sets, 54-60 (§ 2.4)
Measure function, 211, 212, 217; of L. SCHWARTZ, 218
Measure preserving transformations, 61f., 91
Metric, of denumerable sets, 52; of sets, 48-50 (Definition 2.4); of space (*B*), 212
Metric density, of sets, 110, 114
Metric separability of sets, 50-54, 59, 115, 118, 191, 193
Monotone functions, 119, 129; with everywhere dense discontinuities, 119, 138 (Problem 5.7); continuous but not absolutely continuous, 129 (Example 5.3)

Non-absolutely convergent integrals, 90
Non-dense, 13, 14, 16, 138 (Problems, 5.8, 5.9), 148, 153
Non-denumerable, 15, 16, 17; irrational numbers are, 15
Non-differentiable functions, of BESICOVITCH, 171-184; of WEIERSTRASS, 167-174
Non-measurable sets, 61-64, 95-96, 186 (Example 7.1)
Norm, of a function, 212
Numbers, algebraic, 17, 18; extension of number systems, 10; geometrical representation of, 4; irrational, 9; rational 7-15; real number system 10-12; systems of, 3; transcendental, 18

Open interval, 13; denumerability of a set of, 47, 48; half open, 13
Operations, 4, 5, 10, 18; addition, 4, 18 (Problem 0.1); of division, 4, 5; on integers, 4; on irrational numbers, 10; of multiplication, 4, 18 (Problem 0.1); on rational numbers, 7; on sets, 154-158
Order relations, for integers, 4; for rational numbers, 7; for real numbers, 10

PERRON integral, 162
PIERPONT integral, 74
Principle of selection (axiom of choice, ZERMELO axiom), 34, 64, 97
Points, of bounded variation, 137 (Problem 5.2); of non-summability, 147, 148, 149, 154

Rational numbers, 7-15; denumerability of, 14
Real numbers, 12, 13; non-denumerability of, 15, 16
RIEMANN integral, definition of, 69; existence of, 70-73; relation to LEBESGUE integral, 86 (Theorem 4.9)
RIEMANN-STIELTJES integral, 204; derivative of function defined by,

209; function defined by, 209; integration by parts for, 209-211; mean value theorems for, 206-209; properties of, 205; measure function defined as, 211, 212

Saltus, 34, 44, 118
SCHWARZ's inequality, 107 (Problem 4.6)
Sequences, CAUCHY, 24; integrability of, 92, 97; limits and bounds of, 20f.; lower and upper limits of, 20f.; monotone, 23; of sets, 56f.
Sets, 13; bounds of, 20f.; CANTOR ternary, 16; complement of, 46; closed, 26, 46, 55; dense, 13; denumerable, 14, 15, 18, 46, 47; functions of, 125, 131; LEBESGUE integral as a function of, 125, 131; isolated, 26; infimum of, 20, 21; linear, 45; limits and bounds of, 20, 21; measurability of, 55-60; measure of, 54; metric density of, 114; metric properties of, 48f.; metric separability of, 52-54, 115, 118; non-dense, 13, 14, 16, 138 (Problems 5.8, 5.9), 153; null, 52; open, 26, 46, 54; of open intervals, 47; product of, 45; of real numbers, 13; supremum of, 20, 21; symbols for, 13; theorems on metric separability of, 50-54, 59, 115f., 191, 193
Set-functions, 125, 131; derivatives of, 125, 126; additive, 131; completely additive, 131; absolutely continuous, 131; examples of set-functions which are not completely additive, 131-133; monotone, 133; of bounded variation, 133; additive and of bounded variation as the difference of two non-decreasing set-functions, 133; if completely additive then of bounded variation, 135
Space, of bounded functions, 211; complete, 213; of continuous functions, 216, 217; of indefinitely differentiable functions, 219
STIELTJES integral, 204, 211 (*see* RIEMANN-STIELTJES integral)
Summability, definition of, 74, 88f.; of derivatives of function of bounded variation, 127-129 (§ 5.7); of bounded derivatives, 145; of functions over sequences of sets, 87, 90, 91
Summable, 74
Supremum, of functions, 31, 32, 35; of sets, 20
Surface area, 130

Total variation, 137 (Problems 5.1, 5.3)
Transcendental numbers, 18
Transformation, measure preserving, 61, 62, 96
Translation, of a set, 61

Uniform continuity, 35
Uniform convergence, 36, 37, 38, 40, 42, 92; continuity of limit function of uniformly convergent sequences, 37 (Theorem 1.13); definition of, 37, 38; of functions of two variables, 40 (Theorem 1.16); integrability of uniformly convergent sequences of functions, 92 (Theorem 4.13); measure of non-uniform, 43 (Problem 1.18); WEIERSTRASS test for, 42
Union, of sets, 45, 46
Upper bounds, of functions, 31, 32, 35; of sets, 20
Upper derivatives and derived numbers (*see* derivatives and derived numbers)

Upper limits, of functions, 32-33; of sets, 21, 22, 23
Upper and lower derivatives, 122 (*see* derivatives)

Variation, (*see* total variation and bounded variation)
VITALI covering theorem, 111, 112; in two dimensions, 112, 113

WEIERSTRASS test for uniform convergence, 42 (Problem 1.8)
WEIERSTRASS non-differentiable function, 167-174

YOUNG integrals, 74

ZERMELO axiom (axiom of choice, principle of selection), 34, 64, 97

INDEX OF AUTHORS

(Square brackets refer to bibliography, numbers to pages, the notation vii, viii to the preface)

ABEL, 42, 43
ADAMS, 130

BAIRE, 60, 61
BANACH [3], 212
BESICOVITCH, 130, 171; [5], 188
BIRKHOFF, G. D., 100
BIRKHOFF, GARRETT, 100
BLUMBERG, 202
BLYTH, viii
BOLZANO, 26
BOREL, 28
BURKILL [11], 188; 199; [12], 188
BUSEMANN, 114

CARATHÉODORY, 64, 112, 130; [15], 119
CAUCHY, 43, 213
CELLERIER, 168
CHOW, 203
CLARKSON, 130
COURANT [19], 12
COXETER, viii, 3
CROSBY, viii

DEDEKIND [20], 12
DENJOY, 158, 159, 161, 162
DIRICHLET, 43

EGOROFF, 65

FAN, 74
FATOU, 97
FELLER, 114
FOURIER, vii

GEÖCZE, 130
GOURSAT [22], 42, 43, 80
GRAVES, vii

HAHN, 131; [24], 64
HALPERIN, viii, 219
HARDY, 9
HEINE, 280
HILDEBRANDT, 74
HOBSON [28], 12, 158, 162, 204, 209; [29], 109, 168
HOPF, 100
HUNTINGDON [31], 12
HUREWICZ, 100, 105

IMMEL, viii

JEFFERY [33, 34, 35], 45, 74; [35], 189; [36], 75

KESTLEMAN [37], 64
KHINTCHINE, 158, 159
KOOPMAN, 100

LANDAU [40], 12
LEBESGUE, vii, viii, 45, 66, 74; [41], 162
LINDEMANN, 18
LORENTZ, viii
LUSIN, 77

MACPHAIL [42], 75; [43], 130
McSHANE [44], 162
MORREY, 130
MORSE, 172; [46], 130; [47], 130

VON NEUMANN, 100

PEPPER, 172
PIERPONT, 74

RADÓ, 131
RANDOLPH [52], 130; [53], 45
REICHELDERFER, 131
RIEMANN, 66, 69, 74, 86
RIESZ, vii
ROBINSON, viii; 3
ROSENTHAL, 131
RUSSELL, 3

SAKS [58, 59], 158, 169, 172; [60], 190
SCHWARTZ, 204, 219
SCHWARZ, 107
STIELTJES, 204, 209

TITCHMARSH [62], 43, 65, 107, 108, 163, 168
TONELLI, 130

VAN VLECK [63], 64
VITALI, 110, 142

WEBBER, viii
WEIERSTRASS, 26, 27, 42, 167, 168, 183
WEINER, 100
WIDDER [66], 204
WRIGHT, 9

YOUNG, 74

ZERMELO, 34
ZYGMUND, 114

Lightning Source UK Ltd.
Milton Keynes UK
UKHW020019210722
406167UK00009B/853

9 781487 592042